102 070 510 8

What
Abou

ONE WEEK
LOAN

This book is due for return on or before the last date shown below.

D1333910

# What Is To Be Done About Law and Order?

Crisis in the Nineties

John Lea and Jock Young

Pluto Press

LONDON • BOULDER, COLORADO

First published 1993 by Pluto Press
345 Archway Road, London N6 5AA
and 22883 Quicksilver Drive, Sterling, VA 20166-2012, USA

www.plutobooks.com

British Library Cataloguing in Publication Data
A catalogue record for this book is available from the British
Library

Library of Congress Cataloging in Publication Data
Applied for

ISBN    0 7453 0735 3  hardback
ISBN    0 7453 0398 6  paperback

Printed on demand by Lightning Source

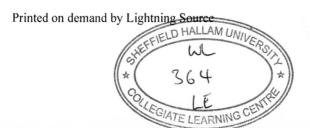

# Contents

*To the memory of Dave Cowell*

# Introduction: Ten Years On

Since its publication in 1984, *What Is To Be Done About Law And Order?* has become the founding text for 'left realist' criminology. Left realism originated as a political platform – an injunction to the political left to 'take crime seriously' – rather than as an academic theory. It is concerned both with the crimes of the powerful – organized crime and the crimes of powerful corporations and the state, (see Lea 1992; Pearce and Tombs 1992) and with the problems of street crime, such as mugging, burglary and interpersonal violence, activities which together have a real and destructive impact on the poor and working-class communities who are least able to cope with them.

When *What Is To Be Done?* was first published, our views attracted a good deal of polemical criticism. With the passing of time, however, our analysis has come to be seen as far less controversial, in relation both to the seemingly inexorable increase in street crime, and to the economic and social deprivation which is its backdrop, and the prolonged and deepening crises of policing. Our views have developed in subsequent publications, and some indication is given in the references at the end of this Introduction. We are grateful to Pluto Press for the opportunity to republish *What Is To Be Done?* and for the opportunity to include some brief comments on the relevance of its arguments for the contemporary situation.

## RISING CRIME AND ITS CAUSES
Since the publication of *What Is To Be Done?* levels of street crime in England and Wales have continued to rise. Crime rose

by 35 per cent during the period 1980–5 and by 25 per cent over the period 1985–90. However, percentage figures do not always enable us to grasp the nature of the problem. Thus, crime rose by 68 per cent over the period 1955–60 and by 49 per cent during 1960–5, both larger percentage changes than for the 1980s. But if we look at the actual quantitative increases the pattern is rather different. During 1955–60 crimes per 100,000 of the population rose by 702 and during 1960–5 by 856. But when we turn to the 1980s we find a much higher numerical increase although a smaller percentage rise. Thus from 1980–5 crimes per 100,000 increased by 1,766 and during 1985–90 by 1,745. This is what is exceptional about recent periods: large numerical increases added to the already large crime levels of the 1960–80 period.

It is often argued that such rises in recorded crime are more a reflection of increased reporting to the police than of real increases, and that all that has happened is that the 'dark figure' of unrecorded crime has been somewhat reduced. In *What Is To Be Done?* we were able to refer to the first Home Office British Crime Survey (BCS) to show an estimation of the size of this level of unreported crime. It is clear that a constant level of unreported crime would have long ago been eaten up by the exponential increases in the official crime statistics. Subsequent sweeps of the BCS have shown real and considerable increases in crime levels – although not nearly as large, overall, as police figures, thus indicating significant increases in reporting rates. Thus BCS figures show that for comparable crimes, the increase over the period 1981–1991, was 49 per cent compared to a 96 per cent increase in crimes known to the police. (Mayhew et al 1993) Yet such an overall divergence conceals important parallels. For acquisitive crimes (burglary and theft), which make up the vast majority of crimes considered – 79 per cent – there is no divergence whatsoever, whereas for crimes of violence there is a significant difference and for vandalism little relationship at all, over the ten year period. Evidence from the United States, where victimization surveys have been in use for a longer time, indicates a close relationship over time between victimization survey data and police recorded crimes, suggesting a close correlation between changes in the level of crimes known to the police and changes in the real level of crime (Field 1991). It is no longer possible to argue, with Geoff Pearson, that: 'What is usually known as the "dark figure" of crime is such an imponderable that all statements about movements in the levels of crime (whether up or down) are largely a matter of guesswork ... There is no way of reliably counting the size of this "dark figure" ' (Pearson 1983 p. 22). On the contrary, our knowledge of the 'dark figure' through social survey methods shows that the actual impact of crime is even higher than that revealed in the figures.

What are the causes of such large increases in crime? In *What Is To Be Done?* we gave great emphasis to the role of relative deprivation. We argued that crime is not caused by levels of absolute poverty or unemployment but by people's perception of unjustified inequalities, and of being excluded from the 'glittering prizes' of capitalist society – be they material wealth or individual status and prestige – and marginalization from legitimate channels for redressing the balance. This emphasis on the centrality of relative deprivation as a cause of crime was important to our argument on two counts.

First of all, it provided an explanation of the continually rising crime rates during the post-war boom when income levels and employment generally were rising. With the welfare state and mass education spreading a mythology of 'equality of opportunity' and the mass media broadcasting a message of generalized wealth and lifestyles to match, the sense of frustration and failure on the part of those sizeable numbers of people left behind could only increase. In this sense relative deprivation is endemic in modern capitalist society. The development of the consumer culture and at the same time the relentless breaking down of older community values, which to some extent shielded traditional working-class communities from relative deprivation, are a result not of deviations but of the core dynamics of capitalism. Secondly, relative deprivation fitted into our understanding of the innovative character of criminal subcultures. Rather than crime being the response of automatons to material conditions, the unemployed and deprived young people in the inner cities, in turning to lifestyles and activities which involved crime, were adapting to situations as they found them with the materials at hand. In deploying these ideas we were following in the footsteps of such classical accounts as that of Cloward and Ohlin in their study *Delinquency and Opportunity* (1960).

Since *What Is To Be Done?* our views on the explanation of crime have developed and taken on a more integrated perspective, of which relative deprivation and the exclusion from legitimate channels of achievement form only one component. We understand the level of crime as resulting from the interaction of potential offenders, potential victims, actions of the state and criminal justice system, and levels of informal community and family social control (Lea 1992, Young 1992).

### Offenders

The number of potential offenders in a society is a result, partly, of the level of relative deprivation as outlined in *What Is To Be Done?* The importance of the theory of relative deprivation is that it cures any tendency to mark out crime as purely an activity of an 'underclass' of young unemployed. The feeling of *relative* deprivation can be felt at all levels of the social structure and is a major spur to white-collar crime (Box 1983). Organized crime has certainly been interpreted this way, especially in America where Daniel Bell once described it as the 'queer ladder of social mobility' which seeks illegal means to perfectly normal goals of social respectability and wealth. The origin of the BCCI banking scandal of 1991 lay in a similar process whereby a group of Third World bankers found themselves marginalized by the western dominated banking system. To accumulate wealth and power from outside the channels of legitimate finance, dominated by the western and Japanese banks, would soon bring the BCCI face to face, whatever the personal motives of its directors, with the phenomenon of drugs money. Heroin and cocaine are, next to armaments, the most profitable commodities in world trade and, by virtue of their illegality, remain outside the official world banking and financial systems.

Relative deprivation is not, of course, identified solely with economic crimes. The crimes of the poor are not simply concerned with achieving the necessities of life. The group that most conforms to this pattern is women, often single parents, involved in shoplifting in food stores. However, an adaption to relative deprivation, especially but not exclusively for young men, may involve the accumulation of status goods such as a particular type of clothing, trainers, video recorders and other things necessary to achieve a certain status – a status which itself is part of an adaption to exclusion from the mainstream achievements of society.

At all levels of the social ladder relative deprivation is related to other equally criminogenic factors similarly rooted in the structure of capitalist market society (Currie 1990). The pure egoism encouraged by capitalist culture, unmediated by traditions of class solidarity, permeates the business and political elites of capitalist countries, and those who have tried to emulate them. An obvious example was the Bhopal incident in India during the 1980s in which the actions of a large multinational company, wilfully ignoring safety questions in the egoistic pursuit of profit, resulted in the poisoning of thousands of working-class people (Pearce and Tombs 1989). This type of rampant egoism filters down to the young unemployed inner-city mugger who is prepared to injure or even kill someone for money or personal valuables.

But, of course, in times of economic recession when large sections of the population become economically marginalized through no fault of their own, relative deprivation will soar as more and more people come to be cut off from the levels of consumption and social provision which they have come to see as their right. They have absorbed the ideology of late twentieth-century capitalism that citizenship involves a considerable measure of property ownership. They have – despite a decade of Thatcherism – retained the post war Keynesian notion that unemployment and poverty are not a fact of nature but the product of inept government.

They will not, to the same extent as during the 1930s, view their predicament as a product of the inevitable laws of the market place.

We can talk, therefore, of the relative deprivation characteristic of periods of prosperity and that characterizing periods of recession. The discontent and frustration which fuels crime, although far from absent during the former, weighs more heavily during the latter as witnessed by the even greater volume of crime added to yearly rates between 1980 and the present when compared, say, to the period 1960 to 1970.

### Victims

Equally important in crime levels is the supply of victims. Changes in public behaviour affect the supply of opportunities to commit crime. Increased affluence has increased the level of car ownership and at the same time the amount of time spent outside the home in the pursuit of leisure. This has resulted in more homes unguarded and at the same time more people vulnerable to crimes of violence committed in public places. The proposition that increased time spent outside the home increases vulnerability to violence is truer of men than women, since the majority of violence committed against women takes place in the home. At the same time public places have become increasingly unsafe for women and the rise in female employment outside the home – often involving unsocial hours – increases vulnerability to crime in public places while also increasing the vulnerability of the home.

In addition to physical vulnerability, cultural values themselves provide labels which increase vulnerability by enabling offenders to elaborate their own justifications. Social groups defined as 'outsiders' may become particular targets for crime. Such isolation increases the vulnerability of victims by assuring attackers that the victim is likely to get little support, e.g. from neighbours in cases of racial harassment on housing estates. A rapist attacking a lone women may feel he is partly justified in that she is 'asking for it' just by being on her own. These cultural values are embodied in institutions which, by linking individuals together in social relations, effectively link potential offenders to potential victims. A man beating his wife or lover as a response to the stresses of family life may feel that such violence within the family unit is a 'purely personal matter' and has nothing to do with crime.

## Community

The fragmentation of communities through economic decay and increased long-term unemployment reduces the level of collective social control over potential offending at the same time as levels of egoism and relative deprivation may increase. Institutions whose functioning was formerly an extension of community cohesion, like the family and the school, may similarly weaken. In this sense the causes of crime are thoroughly intertwined with all the social and economic problems of decay and the structural changes currently taking place in advanced capitalist societies.

The family in particular has been considerably weakened in the recent period as structural unemployment diminishes the economic capacity to form stable families and puts great pressure on those who do find employment to work long hours and therefore to be unable to maintain adequate supervision of children and young people. To blame the family for rising crime, as conservatives frequently do, is to commit what Elliot Currie (1985) calls 'the fallacy of autonomy': the belief that the family is separate from the problems of unemployment and lack of income support which derive directly from the conditions in wider society and government policies.

## The Criminal Justice System

Finally the criminal justice system itself can have an effect on crime rates, on real crime rates that is, quite apart from the question of recording the level of crime or reclassifying acts as crime or non crime through changes in the law. The growing inefficiency of the police as a crime control organization, for the reasons detailed in *What Is To Be Done?*, itself has an effect in increasing crime through potential offenders realizing that the likelihood of being apprehended is becoming continuously lower for many types of offence. In some inner-city areas, for example, the clear-up rate for burglaries during the 1980s fell as low as 8 per cent, effectively reducing the likelihood of detection to minimal levels. This has undoubtedly contributed to further increases in crime levels.

But in addition the criminal justice system, by acting in an unfair and prejudiced way in relation to certain groups, can itself become an important factor in undermining respect for the law, and precipitating crime.

Right-wing politicians and criminologists naturally attempt to disassociate crime from the economic and political structure of society and lay the blame firmly on the individual. It is the individual offender who is at fault because of a wilful wickedness or a biological predisposition to crime; the victim who is to blame for not taking sufficient precautions; and the family which is to blame for insufficiently vigilant supervision of young people. Where it is admitted that the criminal justice system is at fault the problem is seen as simply a problem of 'bad apples' within, of rogue police officers bringing the system into disrepute. All this adds up to the strategy of a denial of the social causes of crime; of disconnecting crime from social and political structure.

RACE AND CRIME

The debate about the relationship between race and crime has in the last few years focused around the explanation of the 'disproportional' number of certain ethnic groups, blacks in particular, in the prison population. In many advanced industrial countries – such as Britain, France, the Netherlands and the United States – there is a considerably higher proportion of blacks in prison than in the general population. In England and Wales in 1989, for example, 10.5 per cent of the male prison population compared to 1.2 per cent of the total male population were of West Indian, Guyanese or African descent (Fitzgerald 1990).

Figures such as these often evoke a one-sided interpretation – either that they reflect racial discrimination within the criminal justice system or, conversely, that they merely reflect the dispro-portionate involvement of blacks in crime (Wilbanks 1987).

One of our main arguments in *What Is To Be Done?* was to the effect that neither of these interpretations is feasible. Different sections of the population, because of their economic and social positions, have differing rates of crime. At the same time, the criminal justice system reacts in a discriminatory manner towards certain sections of the population. To argue otherwise entails the belief that crime is a completely 'democratic' process in which all social groups (black, white, rich, poor, male, female, young, old) commit crime in exactly equal proportions, or that the rule of law really is so socially blind that it acts towards all social groups with invariable impartiality. There is no evidence for either argument. The question is not that of choosing between *either* variations in criminal behaviour *or* discriminatory responses by the criminal justice system, but rather of weighing the balance between them. Research on this question, although intensive, particularly in the United States, is far from conclusive (MacLean and Milanovic 1990), but the evidence so far and the logic of social reality both demand that we make the following conceptual clarifications.

### Race

The classification of people into 'races' based on a combination of skin colour and other physical features simply does not correspond to the actual lived realities within which different subcultures exist. 'Black', for example, in Britain groups together Afro-Caribbeans and various peoples of African origin with totally different lifestyles and behaviour patterns. In the United States such a classification takes on an even more bizarre form where Hispanics are frequently classified as 'whites' and their crime and imprisonment rates compared to those of 'blacks' which includes Afro-Americans and Afro-Caribbeans (Lynch 1990). Similarly 'Asian' involves even more of a cultural heterogeneity, with Bengalis (who in Britain have a generally worse economic predicament than Afro-Caribbeans) classified along with Pakistanis and Indians who have a class structure ranging from the very poor to the very wealthy. Such unreal groupings create crime figures which cancel out differences and conceal variations.

*Class, Age and Location*
Consequently, it is important to separate out factors relating to ethnicity from those concerned with class and age. The types of crime for which people are sent to prison are predominantly those committed by working-class people (Reiman 1979) and offenders are overwhelmingly youthful. Ethnic groups which are predominantly working class and youthful are thus bound to have higher crime and imprisonment rates, particularly if they live in inner-city areas, a third predictor of high rates of offending. The influence of ethnicity must therefore be rigorously separated out from age, class and geographical location. It is quite ridiculous to compare the social behaviour (whether crime rates, educational achievement or health) of 'whites' and 'Afro-Caribbeans' when class and age composition and geographical location differ widely within each of these groups. This is particularly true if one goes on to ascribe high crime rates, low educational achievement, etc. solely to the effects of ethnicity. As far as imprisonment rates are concerned, as Jeffrey Reiman, in his analysis of the US statistics, points out: 'Blacks who travel the full route of the criminal justice system and end up in jail or prison are nearly identical with whites who do. For example in 1972, 47 percent of black jail inmates and 43 percent of white jail inmates had pre-arrest annual incomes of less than $2,000' (1979, p. 98). He indicates how mortality statistics show a similar pattern. Statistics by 'race' are abundant in the US and increasingly in the UK, while class statistics are relatively rare. Yet even our own limited research provides some indications that when class is taken into account, the disproportionality of black and white encounters with the police – as in stops in the street for example – is considerably reduced (Crawford et al. 1993).

*Class and Race*

Having said this, it is incorrect to collapse racism into 'classism'. The effect of racism, for example, may be to concentrate a disproportionately large part of the black population in the poorer sections of the working class. Thus the American sociologist William Wilson, in his study *The Truly Disadvantaged*, shows how the effect of past discrimination, through the denial of job opportunities in new expanding occupations, is to hold working-class black Americans in those parts of the cities long deserted by industrial employment.

*Cancelling Out*

A final important consideration concerns the fact that racism may have conflicting, mutually cancelling effects. The police and courts may, for example, take less seriously crimes committed against blacks. For other crimes, however, particularly where the police are proactive, acting on their own account rather than in response to public demands, there may be an over-representation of black offenders. Drug offences are a good example. Al Blumstein (1982) in his classic study suggests that precisely such a process occurs. This process will obviously vary by the type of offence and the relationship between offender and victim. Indeed, Lynch and Patterson (1990) suggest that the various combinations of black against black, white against white, black against white, white against black, will all produce differential reactions by the criminal justice system. Racial discrimination may, therefore, result in both under-representation and over-representation, depending on these factors. The net result of the two processes may be to cancel each other out so that a perfectly 'proportional' criminal justice system could in fact be the result of discriminatory practices.

With the above comments in mind, the disproportionality question and its relationship to racism becomes more complex than the current debate often allows. In *What Is To Be Done?* we stressed the reinforcing rather than the counteracting factors: that racial discrimination accentuates the level of relative deprivation and marginalization and hence leads to higher crime rates, while at the same time police racism results in a disproportionately high level of ethnic minorities stopped and searched or arrested. What is certain is that the simple call for a reform of the criminal justice system, however welcome, would, because it *avoids* the basic issues of racism and economic deprivation, have only a limited, although welcome, impact on the proportion of ethnic minority people in prison (Hood 1992).

### MILITARY POLICING

An important part of our analysis in *What Is To Be Done?* was concerned with the analysis of policing strategies. We identified a long-run tendency to move away from what we called 'consensus' policing in the direction of what we called 'military' policing. It is important to understand that we never asserted that consensus policing actually existed. It was rather to be seen as an ideal type, part of the mythology of British policing from which to identify the direction of movement. What we were concerned to argue was that a combination of rising crime rates, changes in police technology, and police prejudice against poor and ethnic minority groups accentuates the alienation between police and poor communities, such that the police work less and less with the community, acting on information received from the community and by methods which the community accepts, and increasingly against the community, by methods which further alienate the community from the police and resemble more the activities of an occupying army than a police force. The situation as we portrayed it in contemporary Britain was a form of consensus policing for the middle-class suburbs and inner-city enclaves combined with high profile military policing for the working-class inner cities and peripheral housing estates.

In later work we developed the distinction between consensus and military policing in a more elaborate form.

The causes of the shift towards military policing in the inner cities and peripheral housing estates we saw as a combination of economic decay and rising crime, police racism and the stereotyping of young people from these areas as criminals *tout court* and developments in police technology which put more officers in cars and fewer on foot patrol, with a resultant decline in contact with the community.

| Subject | Consensus policing | Military policing |
|---|---|---|
| The public | supports the police | fears / is in conflict with the police |
| Information from the public | large amount, specific, relevant to crime detection | small amount, general and low quality |
| Mode of gathering information | public initiated, low use of surveillance technology | police initiated, high use of surveillance technology |
| Police profile | low, integrated with community, police as citizens | high, police as outsiders, marginalized, high use of force and militarized units |
| Targeting by police | of specific offenders | of social groups, stereotyped populations |
| Style of police intervention | individual, consensual, reactive | generalized, coercive, proactive |
| Typical example | English village | Northern Ireland |

*Source:* Kinsey et al. 1986, p. 43.

During the 1980s, particularly following the riots of 1981 and 1985, police forces made conscious efforts to restrain some aspects of the drift to military policing by reducing the reliance on large 'stop and search' operations in favour of more 'targeting' of suspects and locations. At the same time efforts were made in the direction of 'community policing' and putting more officers back on the beat combined with various exercises in 'human relations' or 'meeting the public' to hold in check the worst excesses of police stereotyping. Such measures, together with the increased emphasis on crime prevention, have had little or no effect on crime rates and they have simply slowed, rather than reversed, the drift to military policing. As long as the basic combination of economic decay, rising crime and lack of local democratic control over policing persist in the inner cities and poorest areas, then a shift towards consensus policing is a utopian dream. Whatever the training programmes say, the pressures generated by the ghettoised police subculture to stereotype ethnic groups, working-class young people and inner-city areas will continue. The most likely outcome of police reforms of the late 1980s will be to accentuate the division between the policing of the suburbs and middle-class areas and that of the inner cities and fringe housing estates.

A graphic vision of the future – not just for the US but for all large cities in the industrialized west – was provided during 1992 by the riots in Los Angeles which followed the acquittal by a white suburban jury of three white police officers accused of beating a black person, Rodney King. The acquittal, in the face of video recorded evidence of the beating, resulted in the worst riots this century in the United States. In the Watts riot in Los Angeles in 1965, 35 were killed, 1,000 injured and 4,000 arrested. This time 58 were killed, 2,383 injured, and 12,000 arrested.

In Los Angeles the division between consensus policing of the white (and black middle-class) suburbs and military policing of the poor black and hispanic inner-city ghettos has reached extreme dimensions in which the Los Angeles Police Department (LAPD) concentrates on the latter and leaves the former increasingly to private security companies and crime prevention measures. These private police forces have taken over the labour-intensive roles of guard duty, residential patrols, while LAPD concentrates on aerial surveillance, maintenance of major crime databases, and para-military responses to inner-city crime. Virtually all the affluent suburban homeowners' associations contract private policing and in LA County the private security industry has tripled its sales and workforce from 24,000 to 75,000 over the last decade.

The result of this division of labour between middle-class suburbs entrenched behind electronic fences and patrolled by private security, and a police force whose main task is to prevent the ghettos 'boiling over' is that military policing becomes the whole *raison d'être* of policing. LAPD is basically a high-tech military force (many of whose members are ex-marines). The key weapon in the arsenal of militarized policing is the mass raid and stop and search operation in which LAPD specialises. These tactics reached a peak in the late 1980s. The rationale for this style of policing was of course the growth of the cocaine and 'crack' economies in inner-city Los Angeles supervised by large teenage gangs with names like 'Bloods' and 'Cripps'.

An account of some of the recent activities of LAPD is given by Mike Davis in his excellent book *City of Quartz* (Davis 1990). In the 1987 'Gang Related Active Trafficker Suppression Program', or GRATS, targeted 'drug neighborhoods' were subject to raids by up to 200–300 officers to 'stop and interrogate' any one suspected of gang membership. During a two-month period – February and March 1987 – nine such sweeps resulted in nearly 1,500 arrests. In the following year, 1988, GRATS was succeeded by the HAMMER 'supersweep' operations in which 10 square miles were swept by 'thousand cop blitzkriegs' and more black youths arrested than at any time since the Watts riot of 1965. In one such excercise, resembling the 'search and destroy' operations of the Vietnam war, thousands of surprised teenagers were forced to 'kiss the sidewalk' or spreadeagle against police vehicles while officers checked them against computerised files of gang members or entered their names in the database. The result was 1,453 arrests mostly for trivial offences like juvenile curfew violations and parking tickets.

At the same time as such military policing strategies were being questioned as counter productive in terms of low arrest rates and maximum antagonization of the public, they were reaching a peak in Los Angeles. Such tactics have, of course, been widely questioned in the US. At the time of writing, Daryl Gates, the outspoken and allegedly racist chief of LAPD is being replaced by Willie

Williams, a senior black officer from Philadelphia who is committed
to a much more 'community policing' style. In an interview with
*Time* magazine (11 May 1992) Williams said: 'very important in
terms of planning are your contacts with community people.
These people are your best front line of communication.'

Williams' success depends, however, not only on whether he
can break the back of the racist macho-culture of the white-
dominated LAPD, a daunting enough task, but whether he can
succeed in the face of the economic and social forces which have
produced the division between suburbs and inner city and allowed
the drugs economy to lay waste to much of the latter. From our
standpoint the further, crucial issue is whether these economic and
social forces are moving in the same direction in the UK and western
Europe in general.

MARGINALITY, VIOLENCE AND THE UNDERCLASS
In *What Is To Be Done?* we argued that one of the consequences
of military policing was that the distinction between offenders and
the rest of the community became blurred. As the police label entire
populations as 'criminal' so the population responds by labelling
the police as the enemy. This combines with the marginalization
of poor communities from effective channels of political representation and protest, such that the only form of available response
to military policing becomes periodic riot. At the same time marginality combined with relative deprivation is one of the key
causes of crime in poor communities. The turn to criminal
activities as a result of relative deprivation is likely where there
are no other mechanisms, either individual or collective, for
redressing the frustrations to which relative deprivation gives rise.
From a police standpoint, riots and protests become indistin-
guished from crime, even though the causes of some riots may
well lie in people's frustration with the failure of policing to deal
with crime! The result is a further alienation of the community
from the police and a reinforcement of the basis for further rioting.

The most potent source of marginality itself we identified as
growing youth unemployment, the growth of a generation of

young people in the inner city and poor areas who were not simply unemployed but who had never worked and were thus marginalized from traditional working-class forms of political integration based on workplace trade unionism and Labour politics. The weakening of trade unions through Tory government legislation combined with the increasing middle-class orientation of Labour party politics during the 1980s has reinforced this marginality, quite apart from the growing economic crisis of the inner cities.

But let us return for a moment to the United States, to the preconditions for the 1992 Los Angeles riots. The first thing that strikes us is a sense of *dèja vu*. The Kerner Report into the 1967 riots in many major American cities called for an increase in community policing and for economic measures to alleviate marginality and unemployment in the ghettos.

But what happened was that some measures, such as affirmative action, facilitated the growth of a black middle class while the end of the post-war boom from the mid 1970s onwards meant that none of the 'Keynesian' job creation recommendations of the Kerner Report were implemented. The liberalism of the Kennedy and Johnson eras was replaced by conservative Nixon and Reagan administrations determined to cut federal spending and taxes to appease the suburban white middle class who no longer lived in the inner city and saw no reason why they should pay taxes to fund development projects or welfare targeted to the ghetto poor. At the same time the rise of neo-conservative poverty theorists like Charles Murray provided ideological cover through a return to a 'culture of poverty' theory. As the American sociologist William Wilson points out (Wilson 1987), in the face of the New Right liberal reformism went into crisis, hiding its head in the sand through a denial of high crime rates in the ghettos.

Meanwhile poverty in the US continued to increase. The Kerner Commission of 1967 calculated that 32 per cent of non white families and 9 per cent of white families were below the poverty line in 1964. By 1985 11 per cent of whites and 31 per cent of blacks were below the poverty line: the aggregate figures had hardly changed.

But in the core inner cities things got a lot worse. In these areas in 1969 13 per cent (8 million people) were below the poverty line. By 1985 this had reached 19 per cent (14.2 million). The increasing impoverishment of the inner cities was accompanied by racial concentration as whites, accompanied by a small but significant black middle class, moved to the suburbs leaving the poor blacks, joined by Spanish speaking immigrants, in the inner cities.

In explaining these developments Wilson lays emphasis on the structural changes in the US economy, in particular the relocation of manufacturing industries outside the central cities and the increased proportion of technical and service employment requiring several years schooling, beyond the qualification levels of the poor. The effect was to reduce the middle-class elements in the ghetto community (churches, stores, schools, recreational facilities). The decline of unskilled jobs in manufacturing reduces entry into the blue-collar workforce and the linking of the individuals into the older, stable political structures of the trade union movement. Wilson comments:

In the 1940s, 1950s and even the 1960s, lower class, working class and middle class black urban families all resided more or less in the same ghetto area, albeit on different streets. Although black middle class professionals today tend to be employed in mainstream occupations outside the black community and neither live nor frequently interact with ghetto residents, the black middle class professionals of the 1940s and 1950s (doctors lawyers teachers social workers etc) resided in the higher income areas of the inner city and serviced the ghetto community. The exodus of black middle class professionals from the inner city has been increasingly accompanied by a movement of stable working class blacks to higher income neighbourhoods in other parts of the city and to the suburbs. Confined by restrictive covenants to communities also inhabited by the black lower classes, the black working and middle classes in earlier years provided stability to inner city neighbourhoods and perpetuated and reinforced societal norms and values. In short their very presence enhanced the social organization of black communities. If strong norms and sanctions against aberrant behaviour, a sense of community, and positive neighbourhood identification are the essential features of social organization in urban areas, inner city neighbourhoods today suffer from a severe lack of social organization. (Wilson 1987 p. 7)

Mike Davis echoes some of these themes in relation to Los Angeles, pointing out that as elements of the black middle class move out of the inner cities and the ethnic composition of the these areas begins to change so the common cross-class experience of discrimination weakens, with the result that certain elements of the black middle class gave political support to the tough military policing strategy of LAPD:

> In past years this pitiless approach to juvenile crime (i.e. massive militarized policing) might simply have been dismissed as the venom of white backlash. But this time there is an unprecedented 'Black-lash' as well. The qualitatively new and disturbing dimensions of the war on the underclass is the swelling support of Black leadership for the approaches of Gates, Hahn and Reiner (the LAPD police chief and other city officials). (Davis 1990 p. 291)

The demand for better inner-city policing has become displaced by a support for military policing as the 'only alternative'.

These American developments depart from our model of the 'vicious circle' of police-community alienation developed in *What Is To Be Done?* There we saw a consequence of military policing with its indiscriminate targeting of black inner-city communities as a factor mobilizing middle-class and older generation black people in support of their youth. The situation portrayed by Davis is one in which the class differentiation of the black community has broken this process with a section of the black middle class supporting the police. The result is that whereas the 1965–7 riots in the US were seen as race riots, the Los Angeles riot of 1992 was much more clearly a class riot: of the marginalized black and hispanic youth who had never been able to enter the labour market.

William Wilson challenges the culture of poverty theory deployed by neo-conservative theorists to argue that the long-term poor develop a culture of apathy and lack of motivation which is quite independent of the material opportunities which present themselves. The poor cannot and *will not* take advantage of opportunities to work even if they occur and, because of this, employers actively avoid investment in the areas where such populations live. This lack of motivation, argue conservatives, is reinforced by liberal policies which undermine any residual work motivation by providing welfare support. The culture of poverty becomes a culture of welfare dependency.

For Wilson 'the *culture of poverty* ... places strong emphasis on the autonomous character of the social traits once they come into existence. In other words these traits assume a "life of their own" and continue to influence behaviour even if opportunities for social mobility improve' (1987 p. 137). By contrast the concept of '*social isolation*' implies that 'as economic and social situations change, cultural traits, created by previous situations *eventually* change even though it is possible that some will linger on and influence behaviour for a period of time. Accordingly ... public policy ... should place primary emphasis on changing the social and economic situations, not the cultural traits, of the ghetto underclass' (1987 p 138).

The concept of social isolation emphasizes the way in which subcultures are shaped by material circumstances though not a simple reflection of them. Rather they are attempts to solve material predicaments in which social groups find themselves. We deploy exactly this concept of subculture in *What Is To Be Done?* In the case of the ghetto underclass the material predicament that presents itself is isolation: the collapse of economic opportunity and, as Wilson points out, not 'welfare dependency' but rather cuts in the levels of welfare support both in the form of social security and unemployment benefits and support for family and community structures which over the last two decades have been systematically undermined.

In the US the chances of any economic and social changes in the inner cities are even more slender now than they were at the time of the Kerner Commission's report in 1968. Federal government spending between 1981 and 1992 fell by 82 per cent for subsidized housing, by 63 per cent for job training and employment aid, and by about 40 per cent for community service and development programmes. The current federal deficit is $400 billion. The state of California already faces a budget deficit of $10 billion and is busy cutting higher education and other social services to the bone. The emphasis of the Bush administration had been on private capital playing its part in renovating the inner cities. Yet all the evidence over the last 20 years is that the private sector has shunned the inner cities. The talk during the Bush years was of Thatcherite 'enterprise zones' and tax havens. Yet as Jesse Jackson, the last black leader with a national voice in the US and still talking in terms of the old philosophy of the Kerner Report, says, new investment in the inner cities 'is the last thing on the minds' of white bankers and middle-class blacks who joined the suburban exodus a decade ago.

These American developments are parallelled by those in the UK, indeed in many major capitalist countries in the west. The economic forces at work are the same – Los Angeles, London, and other cities are all part of the same world capitalist economy. The movement of jobs and opportunities out of the inner cities and older industrial towns has been the main characteristic of the last decade despite Tory rhetoric about enterprise culture and training initiatives. Recent figures from the Department of Social Security show that the gulf between rich and poor has widened massively during the era of Tory governments since 1979. The number of people living below half average income more than doubled – from 5 million to 12 million – between 1979 and 1989, a proportional rise from 9 per cent to 22 per cent. Meanwhile a recent Policy Studies Institute review of government policies to regenerate deprived urban areas concluded that over the last 25 years 'Surprisingly little has been achieved' (*Urban Trends I*, Policy Studies Institute 1992).

Perhaps the best comparison between the US and Britain was made by a *Financial Times* editorial shortly after the Los Angeles riots.

Yet urban deprivation and the existence of an alienated underclass are familiar enough to Europeans. Throughout most advanced industrial economies, unemployment rates of 10 per cent or more are persistent with the underlying rate racketing to a new floor after each recession. The position is much worse in rustbelts and declining inner cities, especially those with substantial ethnic minority communities. Serious riots have afflicted Britain and France in recent years. (*Financial Times* 5 May 1992)

There are, continued the editorial, several differences between western Europe and the USA: greater welfare spending, for example, and the fact that although inequality gaps have been widening, the real wages of the poor have not been falling as in the US. But it concluded: 'Underlying these different circumstances lies a common factor, the decline, in advanced industrial economies of the unskilled labourer' (5 May 1992). It is this decline in the type of employment which enabled young people from the unskilled working class to make the transition from school to work and adulthood, a transition which took the struggle for better living conditions into the conventional channels of trade union and labour politics. Throughout the industrialized capitalist world unemployment continues to rise and youth unemployment continues to increase as a percentage of the total. In the UK today, young people under 25 account for about a third of the total population.

Our analysis of marginality is even truer today than when *What Is To Be Done?* was first published in 1984. Britain saw riots in Brixton, Liverpool and Birmingham in the early and mid 1980s. They were predominantly caused by black youth who, due to discrimination, had borne the brunt of economic decay. But over the last year or two we have seen the spread to white youth as well, with the outbreak of 'joyriding' – racing with stolen cars – on estates like Meadow Well on Tyneside, open fights between police and white youth in Oxford and Coventry and, most recently, in the Hartcliffe area of Bristol. Joyriding is a particularly apt expression of the combination of marginality and relative deprivation, as kids who are denied access to the labour market take the status symbols of the consumer society and test them to destruction!

Marginality and relative deprivation are fundamentally class not race issues. Black youth were to the forefront of the riots in Britain because they were the first to face the cutting edge of the recession, but it is class, not race, that unites the rioters today. At the time of writing there are almost daily reports of confrontations between youth and the police in towns such as Bristol, Blackburn, Burnley, Huddersfield, often lasting several nights and involving, besides unemployed white youth, Indian and Pakistani youth who were absent from the skirmishes of the early 1980s. These events also bridge the spectrum from community antagonism to police treatment of young people to battles – in which in one case firearms were deployed – between criminal gangs and police. It is an inevitable feature of such marginality that, in the absence of effective political representation, forms of protest and forms of criminality begin to fuse, not simply organizationally but also ideologically.

## POLICE ACCOUNTABILITY

The position we adopted in *What Is To Be Done?* was that only a thoroughly democratized and politically accountable police force could respond effectively to the needs of working-class communities in the area of crime control. Our advocacy of police accountability to elected local authorities had two essential strands, the first of which was part of a general argument about demarginalization. If riots were a symptom of the fact that the existing institutions of central and local government, political parties and trade unions no longer gave an effective voice to growing sections of the unemployed and youth of the inner cities, then the struggle for local democratic control of wide areas of state, welfare and planning could be seen as a struggle for political inclusion. If growing numbers were no longer linked to the political system through national organizations then the localization of effective decision making was an appropriate response in terms of which a local public sphere or political culture could be re-established. The campaign for police accountability was part of this strategy.

But our analysis of policing had given emphasis to the role of information flow from public to police as a key ingredient of police effectiveness and indeed of the whole character of policing strategy. In this context the argument for accountability was an attempt to link democracy with efficiency. The public will provide information to an institution they trust, and they will trust it if it is politically answerable to the community.

Various arguments were brought against our position, of which the most important was to deny that fragmented marginalized communities with high crime rates had much information about crime to give. As we argued in a later publication (Kinsey et al. 1986), this was simply not the case – the inhabitants of poorer areas with higher than average crime rates have a much greater level of witnessing crimes than do those in more well-off areas with little crime (ibid. p. 49). There are of course crimes of which there is little public knowledge, for instance, domestic violence, child abuse and serial killing. In the case of the first two the victims themselves know, and the issue is that of providing conditions in which they will feel able to report the incidents. Police domestic violence units have made some minimal incursion into this problem, and organizations like Childline have shown that many children can be persuaded to report crimes committed against them. In the case of serial killers, knowledge is of course unavailable and it is here that traditional police detective and forensic methods come into their own, although in some instances, such as the case of the Yorkshire Ripper, those prostitutes who had valuable information were themselves alienated from the police as a result of previous experiences (Kinsey et al. p. 38). The immense difficulty of detecting such crimes is the exception that proves the rule concerning the relationship between public knowledge and police effectiveness.

It might be further argued that in areas like domestic violence or child abuse democratic police accountability would be pointless, as the dominant powers in the community – husbands and fathers – would use the democratic machinery to encourage police to

intervene less rather than more in such crimes. Again, the establishment of a local democratic public sphere should not be thought
of as simply enabling a community to transmit its prejudices to
the police but as a process which itself changes the community.
The opening up of channels of democratic discourse over policing
policy is precisely the sort of environment in which silences about
crimes such as male violence against women can be broken. The
experience of the women's movement testifies to this. Other
forms of crime, such as the power of organized criminal syndicates
to intimidate their victims and enforce a code of silence towards
the police and authorities, are well known. In areas like the
southern provinces of Italy the mafia has long relied on its power
to enforce such submission in the community. But again it has
been the development of a more democratic atmosphere, and the
foundation of an explicit anti-mafia political party in Sicily which
has enabled many individuals to break their silence concerning
the violence perpetrated by the mafia.

*What Is To Be Done?* was published in the middle of the Thatcher
years. The campaign for police accountability, which had been
gathering pace at that time, subsided after the abolition of the
GLC and the metropolitan authorities, and the ground was cleared
for the Tory government to shift the terms of mounting public
criticisms of the police away from the issues of democratization.

First some of the main criticisms of the police, in particular the
role of stop and search, were taken note of, and the 1984 Police
and Criminal Evidence Act became effective in 1986 together with
a new code of police behaviour and more stringent rules for the
conducting of street stops. The number of stops obligingly fell for
a while though, as Home Office figures released in July 1992
showed, they have risen almost threefold since 1986. The stops
seem no more effective in terms of actual crime control than they
ever were. According to the Policy Studies Institute 1983 investigation into the Metropolitan Police, only 11 per cent of stops
resulted in actual arrests. In the 1992 Home Office figures the level
was just 15 per cent (*Guardian*, 4 July 1992). If the aim has been

to remove one of the worst features of 'military policing' without recourse to democratic accountability of police to local communities, then it has failed.

A second strand of Tory policy from the mid 1980s onwards was to sidetrack the movement for accountability into various forms of community policing involving increasing the number of officers on foot patrol who make it their business to get to know the community, and 'police–community liaison' panels and groups in which small, usually totally unrepresentative, groups of 'citizens' discuss problems with local police commanders. The aim of these panels has been to try to give a semblance of democratic legitimacy to police without in any way increasing their actual accountability. Research on such liaison panels has concluded that they are little more than talking shops (Morgan 1989).

The main aim of government policy has been ideologically to reorganize the police accountability debate away from issues of democratization in the direction of the market-oriented issues of 'efficiency' and 'value for money'. Despite a resistance among traditional conservatives to seeing the police and the criminal justice system from the same standpoint as the Health Service or the Gas Board – as an inefficient bureaucracy which must be trimmed down and either privatized outright or at least submitted to market-based criteria of efficiency – the government persisted in this direction. During the Thatcher years New Right think tanks such as the Adam Smith Institute turned with enthusiasm upon the criminal justice juggernaut and marked out those areas which could be seen unproblematically as candidates for privatization. The prison system was the obvious candidate and currently the growth of private prisons seems to be a firmly established policy.

As far as the police were concerned, while any hairbrained schemes for wholesale privatization had to be ruled out of court, the question of technical efficiency became a key ingredient of government thinking in this area, and the concern with efficiency was a key factor working against any simple strategy aimed at building an authoritarian political consensus around policing and crime control. While the notion of an 'authoritarian consensus' built around policing and law and order may have been to the forefront of Tory thinking in the earlier part of the decade, by the mid 1980s it would seem to have been understood that no consensus could be built, particularly in the inner cities, around an institution which had gone so far down the road of legitimation crisis. It is not easy to argue for a consensus led by an institution almost universally regarded as inefficient and in serious need of reform and restructuring, not just by the public but by a large section of senior police officers. Home Office injunctions to police forces to develop 'performance indicators' because 'even they' must show value for money in the disposal of resources and submitting police accounts to the Audit Commission are not the stuff out of which an authoritarian consensus is built.

The recent symbolic collapse of police legitimacy has taken the form of the overturning of a number of serious terrorist convictions of the 1970s together with more recent cases such as that of Winston Silcott largely because of the way police investigations were handled. That these cases have had such an impact – quite apart from the detention of innocent individuals for over a decade – is undoubtedly because they came to symbolize the police illegalities which had penetrated the consciousness of widening sections of the public in the preceding years. The result is both a Royal Commission on the criminal justice system as a whole and a special inquiry, announced by the Home Secretary Kenneth Clarke at the 1992 Police Federation Conference, into police organization and structure.

If the aim of the government is to rescue police legitimacy through a 'trimmed down' and efficient force giving value for money and meeting its performance indicators, it is likely to be at the expense of the poor communities. Increases in clear-up rates will be more effectively achieved in middle-class areas where there is a willingness to cooperate with the police. In poor areas where police community relations are at a low ebb, an increase in 'community policing' by making the police more visible may increase antagonism as much as ameliorate it, despite the efforts of a minority of dedicated officers.

The distance between police subculture and that of poor communities will not be reduced by such strategies, but by democratic accountability which will have an effect in changing not only the culture and forms of communication of communities themselves but also in opening out the equally ghettoised mentality of the majority of police officers which the various exercises of the last few years in 'corporate image' management, codes of conduct, statements of purpose, 'meet the public' operations (as in the Metropolitan Police 'Plus Programme') have done little or nothing to change. Thus the drift towards military policing in the poor areas of our cities, which we outlined in *What Is To Be Done?*, will continue. In such areas military policing – the periodic mass drugs raid with a sizeable arrest rate, the occasional stop and search operation in an area well targeted by intelligence gathering, driving the burglars, street-robbers and drug-dealers underground for a short while – is probably what cost-effectiveness and value for money will dictate.

A final component of government strategy was to depoliticize crime as much as possible by shifting the focus from the police to the responsibilities of the public through promoting the growth of Neighbourhood Watch and other crime prevention activities. The appropriate theorization appeared in the guise of what has come to be called 'administrative criminology' popular in Home Office circles in the second half of the 1980s. Administrative criminology has a paradoxical affinity with many aspects of left idealist thinking about crime. Both stress the exaggerated fear of crime on the part of the public, pinpointing the mass media as the source of undue anxiety. Both seem to relegate the police to a marginal role in the fight against the majority of crime. For the new administrative criminologists the police can do little against the majority of crime which is both minor and opportunistic. Indeed the police should restrict their role to dealing with 'serious' crime (in which they are seen to be effective) and to the more symbolic role of maintaining public order, while for left idealists the police cannot and indeed never have had the intention of controlling crime, being rather more concerned with the maintenance of the present inequitable social order. Either way, the result is a circumvention of the police. For the administrative criminologists situational crime prevention was the most appropriate way to deal with 'street' crime, while left idealism is concerned with a politics of exposing police malpractice but avoiding advocacy of any policies that might seem to allocate a role in crime control even to a reconstructed and democratized police force.

Left idealism has meanwhile seen crime prevention as part of a well-orchestrated strategy of surveillance and political control. Thus for Paul Gordon 'Neighbourhood Watch is clearly aimed at mobilizing support for the police among the middle class and "respectable" working class and, at the same time, as a means of gathering low level intelligence' (Gordon 1987 p. 139).

Crime prevention has proved largely ineffective in controlling the rise in crime, and the quality of 'intelligence' it gathers is dubious. The entire weight of research (Rosenbaum 1988, McConville and Shephard 1992) suggests that such schemes as Neighbourhood Watch make little difference to crime rates, that they are short lived as effective institutions, that police subculture is generally antagonistic to them, and that they are easiest to set up in middle-class residential areas where crime rates are low but where there is concern that they are rising, and where there is already a sizeable level of support for the police. In poor inner city and peripheral housing estates blighted by crime and drugs, where police–community relations are virtually non existent, this type of crime prevention is not working.

We conclude by re-emphasizing our commitment to democratic policing in terms of the wider perspective that we introduced at the beginning of our discussion.

## The Police

Democratic accountability of policing to properly elected local government bodies who have responsibility for the direction of policing policy increases public support and willingness to give information about crime to the police, and creates the basis for a more open police force and a breaking down of the ghettoised 'them and us' view of the public which still by and large characterizes police culture.

## The Community

Democratic accountability enables the community to institutionalize meaningful political debate about what its crime problems are and how best they are to be dealt with. It enables minorities and disadvantaged groups within the community – women, the old, ethnic minorities, young people, gay and lesbian people – to have a direct local debate and discuss the similarities as well as the differences in the problems they face. The result will be the possibility of a more consensual and more effective system of community social control and prevention of crime. The extension of democracy is of course only possible on the firm foundation of economic development: of jobs that have a future and that provide a fair income, housing and living conditions of which people can be proud, an education system that provides training for democratic participation, and a proper system of welfare support for communities and families. These measures provide the material basis for a strong community and ameliorate criminogenic conditions.

## Victims

Democratic accountability integrates the victim and the rest of the community. Victim groups will be able to mobilize and present their problems to the rest of the community rather than simply lobbying a faceless central government, a powerless local government, or a local police force whose response will be determined purely by the presence or absence of imaginative and sympathetic senior officers. This requires resources for adequate levels of victim compensation and a framework of victim–offender mediation and reconciliation schemes where appropriate.

## Offenders

Democratic control can lay the basis for a demarginalization of the offender. Strategies for community alternatives to custody –

which are taking an increasingly punitive form under the present government – can be widened out to include ex-offenders discussing the impact of their crimes with community groups, school kids, etc. In this context the reform not only of policing but also of sentencing is necessary to secure fair and equal treatment and to exploit alternatives to imprisonment to their fullest extent. Such policies exist at present, of course, but an overall democratization of crime control would provide the basis for their extension and consolidation, for what John Braithwaite (1989) calls 'reintegrative shaming'. Only a strong, secure and democratically organized community can hope to reintegrate its offenders.

Such policies look perhaps further away now than they did in the early 1980s. The difference between then and now is the decimation of local government funding and the closure of the Greater London Council and the Metropolitan Authorities. The future does not look bright. The most likely results of government policy will be an exacerbation rather than an amelioration of the tendencies we first outlined in *What Is To Be Done?* – cost-effective, episodic military policing in the increasingly impoverished inner cities and peripheral housing estates, and cost-effective community policing in the suburbs, and the creation of Los Angeles in London, Liverpool, Birmingham, Manchester: patchwork conurbations where poverty, crime and harsh policing exist side by side with affluence and consensus policing.

John Lea
Jock Young
August 1992

# References

Blumstein, A. 1982. 'On the Racial Disproportionality of the United States Prison Population' *Journal of Criminal Law and Criminology* p. 73.

Box, S. 1983. *Crime, Power and Mystification*. Tavistock.

Braithwaite, J. 1989. *Crime, Shame and Reintegration*. Cambridge University Press.

Cloward, R. and Ohlin, L. 1960. *Delinquency and Opportunity*. Free Press.

Crawford, A. et al. 1993. *Crime in the Inner City*. London, Routledge.

Currie, E, 1985. *Confronting Crime*. New York, Pantheon.

Currie, E. 1990. Crime in the Market Society: lessons from the United States. Paper to Conference on Crime and Policing. Islington.

Davis, M. 1990. *City Of Quartz: Excavating the Future in Los Angeles*. London, Verso.

Field, S. 1991. *Trends in Crime and their Interpretation*, London, HMSO.

Fitzgerald, M. 1990. 'Crime: an Ethnic Question?' *Home Office Research Bulletin 28* pp. 23–37

Gordon, P. 1987. 'Community Policing: Towards a Local Police State?' in Scraton, P. ed. *Law, Order and the Authoritarian State*. Milton Keynes, Open University Press.

Hood, R. 1992 *Race and Sentencing*. Oxford, Clarendon Press.

Kinsey, R. et al. 1986. *Losing The Fight Against Crime*. Oxford, Blackwell.

Lea, J. 1992. 'The Analysis of Crime' in Young, J. Matthews, R. eds. *Rethinking Criminology: the Realist Debate*. London, Sage.

Lynch, M. 1990. 'Racial Bias in Criminal Justice' in MacLean, B. and Milanovic, D.

Lynch, M. and Patterson, E. 1990. 'Racial Discrimination and the Criminal Justice System' in MacLean, B. and Milanovic, D.

MacLean, B. and Milanovic, D. eds. 1990. *Racism, Empiricism and Criminal Justice*. Vancouver, The Collective Press.

Mayhew, P. and Maung, N. 1993 *The 1992 British Crime Survey*. London, HMSO.

McConville, M. and Shephard, D. 1992 *Watching Police, Watching Communities*. London, Routledge.

Morgan, R. 1989. 'Policing By Consent: Legitimating the Doctrine' in Morgan, R. and Smith, D. eds. *Coming To Terms With Policing*. London, Routledge.

Pearce, F. and Tombs, S. 1989. 'Union Carbide: Bhopal and Hubris of Capitalist Technocracy' *Crime and Social Justice* (June).

Pearce, F. and Tombs, S. 1992. 'Realism and Corporate Crime' in *Issues in Realist Criminology* (ed) R. Matthews and J. Young. London, Sage.

Pearson, G. 1983. *Hooligan*. London, Macmillan.

Reiman, J. 1979. *The Rich get Richer and the Poor Get Prison*. New York, Wiley.

Rosenbaum, D. 1988. 'A Critical Eye on Neighbourhood Watch: Does it Reduce Crime and Fear? in Hope, T. and Shaw, M. eds. *Communities and Crime Reduction*. London, HMSO.

Wilbanks, W. 1987. *The Myth of a Racist Criminal Justice System*. New York, Brooks-Cole.

Wilson, W. 1987. *The Truly Disadvantaged*. Chicago, University of Chicago Press.

Young, J. 1992. 'Ten Points of Realism' in Young, J. and Matthews, R. (eds) *Rethinking Criminology*. London, Sage.

**What Is To Be Done
About Law and Order?**

The text pages start at page 11 – pages 1–10 of
the original have been replaced by the new introduction
which has roman numerals.
The introduction is not indexed.

# 1  Is Crime a Problem?

We are caught between two opposing views on crime: the mass media and a substantial section of right-wing opinion are convinced that the crime rate is rocketing, that the war against crime is of central public concern and that something dramatic must be done to halt the decline into barbarism. The left, in contrast, seeks to minimize the problem of working-class crime; left-wing criminology has – with a few notable exceptions – spent most of the last decade attempting to debunk the problem of crime. It has pointed to the far more weighty crimes of the powerful, stressing how the working class has much more pressing problems. It sees the war against crime as a side-track from the class struggle, at best an illusion invented to sell news, at worst an attempt to make the poor scapegoats by blaming their brutalizing circumstances on themselves. A new left realism about crime must seek to navigate between these two currents. It must neither help fan moral panic nor must it make the serious political mistake of neglecting discussion of crime – leaving the running to the conservative press. But it must be objective and try to assess the actual threat of crime: its impact, its relative impact compared with other social problems, and who its targets are.

We have chosen to focus largely on what are conventionally thought of and defined as crimes, but not because we are unaware of the severe and perhaps greater impact of crimes committed by the upper and middle classes. Thus we will consider assault against the person rather than crimes at work due to violation of safety regulations; burglary rather than income tax evasion; theft of motor cars rather than corporate criminality. Our

emphasis on official crime is not accidental – it aims to·redress
the balance in radical thinking.

Radical criminology and exposé journalism, over the last two
decades, have done a vital job in showing up the calculated
violence and cupidity of the powerful. But in their attempt
to counter the mass media they have evolved a blind spot about
the crimes which most of the population see as worrying. Even
more problematically, they have suggested that these public
concerns are creations of the media. We will argue to the contrary that there is an only too real problem of crime in this
country. But first of all, let us clear up the problem of what
criminal statistics really mean, for without a sense of their construction and their basis (both in value judgements by people
*and* in objective actions in the world against people), we will
be unable to grasp their true significance.

Consider the following headline from the *Guardian*, 22 July
1982: YEAR OF STREET DISTURBANCE SAW 11% RISE IN
SERIOUS CRIME. The first and paramount thing to realize about
crime statistics is that they are not hard facts. They look hard;
the figure of 11 per cent seems precise enough. But the fact that
a piece of information is given a numerical value – even if it has
decimal places in it – does not mean that it is of the same order
as, say, the statement 'the house was 20.6 metres high'. For the
height of the house is open to very little variation in *interpretation*
(you might argue over what points you are measuring from) and
the resources used to measure it would make very little difference
(apart from in your degree of precision), but criminal statistics
are another matter. Both the interpretation of whether or not an
act is criminal and the resources available for labelling acts as
criminal make an enormous amount of difference to the final
statistic. Nor is this a result of an imperfect world where, if only
we had more tightly written laws and a lot more police, we could
arrive at the 'true' crime rate. Rather, it lies in the nature of
crime itself that there is an important level of human inter-

pretation in the definition of what is criminal. Moreover, this is logically necessary and morally desirable.

Laws are written in general ways so that they have to be interpreted to fit specific events. What, for instance, is the meaning of 'pornographic'? How grievous is an injury before it becomes 'grievous bodily harm'? What is 'murder' and what is 'manslaughter'? The very basic questions of whether an act fits into the categories set down by the law and whether or not it was intentional are all quite necessarily and justifiably subject to interpretation: it makes a great difference to the agent whether his action is defined as murder or manslaughter. This is strikingly brought out if one compares definitions of crime in different countries, or even if one notes the changes that occur over time in the same country. For example, as far as the latter is concerned, Professor McClintock writing about England and Wales has argued very convincingly that:

> One of the main causes for an increase in the recording of violent crime appears to be a decrease in the toleration of aggressive and violent behaviour, even in those slum and poor tenement areas where violence has always been regarded as a normal and acceptable way of settling quarrels, jealousies or even quite trivial arguments. (McClintock, p. 74)

Much the same conclusion was arrived at by President Johnson's Commission on Law Enforcement in the United States (see Winslow, p. 50). Thus, something as important as the measure of serious crimes of violence varies according to the subjective tolerance and assessment of the public. Not that this detracts from its reality, for serious crime *really* is what people at a particular time define as serious.

The second condition which underlines this problem of definition is a material consideration: the amount of the resources at the disposal of the police and the courts to deal with crime. For to implement the simple 'law-and-order' requirement in every case of illegality that occurs not only begs the definitional question but ignores the stark facts of limited resources. The statute book is full of laws that no one in their right mind would think worth enacting or where, as in the case of Mary Whitehouse prosecuting the editor of *Gay News* under the archaic laws against blasphemy, a statute is resuscitated for very particular political purposes. Furthermore there is such a sheer quantity of law that there would need to be a police and judicial system of unparalleled proportions to cope with it. Fortunately, and realistically, we exist in a world of limited resources. Because of this, choices have to be made as to which crimes to act against and this too involves a subjective decision, not a technical, object-ive choice which could be arrived at by studying the statute books and then assessing the social problems which exist in the world.

Thus, instead of the notion of statistics which have a reality independent of those who formulate, generate, and collect them, we have, in fact, a number which is a joint product of sub-jective assessment, material resources and – as defined in these terms – troublesome behaviour in the world. Choices, then, have to be made and these choices involve political decisions. From the politics entailed in getting a law on to the statute book, to the decisions concerning how to interpret it, to the exercise of police discretion in its application, to the public responses to it – all these stages involve politics and all involve a struggle.

Let us examine the stages through which an act deemed illegal reaches the pages of the annual criminal statistics:

Acts known to the public

↓

Crimes known to the public

↓

Crimes reported to the police

↓

Crimes registered by the police

↓

Crimes deemed so by the courts

↓

The 'official' statistics

At each of these stages subjective interpretations enter: does the member of public concerned think it worth reporting to the police (that is, is it a real crime and even if it is, will the police do anything about it)? Do the police think it a real crime worthy of committing resources? And does the court concur? At each stage there is a subjective interpretation, very often involving conflict (for instance, the police may think the crime not worth bothering about but the member of the public will) and often a reclassification (for instance, the crime begins as suspected murder and ends up as manslaughter). The hard figures, then, presented to us by the police and media as the state of play regarding crime in the country have to be interpreted with extreme caution. It is not that they are meaningless; they do reflect public, police and court definitions of crime, the disposal of limited resources, and the extent of infractions thus defined; but what they do not do is tell us about an independent entity called 'crime', because by its nature no such *fact* exists.

To illustrate the unrealistic nature of statistics, note the revealing observation in the *Police Review* on the prosecution of homosexuals prior to the Sexual Offences Act of 1967 (see Chapman, chapter 4):

Vice is of greatest concern to the Police when it is of a kind which can lead to crimes such as grievous bodily harm, robbery and blackmail. This is why most Forces keep a close watch on importuning by men, in spite of the current demands that homosexual acts between consenting male adults should no longer be regarded as offences against the criminal law. Manchester is evidently one of the Forces which believe that the law should be strictly enforced, and some figures included in the Chief Constable's annual report in fact reveal a radical change of policy during the past few years. In 1955 there was one prosecution for importuning, in 1956 and 1957 there were none and in 1958 there were two. Mr A. J. McKay was appointed Chief Constable at the end of that year, and the number of prosecutions rose to thirty in 1959 and 105 in 1960, to 135 in 1961, to 216 last year. The inescapable conclusion to be drawn from these figures is that until 1958 a blind eye was turned on importuning and that prosecutions were not encouraged by the Chief Constable. (*Police Review*, 3 August 1963, p. 721)

Now no one in their right mind would believe that the number of homosexual acts in Manchester increased one-hundred-and-eight-fold between 1958 and 1963, yet that is exactly what the official statistics would tell one. That is what a headline writer in a newspaper could have construed from perusing the Chief Constable's report. Yet, of course, the 'staggering' increase had a great deal to do with the predilections of the Chief Constable and very little to do with the changing desires of gay men.

We have pointed out the subjective and political nature of the 'official' criminal statistics. This is not to suggest that the crime problem lacks reality; far from it. It is to say that we must handle the figures with caution, and, most importantly, that we must develop a sense of realism. We must avoid both the alarmism which takes the figures simply at their face value and the sense of false calm which insists that the same statistics are a mere product of police practices, which is a total misapprehension of the actual threats to life and property which confront the mass of the population.

The public are bombarded by crime news daily in the mass media: it is a staple of news, and it is therefore legitimate to ask to what extent our fears are exaggerated and distorted. For there are many who would argue that the public alarm about crime is a distraction fabricated by the powerful to take attention away from the real problems of society. We will argue against this, but not in a dismissive fashion. For as we have seen, the 'crime rate' is not a simple, obvious fact and the public fear of crime contains both realistic and fantastic elements. With this in mind we have asked a series of sceptical questions regarding the statistics in order to develop a realistic approach to their use.

1 ISN'T THE CRIME RATE EXAGGERATED?
Besides the official statistics of crimes known to the police, there are two other chief ways of measuring the rate of crime: self-report studies, where offenders list their misdemeanours, and victimization surveys, where the victims themselves note the crimes committed against them. Self-report studies are obviously flawed by the unwillingness of people to admit their guilt even anonymously, but victimization studies, despite minor problems, are of much greater validity (see *Crime Statistics England and Wales*, HMSO, 1980, Appendix I). In victimization studies you simply ask a sample of the population, using a check list, how many crimes have been committed against them in the last year. Although there are reasons why people would still conceal or exaggerate their victimization (for example, embarrassment because the crime involved a member of the family, or wariness because of a fake insurance claim), victimization studies have obvious advantages over the official statistics. By contrasting victimization surveys with the official statistics we have a fair estimation of the so-called 'dark figure', the proportion of crimes unknown to the police. Victimization studies have been carried out in a large number of countries, including Australia, Canada, Israel, the Netherlands and Sweden. In all cases the dark figure has been shown to be considerable, to be an underestimate, and to vary between offences. For example, in the most extensive study ever undertaken, the American National Crime Survey, the percentage of victimizations reported to the police in the case of rape was 49 per cent, purse-snatching 38 per cent and robbery with violence 65 per cent (see *Criminal Victimization in the United States*, 1978, Table 87, p. 72).

Up till now in Britain we have had to rely on American evidence despite a few very useful local studies, but in 1981, after much political debate, the Home Office spent a quarter of a million pounds on an extremely thorough victimization study. We reproduce a diagram of their findings (Figure 1.1) which

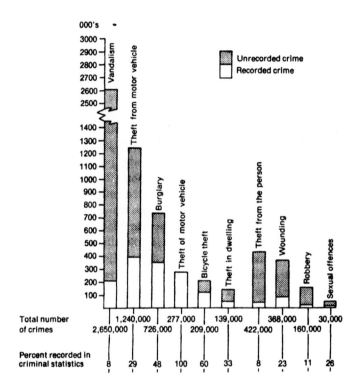

Figure 1.1. Levels of recorded and unrecorded crime, 1981

show that only a quarter of sexual offences, a half of burglaries, and a small proportion of vandalism are recorded, yet all car thefts are. Taking crimes of violence together – sexual offences, robbery and wounding – there were five times as many incidents as were recorded; taking incidents involving property, four times. The researchers insist that these figures are only estimates, but add that if anything they are underestimates because of respondents' forgetfulness or reluctance to admit offences against them. Victimization reports which occur through official channels – such as the Home Office research project just cited – are bound to cause concern and concealment among a significant proportion of the respondents. If the crime involved an acquaintance (for instance, marital rape, or violence between friends), or was part of an illegal enterprise in which the individual had been involved, or simply 'better forgotten' – all these situations would cause the respondent to falsify his returns.

But there are even more fundamental reasons for such underestimation. As Steve Box (p. 62) notes:

> People can report having been victims of crime only if they know they have been victimized. However, in many instances of corporate crime, white-collar crime, and other forms of respectable and not so respectable crimes, persons remain totally unaware that they are victims. Since most of these crimes are serious in that they involve vast sums of money and frequently result in human suffering, then victimization surveys fail in a decisive way to reflect the amount of crime being committed. At the moment, it appears that these surveys are viable only for measuring 'conventional crimes' such as rape, robbery, assault, burglary and larceny. In this sense, their deficiency resembles that of official statistics.

Not only quantitatively, then, but also qualitatively there are considerable reasons for seeing the dark figure to be much larger than is imagined – even by victimization studies.

Against this it must be pointed out that although all burglaries or assaults, for example, are not reported to the police, the

crimes which are tend to be more serious than those which
are not. As Sparks, Genn and Dodd (p. 81), commenting on
their own pioneering victimization study in London, put it:

> Our respondents reported substantial numbers of incidents which
> appear to involve crimes against them. But many of these incidents
> were manifestly not of a serious kind . . . many were not reported to the
> police, and would probably not have been treated by the police as
> crimes even if they had been reported.

It would be grossly inaccurate, therefore, merely to multiply
the official rate of crime by a ratio calculated from victimization
studies and arrive at a final 'real' crime rate which made
allowances for the dark figure. Not only does this not give due
weight to the relative seriousness of offences, it evades the
methodological question which we discussed earlier: who is it
who defines a crime as serious enough to demand police action?
The obvious danger is that the victimologist takes it upon himself
or herself to define which crimes deserve attention, so that the
dark figure becomes a construction of these definitions rather
than of the promptings of the people interviewed. While keeping
this in mind, there no doubt exists a dark figure of crime which
a wide consensus of people would agree upon, which is of considerable size and consists of crimes of a serious nature. Such
a figure considerably supplements the existing official statistics.
Thus, far from the official crime rate being exaggerated, it is
undoubtedly the case that over a wide range of offences there
is a serious underestimation both quantitatively but also qualitatively concerning particular types of crime. And the victimization studies themselves do not fully encompass the dark figure
on either of these counts.

There are very important lessons to be learnt here as regards
policy. Because of the simplistic yet prevalent belief that official
crime statistics accurately reflect levels of crime it may be that
a rise of the official crime rate is a reason for congratulation
rather than dismay. It may reflect, first of all, greater public

awareness of a particular crime and, secondly, greater police efficiency. Thus the recent rise in the *official* rate of rape in the United States may be the product of the Women's Movement encouraging a greater proportion of women to report their victimization and the progress in obtaining all-female rape squads within the police to deal with the offence; the figures, which we will examine later, have escalated to an extent which cannot be explained by the simple diminishing of the dark figure of crime. But, as far as short periods are concerned, we must be extremely careful in our assessment of the relevance of statistics to police efficiency or, indeed, the lack of it. For example, the Lambeth police have recently claimed that there has been a decline in the crime rate in Brixton. This has been widely welcomed in the mass media. But before we sit back and join in the praise of new police methods, we should note that this might represent merely a temporary withdrawal of intensive policing in the area. After all, given that street crime is often unreported, a change in the official rates for such crime is *very easily* influenced by changes in allocation of police resources. And we can quite easily understand that the new and 'softer' system of policing currently being employed in Brixton would almost invariably result in changes in the official crime rate irrespective of changes in the real rate. It might merely mean that the police in Brixton were holding back and arresting fewer people during their public relations exercise. That is, just as the intensive policy which preceded Swamp '81 (see pp. 175–9) was *bound* to give rise to an increase in recorded crime, the soft methods are very likely to give rise to a decrease.

## 2 THE CRIME RATE MAY BE UNDERESTIMATED, BUT ISN'T IT COMPARATIVELY LOW ANYWAY?

The homicide rate of England and Wales is 1.1 per 100,000 of the population; against the rest of the world it compares very favourably (see Table 1.1). In the first place one should,

Table 1.1. *Homicide rate per 100,000 of population*

| | |
|---|---|
| Australia | 1.8 |
| Brazil | 10.8 |
| Canada | 2.5 |
| Colombia | 25.5 |
| Czechoslovakia | 1.1 |
| Germany (West) | 1.1 |
| Greece | 0.7 |
| Guatemala | 14.0 |
| Hungary | 2.6 |
| Israel | 4.5 |
| Japan | 1.5 |
| Mexico | 22.0 |
| The Netherlands | 0.9 |
| New Zealand | 1.6 |
| Scotland | 1.5 |
| Switzerland | 0.7 |
| United States | 10.3 |

as argued previously, treat these figures with healthy scepticism. The differences in recording practices and reporting to the police between, say, the Netherlands and Colombia are, of course, immense. But, allowing for the fact that countries with very high homicide rates probably have a *larger* dark figure of murders than those with lower, we can note the very striking contrast between most of the advanced industrial countries and some – though by no means all – of the Third World nations. The only exception is the United States which has an extraordinarily high homicide rate for a developed country. As in many other instances, it should be noted that the States is an exceptional rather than a typical capitalist country. Warnings of a crime rate which is heading in the direction of America should be taken with a pinch of salt. The extreme heterogeneity of its population and the overwhelming competitiveness of its ethos make it a maverick nation in terms of quantity of crime, although qualitatively the class, age and gender breakdown of victims and offenders is often remarkably similar. As Ian Taylor puts it (p. 18):

> The inner city and 'downtown core' of the average British city may be unpleasant, litter-ridden and generally unsettling and ugly, especially at night, but there is no firm evidence to suggest that these areas are dangerous in the sense that the downtown areas of Manhattan, Detroit and Philadelphia quite certainly are ... In 1975, for example, there were 1,645 murders and non-negligent manslaughters in New York City, 818 in Chicago, 633 in Detroit, 554 in Los Angeles and 434 in Philadelphia, with an overall total of 18,642 murders known to the police in the United States as a whole. In 1979 there was a total of 629 murders in the whole of England and Wales.

England and Wales have an extremely low rate of homicide – lower, for instance, than Australia, Czechoslovakia and New Zealand among the advanced industrial countries – and the incidence of this most serious crime is reflected in other areas of criminal activity.

Further, it should be pointed out that, as with all countries, homicide constitutes a very small portion of violent crime, violence a very small portion of serious crime, and serious crimes, in turn, only a fraction of the total crime rate (see Figure 1.2). First of all, homicides are a mere 1 per cent of all acts of serious violence. Secondly, serious violence is a comparatively rare example of serious crime: it constitutes only 3.4 per cent of all serious crimes.

Let us look at an edition of the *Daily Mirror* (29 March 1982). This devotes five of its thirty-two pages to articles with headlines such as OUR VIOLENT CITIES: BLOODY, BATTERED, FRIGHTENED (front page, with a picture entitled THE FACE OF TERROR), or A BOOT IN THE FACE SPOILT SISTER SANDRA'S NIGHT: FOR NO REASON THIS BLOKE SHOVED A BEER GLASS IN GERRY'S FACE (juxtaposed, incidentally, with a headline KICK OUT THE REDS). This is exaggeration. It purposely takes what is a serious problem and presents it as a

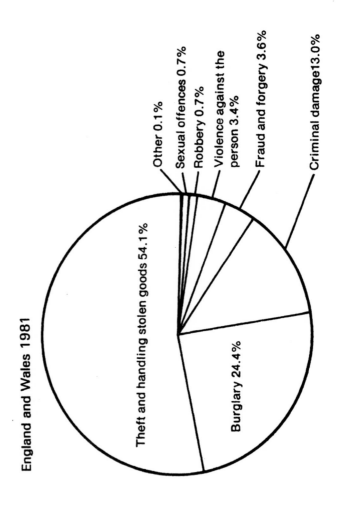

Figure 1.2. Notifiable offences recorded by the police by offence group

typical problem. Whatever this achieves in promoting the sale of newspapers, it certainly creates quite detrimental effects on public consciousness and fear of crime. Over against this we have *The British Crime Survey* (p. 15) which informs us that the average person can expect: a robbery once every five centuries; an assault resulting in injury (even if slight) once every century; the family car to be stolen or taken by joyriders once every sixty years; a burglary in the home once every forty years.

We would be as critical of those who underestimate crime as of those who sensationalize it. For example, Chris Harman, in an otherwise well-argued article on mugging in *International Socialism* (Summer 1981), comes out with the statement:

> The average Londoner still has to live in the city two thousand years before having an even chance of being mugged and even then the odds are three to one against a weapon being used. (p. 21)

It is useful to follow up the source which Harman uses to glean these figures: Michael Pratt's *Mugging as a Social Problem*. In fact, if we look at the argument in this text we find precisely the opposite point being made. Pratt notes that the chances of being mugged in London are, on the basis of the official statistics, 1 in 2,000 per year. But then he goes on to point out that in certain areas this is at least 1 in 1,000 or quite possibly 1 in 500. And, Pratt argues, if you take into account the dark figure of unreported crime you would arrive at a figure of perhaps 1 in 200 in certain areas. Now this is not an insubstantial figure, and however cautious we may be in interpreting it, it points to the need to take into account, when considering the risk of victimization, both the dark figure and the problem of the localization of crime. For extremely powerful reasons, some of them economic (unemployment, bad housing, etc.), some of them social (for instance, the generation by councils of 'bad' estates and the movement away of the law-abiding), crime may be exceedingly localized. Furthermore, any generalization about the objective threat of crime must acknowledge the problems of dark figures and of localization and their interaction. For it is precisely in areas with very high crime rates that crime reporting is least. Thus it is often near to useless to talk of comparisons on a national level which may hide wide-scale variations – compare in the US Salt Lake City to New York City or in the UK Reading to Glasgow – or even to talk of boroughs (Hackney and Hampstead, for instance) and certain areas which are relatively crime free, and other areas, or problem estates, with extremely high concentrations of crime.

Crime is concentrated not only in certain areas but also within certain groups. For instance, in Britain you are twice as likely to be burgled if you are an unskilled worker than if you are a professional, and over four times as likely if you are under twenty-four than if you are over sixty-five (*General Household Survey 1980*, Table 4.4, p. 80; London: HMSO, 1982). And, in terms of serious crimes against the person in the United States, you are more likely to be victimized if you are black rather than white (1.5:1); male rather than female (2:1); aged between twenty and thirty-four rather than over sixty-five (5.5:1); earning less than $7,500 rather than over $15,000 (1.4:1) (see *Criminal Victimization in the United States*). We use American figures here as they are by far the most systematically collected – the patterns of victimization are remarkably similar to those of most Western countries although, of course, the quantity of crime and precise proportions differ. These ratios are high in themselves but when several characteristics are combined they become even more striking. For example, a young black male (aged between twelve and fifteen) is twenty-two times more likely to have a violent crime committed against him than an elderly white woman (over sixty-five), and seven times more likely to have something stolen from him. Thus the objective likelihood of serious crime occurring to a person is sharply focused by locality and by the social characteristics of a person. A relatively low official crime rate overall in Britain reflects the dark figure and masks this focusing of its impact.

### 3 THE CRIME RATE MAY BE HIGH FOR CERTAIN MARGINAL GROUPS, BUT ISN'T IT LOW FOR MOST OF US?

Does this mean that we can resolve the debate about the threat of crime by saying that it is exaggerated in general but has some truth in terms of particular areas and groups of people? If so, then against the position which says that the war against crime is one that involves us all, one could pose a notion of *marginalized crime*, that crime is a serious threat only to those in small marginal localities and in certain social categories. Furthermore, it could be added that there is remarkable symmetry between the characteristics of offenders and victims: there is a remarkable preponderance of young lower-working-class males on both sides of the criminal act. Criminals prey on each other, it could be said: outside of them the vast bulk of the population are in a state of moral panic about crime without basis in terms of real risk of victimization. If this were true, the general proposition that the fear of crime is irrational still holds, with the exception of a minority of social groups in a limited number of localities. The arguments of the radical deviancy theorists of the seventies and the left-wing apologists for crime of today would be left largely untouched.

What is the evidence for this? Chiefly the fact that fear of crime does not seem to be proportionate to the risk of victimization. Let us look first of all at the degree of fear of crime which people have, compared to their actual ratings in the victims league. We reproduce in Table 1.2 the results of a study carried out by James Garofalo on eight American cities. Garofalo's results concur with a wide range of studies (e.g. Clemente and Kleinman), except that the difference between black and white victimization rates is usually found to be higher, which would make the difference in fear of crime more 'rational'. Thus, whereas the poor are realistically more afraid of crime than the rich, and similarly black people more than white, old people and women fear crime much more highly than young people and men, although, on the basis of these statistics, the reverse

Table 1.2. *Estimated rates of victimization and fear of crime among age,
sex, race and family income groups: eight American cities aggregate, 1975*

|  | Rates of personal victimization per 1,000 persons* | Percentage feeling somewhat unsafe or very unsafe |
|---|---|---|
| **Age** | | |
| 16–19 | 125 | 37 |
| 20–24 | 105 | 38 |
| 25–34 | 76 | 37 |
| 35–49 | 51 | 43 |
| 50–64 | 42 | 50 |
| 65 or older | 34 | 63 |
| **Sex** | | |
| Male | 90 | 26 |
| Female | 54 | 60 |
| **Race** | | |
| White | 69 | 41 |
| Black | 72 | 54 |
| **Family Income** | | |
| Less than $3,000 | 93 | 62 |
| $3,000–$7,499 | 78 | 53 |
| $7,500–$9,999 | 70 | 45 |
| $10,000–$14,999 | 64 | 39 |
| $15,000–$24,999 | 59 | 34 |
| $25,000 or more | 56 | 30 |

*Rape, robbery, assault, and larceny with victim–offender contact.

*Source:* Garofalo, p. 652.

should be the case. Exactly the same results in terms of men and
women were found in the *British Crime Survey* (p. 25): see
Table 1.3.

In the United States such evidence is backed up by the claim
that people in general fear crime far out of proportion to the
likelihood of being victimized and that people fear most those

Table 1.3. *Fears of personal safety after dark and risks of 'street crime'*

|  | Percentage likely to be victims of 'street crime' | Percentage feeling very unsafe |
|---|---|---|
| Men | | |
| 16–30 | 7.7 | 1 |
| 31–60 | 1.6 | 4 |
| 61 + | 0.6 | 7 |
| Women | | |
| 16–30 | 2.8 | 16 |
| 31–60 | 1.4 | 35 |
| 61 + | 1.2 | 37 |

crimes which are least likely to occur to them. That is they fear crimes of violence more than property crimes (see Conklin). In England and Wales there is a little more 'rationality' on this score, but not much (see Table 1.4). How, then, is such a state of misrepresentation explained? Not surprisingly the mass media are cast as the villains of the piece – as they are in so many other examples of 'irrationality' which the commentator disapproves of. Thus, for example, the mass media are blamed for the false consciousness of the working class or the incidence of sexual crimes and of violence. The focus on crime, characteristic of

Table 1.4. *Rate and fear of crime*

|  | Rate of crime per 100,000 population | Fear of crime (per cent) |
|---|---|---|
| Vandalism | 1,490 | 1 |
| Assault | 396 | 16 |
| Sexual Attacks | 16 | 23 |
| Mugging | (42)* | 34 |
| Burglary | 410 | 44 |

* Mugging is not a legal term, but all incidence of robbery is 42 per 100,000.

the mass media in capitalist societies, is added to their sensationalism and distortion of both the likelihood of risk and
the nature of the crimes most likely to beset any individual,
and gravely distorts public knowledge. This is particularly true,
it is argued, where direct knowledge of crime is *in fact* lacking,
because *in reality* it is restricted to the margins. As Ramsay
Clark, the former Democratic Attorney-General of the United
States, remarked: 'Most lives in America are unmarred by serious
crime. The only meaningful impression such people can have
about the incidence of crime is made from the press, other
communications media and the police. As crime becomes more
topical, the tendency of distorted impressions to mislead increases' (Clark, p. 45). Indeed, the Attorney-General went on
to doubt the existence of a crime-wave at all.

The final conclusion in this chain of reasoning is of interest.
It is that such an irrational fear of crime has real consequences.
Fantasies transform reality. For 'fear of crime ... has become
a problem as serious as crime itself' (Clemente and Kleinman,
p. 519). The moral panic about crime empties the streets of
people and thereby facilitates crime by undermining the basis
of its informal control by the presence of people, and reduces
the quality of people's daily lives. We will return to this important point in the next section; suffice it to say for the moment
that it can be argued that such irrational fears are self-fulfilling.
Thus, crime becomes more of a problem in the margins and,
indeed, begins to expand out from them as people and police
begin to define areas as crime-prone and effective intervention
in them dangerous and futile.

Such a theory of the fear of crime has considerable impact
and adherence. Let us recapitulate its basic premises:

(a) *Marginalization:*   Crime exists in the minor margins of
society within distinct criminal areas

(b) *Moral symmetry:*   The offenders and victims of crime tend
to be socially very similar; it is the poor
attacking the poor

(c)  *Moral panic:*    The vast majority of the population have little threat of crime and an irrational fear of it

(d)  *Mass media:*    The mass media engender distortions as to both the quantity and quality of crimes

(e)  *Self-fulfilment:*    The fear of crime has deleterious effects in itself, some of which to an extent tend to fulfil these fears.

Our intention throughout is to maintain a position which neither causes panic about crime nor denies its impact. The problem of crime is satisfactorily tackled neither by the hysteria of the popular press nor by the liberal or left-wing commentators who profoundly underestimate its effect. We must, however, take what is useful from the existing literature. For instance, with respect to the moral panic theory of crime outlined above, we shall point to some severe problems in its argument while at the same time learning from some of its more pertinent points.

### Statistical Problems and the Reality of Fear

The victimization rate for a particular social category obliterates and ignores the extent of variation within it. Thus, to say the victimization rate for women is comparatively low obfuscates the fact that some women have extremely high victimization rates whereas others have very low ones. So, just as we have examined the focusing of crime on certain social categories of people rather than others, we must also look at the foci *within* social categories.

If we take two examples of serious crime we find that the variation is considerable and relates closely to class, age and race. First of all, consider the incidence of rape. The overall figure in the United States, which has comparatively high incidence of rape, is less than 1 in 100,000 of the female population in any given year. Although rape is feared by all women, its incidence varies considerably. Thus a poor black woman in the United States (income under $3,000) is almost six times more likely to be raped than a rich white woman (income greater than $25,000). And if you add age to this you get even greater disparities: for example, a woman aged between sixteen and nineteen is seven times more likely to be raped than one aged between thirty-five and forty-nine. That is, a specific social category of female person – lower class, black and young – is at tremendously greater risk (Kittrie). Thus, whereas the incidence of rape in general is comparatively rare, it is not at all so for particular groups of women. To talk, then, of irrational estimation of risk takes no account of such variation.

Such a variation is brought out even more evidently when we examine a type of crime in which men are, in gross terms, the most likely victims: homicide. Table 1.5 gives the deaths by homicide of men and women in the United States in 1978.

Table 1.5. *US Death by homicide rates per 1,000,000 of the population, 1978*

| All females   | 3.9  |
|---------------|------|
| All males     | 14.2 |
| Black males   | 52.6 |
| White males   | 9.2  |
| Black females | 11.8 |
| White females | 2.9  |

*Source: Statistical Abstract of the United States, 1980* (US Department of Commerce), Table 120, p. 81, and general demographic tables therein.

Now, if we look at the gross differences between men and women we immediately notice how males are considerably more likely to die of homicide than females; this might easily form part of an argument which notes the 'irrational' fears of women with regards to crime. But if we separate out the data by race, a strikingly different pattern emerges. Black females have, in fact, a higher homicide rate than white men; the very low homicide rate of white women, and their larger proportion of the American population, has served to conceal and cancel out this fact. Black females are, in fact, more likely to be killed by homicide than in a motor vehicle accident, as we shall see in the next section. At least one section of the female population has, in all realism, a greater reason to fear homicide than men.

This variation is, of course, not only evident in terms of gender: if we look at age we find numerous wide disparities in the threat of crime based on the usual lines of race and class. Thus, for example, if black rather than white, a sixty-five-year-old person is twice as likely to be a victim of violent crime, twice as likely to be a victim of robbery with injury and five times more likely to be a victim of personal larceny with contact (*Criminal Victimization in the United States 1977*, Table 9, p. 25).

The glib pronouncement that there is a puzzling inverse relationship with regards to age and gender between fear of crime and the actual risk of victimization must, therefore, be subject to considerable reservations. None of this – up till now – explains the greater fear of old people than young people, or women than men, *in general*, but it removes *sections* of women and old people (particularly those who are poor and from oppressed minorities) from this generalization.

## The Myth of the Equal Victim

The comparison of fear of crime with victimization rates has a fatal flaw in its logic. It assumes that all people are equally equipped to withstand the impact of a given crime – that we are all equally resilient and similarly vulnerable. But on the contrary, an act of violence on a young male can be a measure of kudos; on an old man it may be experienced with fear and drastic loss of pride. Or in terms of financial loss, £25 stolen

from a rich person is not equivalent to £25 stolen from a
pensioner. Mike Maguire has recently completed a survey of
the effects of burglary on victims within the Thames valley
area, which well illustrates this point. A few of his examples
give one a feeling of the instances of severe reaction to a break-in:

No. 539   I shall never forget it because my privacy has been invaded. I
          have worked hard all my life and had my nose to the grind-
          stone ever since and this happens. Now we can't live in peace.
          I have a feeling of 'mental rape'. I feel a dislocation and dis-
          ruption of private concerns. I have destroyed everything they
          touched. I feel so extreme about it.

No. 976   They had gone through all my clothes. I felt a real repulsion –
          everything felt dirty. I wanted to move – I had nightmares,
          and it still comes back even now.

No. 536   I went to pieces. I just couldn't believe it. I cried so much I
          couldn't phone the police. I was so frightened. I cried every
          time someone talked to me.

(Maguire pp. 261, 275)

The initial reaction was sharply divided between the sexes:
41 per cent of men felt anger and only 26 per cent shock and
fear, whereas only 19 per cent of women experienced anger
and 62 per cent shock and fear. Such a gender difference was
even more evident in terms of lasting effects. Of the sample,
35 per cent were assessed as experiencing fairly serious to serious
long-term effects: all of them were women. And such vulnerability was further compounded by age. Table 1.6 illustrates
the categories of people seriously affected and dramatically shows
the way victimization is focused by social categories and how
the build-up of several social categories (female, working-class,
isolated, aged) severely and progressively compounds vulnerability. Whereas the reaction of the male, middle-class
intellectual to a burglary might be the imaginative filling-in
of an insurance claim form, that of these women was dramatically
different. It was not the property involved; it was the emotional

Table 1.6. *Vulnerability*

|  | Percentage rated as seriously affected |
| --- | --- |
| All victims | 13.4 |
| Women | 21.4 |
| Working-class women | 24.5 |
| Women living alone | 28.3 |
| Women over 60 | 34.3 |
| Divorcees | 40.0 |
| Widows | 45.8 |
| Widows living alone | 50.0 |
| Working-class widows | 60.0 |
| Working-class widows over 60 | 62.5 |

*Source:* Maguire, p. 268.

upset and violation of privacy which were paramount. As Maguire points out (p. 269): 'The irony is that the event triggering off such responses was often objectively a fairly trivial incident. Most of the victims had lost very little and their houses had not been ransacked; more often than not it was still daylight when they discovered the offence and there was no sign of the offender ... Above all, the impression was of people struggling to recapture a lost sense of security.' Significantly, the strongest reactions were found in people who were already experiencing a high degree of insecurity in their lives. It is this fact of differential social weakness that undermines the idea of matching up objective risks with perceived fears and making easy pronouncements on the 'rational' and 'irrational' nature of responses. It also encompasses an aspect of the fear of crime which is always ignored by those who talk about the irrational over-reaction to crime, namely the significant 'under-reaction' of young males.

But, precisely because people vary in their reactions, it might be argued that at least some of them are victims of moral panic.

In fact the different reactions may be precisely a result of such a 'hysterical' panic. Our task, therefore, should be to 'harden' victims to crime by explaining the relatively innocuous nature of its impact. In reply to this we would stress the only too real objective variations in people's vulnerability. For instance, there are wide differences in wealth, and in degree of social isolation and ability physically to resist personal violence. This is not to deny that panic and hysteria can set in; it is to stress the inequality of victims in the face of criminality.

## The Notion of the Equal Offence

Most commentators have noted an important element of irrationality in the public's fear of crime: fear of crime is far out of proportion to the objective probability of being victimized. Further, the crimes people fear most (personal violence) are those which occur least . . . Mass media, sensational journalism, and the tendency to stereotype crime as invariably violent, all contribute to what may be an irrational fear. (Clemente and Kleinman, pp. 520–21)

Just as the theorists who maintain that fear of crime is irrational imply the notion of the equal victim, they also frequently invoke – and with great emphasis – the idea of the equal offence. That is, they claim that the rational person's fear of offences is proportional to the likelihood of them occurring. According to such strictures, it is odd that people fear violence more than property crime, as the latter is much more likely to occur than the former.

It seems to us that there is scarcely any irrationality in fearing personal violence more than one's property being stolen, and the fact that women, for example, are one hundred times more likely to be burgled than raped is neither here nor there. If a crime is sufficiently frightening its *comparative* infrequency makes it none the less intimidating. And as we have seen, the actual infrequency of many crimes is often disguised by ignoring the dark figure and using global figures. We have already pointed out the fallacy of Chris Harman's pronouncement that it would take two thousand years before a Londoner had an even chance of being mugged (see p. 25). Let us now turn to the sequel he adds to it: 'and even then the odds are still against a weapon being used'. It is tempting to reverse this statement and say that in a full quarter of instances weapons are used! It is scarcely reassuring to know that in a case of street robbery there is a one-in-four chance of a weapon being used against you!

Finally, a very obvious point must be made. The lower rate of crimes against old people and women may, to a large degree, be a product of the precautions taken by them against crime. Both groups, for example, are extremely careful about going out at night; and women in particular are very restricted in their use of public space. Fear of crime and of harassment forces them into their homes, but even there, alas, domestic violence is present. It would be an eye-opener to know what the extent of violence against women would be if they did not take the precautions they do when going out in public. To lecture vulnerable groups that they have a low risk rate when their justified fear of crime forces them to take elaborate precautions against it is both illogical and patronizing.

We have demonstrated that the simple dismissal of fear of crime as irrational when it occurs outside of the ranks of certain marginal groups is wrong. The fears of a substantial number of old people and women, for instance, may be exaggerated but they do have a rational kernel. The mass media may inflame these fears but they do not, necessarily, create these fears in the first place. But is there a way in which we can be more objective with regard to the fear of crime? We believe there is and this can be achieved by, so to speak, a mapping of victimization. To do this we aim to draw a distinction between three dimensions of the crime problem. We feel that this radically alters the notion of marginal criminality without embracing the mass-media notions of the all-threatening ubiquity of crime.

## Dimension One: Crime within the Margins

We have noted how crime is focused in terms of perpetrator
and victim both geographically and socially. It is this concentration which is commonly called a criminal area. This term is
bandied about with casual frequency, but what does it really
mean to say that a part of a city is a criminal area? Obviously
it signifies first of all the localization of crime, but it should
be noted that such localization can involve quite extreme foci.
As Terence Morris put it in his study of Croydon:

> Perhaps the most important fact about areas of delinquent residence
> is that they tend to be small and highly localized. On the Waddon estate,
> for example, both juvenile and adult offenders in 1952 were exclusively
> concentrated in the back streets on the south-west corner of the estate.
> The main road through the centre, and the streets to the north were in
> contrast entirely without individuals who had been charged and brought
> before the Courts. Bearing in mind the differences between these latter
> streets with their rows of parked cars and neatly trimmed hedges and
> the former with cycle tyres hanging from trees and neglected gardens,
> it seemed reasonable to assume that on the housing estate itself some
> ecological segregation had taken place, and if this were so, then it was
> probable that it had been the outcome of housing policy ... The net
> effect of segregation is to create enclaves covering a relatively small area,
> but which contain a disproportionately large number of families belong-
> ing to the social problem group. As a consequence, the street play groups
> in such areas are likely to contain an unduly high proportion of children
> who by virtue of their cultural inheritance are prone to social delin-
> quency. (Morris, pp. 186, 188)

But even within these sharply defined localities one should avoid
the common idea of a criminal area as equivalent to a cultural
area. In London, for instance, there are areas around Stamford
Hill where a substantial minority of Hassidic Jews live, and
similarly in Brixton there is a proportion of people of Jamaican
descent. To call these areas Jewish or West Indian makes some
sense, although unlike the ghettos of North America rarely in

Britain is there a majority of people in a particular area from a particular group. But it is not permissible to refer to criminal areas in this sense, as if crime were a central and typical cultural activity like eating kosher food or curries. For this would signify that crime was an activity of a majority of people most of the time, and of central importance to the economy of the area. In reality crime, even in such high-crime areas, is almost always the activity of a minority of individuals at any *one* time – although of a significant section of such populations at *some* time. Furthermore, such sporadic criminality is rarely the central activity of culture as it is with professional criminals.

Professional criminals are an extremely rare breed of criminal, as any short visit to a prison will confirm. The notion of the criminal area consisting of professionals and apprentices committed to the cult of criminality is grossly inaccurate. Rather, most crime is ill-conceived, amateurish and lacks planning – which is *not* to say that it is petty. For instance, the daily 'spontaneous' outbursts of violence in the margins are in sum more harmful than the infrequent and controlled violence of the small number of professional criminals.

Normal crime in the margins is a transitory affair. Kids, for example, *drift* in and out of delinquency: hardened criminals are the end-points of the process of official labelling and incarceration, not the beginning of it (see Matza). They are an unfortunate minority of all of those who have at some time been involved in crime. The majority of those who pass through the penal system are systematically broken: they are rendered inadequate by the system rather than rehabilitated by it. Furthermore, consistent with the notion of certain social groups being more crime-prone than others, it is virtually impossible to imagine a homogeneous criminal culture in an area, for it would have to involve, for instance, the old, the female and the respectable working-class. It could scarcely be made up of young, lower working-class, adolescent boys! Thus, instead of a homogeneous area – a society of Fagins – we have an area which is a focus of crime, interpenetrated by individuals who at some time may act in a delinquent or criminal fashion.

For all these reasons, the notion of the criminal area as a cultural area must be rejected. But the confusion of comparatively high *rates* of crime with typical behaviour in certain localities is a common stereotype in our society. High rates of crime are not cultures. They may possibly have been so in the Victorian rookeries or, perhaps, they may even be so now in certain parts of New York City – but there is sufficient doubt even in these extreme instances.

This misconceived staple of our culture, however, is one which fascinates the media and transfixes people. Furthermore, it lies at the heart of a certain puzzling finding which has repeatedly cropped up in research projects within 'notorious' criminal areas: that however bad the reputation of an area the people actually living there nearly always see the problem as just beyond their own locality. Thus, John Baldwin and Tony Bottoms in the meticulous study of a problem estate in Sheffield:

> The Blackacre residents were fully aware of the estate's adverse reputation (it is widely regarded by police, social workers, and Sheffield residents generally as a 'problem' estate). They themselves, however, did not believe that the offender rates for the estate were higher than for the city as a whole, nor that criminality had been increasing recently (so far as official figures were concerned, they were clearly wrong on both counts). Furthermore, when asked about 'problems on the estate' before any criminological question was introduced, hardly any spontaneously mentioned crime as a social problem for the area. Very many of the respondents believed (again erroneously) that the 'criminal element' was to be found *elsewhere* on the estate than in their own immediate vicinity. This is a fascinating finding worthy of further investigation; speculatively, it is suggested ... that: the great majority of Blackacre residents are indeed aware that people they know on the estate appear in court with relative frequency, but these tend to be regarded as in some sense exceptional and not really 'criminals'. (p. 182)

And Sean Damer came to a similar conclusion concerning the 'crime-ridden' Wine Alley of Glasgow's Govan:

> The day-to-day life of Wine Alley reflects *not* the den of thieves but rather a complex mosaic of stairhead groups which actually live in mutual ignorance and suspicion. It rapidly became clear to me that the amount of mutual ignorance and suspicion in Wine Alley was far greater than one would expect in such a community. For example, there was an ecological equilibrium in the estate with regard to where the riff-raff were supposed to live. People at the North end of the scheme told me that the riff-raff lived at my end – the South end of the estate – but they knew no one there. My neighbours believed strongly that the North-enders were the hard men and the hatchet-men, while the East- and West-enders believed the same of each other. As everybody *knew* there were antisocial families in the estate, from whom there was a marginal chance of physical, and a real chance of symbolic violence, but as nobody seemed to know exactly where they lived, there was a generalized suspicion directed at the furthest point from them. (p. 195)

Important here is how the fake stereotype of the criminal area – of the wild beasts that live at the margins of the social order – has a whole series of real effects for the community concerned. For example, it demoralizes the inhabitants unduly, it causes exodus from the area at an undue level and leads to over-enthusiastic reaction from authorities (see Armstrong and Wilson).

Local foci of criminal activity create areas characteristic of social disorganization and deviancy and high *comparative* rates of crime, especially amongst the social categories most at risk. Who are the victims of crime within the margins? It is true that the offenders themselves have a remarkable moral symmetry with the social profile of the victims. To be male, to be adolescent, to be lower-working-class – each of these social categories, and particularly their combination, enhance the likelihood of the individual being both a criminal and a victim. But once we take full cognizance of the sporadic drift in and out of crime and of the typical petty criminal, it is impossible to have the satisfaction of appraising a moral scenario where a set-piece of criminal and victims reciprocally and alternately victimize and criminalize each other!

The syndrome of poor housing, unemployment, bad education, poor leisure facilities – relative deprivation on all these levels – produces many adaptions. One of these is dejection and fatalism: the passive acceptance of the here and now. Another is religious commitment: the postponement of the here and now till the afterlife. Another is feeling solidarity and comradeship: an attempt to support one another and to change the here and now. Another is rank individualism: an attempt by physical and moral force to separate oneself as an individual from the brutalizing conditions of the here and now. Street crime belongs to the latter category: it is part of a series of individualistic adaptions which promote the notion of the 'hard' individual – the survivor who knows how to look after himself. It is scarcely a cultural innovation which is another reason for not seeing criminal areas as 'special' cultures. For, as Engels so astutely noted, in its individualism it reflects merely the dominant values of the system as taken up in the particular circumstances of the poor:

> In this country social war is under full headway, everyone stands for himself, and fights for himself against all comers, and whether or not he shall injure all the others who are his declared foes, depends upon a cynical calculation as to what is more advantageous for himself ... everyone sees in his neighbour an enemy to be got out of the way or, at best, a tool to be used for his own advantage. And this war grows from year to year, as the criminal tables show, more violent, passionate, irreconcilable ... This war of each against all ... need cause us no surprise, for it is only the logical sequel of the principle involved in free competition. (pp. 161–2)

Out of the heart of the system arise not only the causes of criminality but also the values which make criminality morally possible. David Matza notes with insight how delinquent values reflect not only the individualism of bourgeois culture but also the machismo, cult of violence, taste for conspicuous consumption, thirst for daring and adventure redolent within it. Hustling, inter-personal violence and stealing are not, of course, as forms of behaviour, equally distributed throughout the population. But rather they are the way that conventional values – somewhat exaggerated and exacerbated – are expressed in the particular brutal circumstances of the poor. The egoism of the speculator at the Stock Exchange is not different from that of the hustler, only the opportunities are much greater; the machismo of the ghetto is scarcely absent from the bar-room talk of upper-class men. Al Capone, that epitome of the successful criminal, understood this well when he talked of business as the 'legitimate rackets' and insisted:

> Don't get the idea that I'm one of those goddam radicals. Don't get the idea that I'm knocking the American system ... Capitalism ... gives to each and every one of us a great opportunity, if we only seize it with both hands and make the most of it. (Balkan, Berger and Schmidt, p. 75)

For all the reasons we have discussed – the impermanent, transient, sporadic nature of street crime, the drifting membership, the localization of crime among a minority of the area, and the structural and cultural links with the wider society – we reject the notion of separate, distinct and autonomous criminal cultures. Areas exist with high crime rates; we retain the notion of criminal areas but reject the way in which these margins have been conceived. To aid in grasping this contrast we have summarized the differences in Table 1.7. Working-class crime, then, is generated both structurally and culturally within the system; it is a part of an individualistic response to the brutalization created by multiple deprivation. *And then it further contributes to this brutalization.* To grow up 'hard', to be willing to stand up against difficult circumstances, only too often creates and contributes towards adverse circumstances for others and, in the last analysis, for oneself.

Table 1.7. *Stereotyped and real crime*

| Criminal area | Stereotype | Reality |
|---|---|---|
| Commitment to crime | Control | Drift |
| Style of crime | Professional | Amateurish |
| Organization of crime | Planned | Spontaneous |
| Time spent on crime | Continuous | Sporadic |
| Impact of crime | Serious | Spectrum: pre-criminal to serious |
| Criminals in the population | Homogeneous | Heterogeneous |
| Criminal values | Alternative | Conventional |

Paul Willis, in his analysis of the subculture of working-class boys, notes how it is at the point of 'seeing through' the reality of the 'shit work' that faces them – their destiny as labourers or unemployed – that they create a survival culture. This, with its individualism, sexism and racism – none of which is at all alien to the dominant culture – is not only a means of economic and personal survival, it is also a trap. The culture, generated by insight and galvanized by the need for survival, is also that which ensnares them both ideologically and materially. The irony of their predicament was well brought out by Ken Pryce when referring to the street culture of young blacks in Bristol:

> People ... become the victims of their own unrestrained irascibility. In their day-to-day interaction with each other they inflict much damage on themselves and on each other, in much the same way that the environment brutalizes them socially and economically. (p. 93)

So a brutalizing environment becomes all the more brutalizing by particular survival responses. Some survival responses are positive, some merely make for acceptance of the world as it is, but those associated with street crime are very largely negative. Thus antisocial crime augments the milieu which creates further antisocial behaviour. Not only are the individuals within the margins further brutalized, but the ethos serves to spread and create crime in the surrounding milieu.

## *Dimension Two: Crime around the Margins*

We have seen that street crime occurs sporadically among certain social categories of people within marginal areas. Its prime victims are those who commit street crime themselves, its second those around them. For such crime is rarely adventurous: it involves the victimization of women, older men, and the 'honest poor' – people who are socially close like the wives of marginal men, or geographically close like the respectable working class who live in the locality. These are groups with relatively low offence rates but, as we have seen, relatively high victimization rates. There are two important points about these groups which must be made now, though we shall return to them later:

(i) These groups are often both socially and economically the weakest in our society. They are the most unequal of victims. Those people are involved who are unable to move away – who, because of poverty or social relationships, are fixed in their propinquity to the margins.

(ii) It is largely true that the highest victimization rates are intra-group, for instance between males, between young people, between blacks, between whites, or between poor people. However, this category of victimization points to the existence of an important category of criminality which is inter-gender (men against women), inter-age (young against old), inter-class (lower working class against upper working class), inter-racial (blacks against whites, whites against blacks, and even both against Asians).

To summarize, we are suggesting that if we look at those people who commit crimes most often and are the most frequent victims we are talking largely of an intra-group phenomenon. This is the crime of the margins. However, around the margins there exists a group of people who are relatively low offenders but relatively high victims. These are also the most vulnerable people in the population.

### Dimension Three: Crime beyond the Margins

If we move socially and geographically away from the margins we note a decline in crime (or rather, street crime). Possibly the accountant in Hendon or Hampstead is fiddling the books more and more avidly than the mechanic in Hackney or Harlesden. But crime in terms of immediate inter-personal violence or burglary is substantially lessened.

Let us look at the graphs of crime: Figure 1.3 is a diagrammatic representation of three types of criminal victimization as they vary by income group. (Here again we have used US figures because of the accessibility of *victim* statistics. These curves, however, reflect reasonably accurately, in shape if not in quantity, the occurrence of various types of crime in most industrial countries.)

The three curves represent, with an almost logical consistency and average, three alternatives:

(a) in terms of the most direct violence, sexually and economically, a concentration in the lower regions – the 'margins' of society;

(b) in terms of direct economic robbery with threat victimization is still highest within the margins, spreads out into the middle income group and is rare beyond the margins;

(c) in terms of simple economic theft whether of money or of motor cars, victimization is proportional to income, and spreads out beyond the margins.

The significance of these curves should not be underestimated. They precisely map the moral parameters of crime and they fly in the face of much conventional wisdom either of the left or of the right. We are *not* all equally threatened by crime as the right would assume; neither are the rich the sole targets

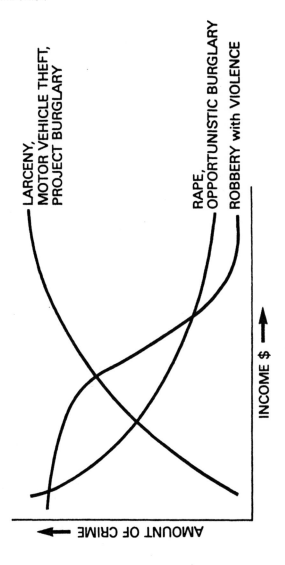

Figure 1.3. Types of criminal victimization by income

of crime as left-wing romantics would presume. The poor suffer disproportionately from all the more serious forms of crime, the middle income brackets suffer more than the rich, the rich suffer only in terms of the least serious forms of crime and those whose impact they can endure, because they are well-healed and well-insured. In addition, they can distance themselves from 'criminal areas' by virtue of their ability to be geographically mobile.

To illustrate this point, it is useful to look at an example where the middle class cannot achieve such social distancing. If we look at the victimization rates of middle-class American blacks who are unable – because of discriminatory housing policies – to escape the inner cities, we see that the general protection which income gives against violence does not apply. Thus a white with an income of more than $25,000 is half as likely to be a victim of a crime of violence as one who earns less than $3,000 per year; a similarly well-off black is only 20 per cent less likely to be a victim.

## *A Reformulation of the Theory of Marginal Crime*

We are now in a position to be more objective about the fear of crime and have accordingly reformulated the theory of marginal crime. Let us recapitulate our findings so far:

(a) *Marginalization*: We have pointed to the differential incidence of crime and victimization among certain groups of people and stressed the localized and sporadic nature of criminal activity. The concept of 'margins' is distanced from the notion of a tight-knit, homogeneous criminal area.

(b) *Moral Symmetry*: We have pointed to the existence of both symmetry and asymmetry in the patterning of victims and offenders. While it is true that the highest offenders are also the most likely victims and that such a relationship is *intra-group*, the existence of the phenomenon of the margins is of great importance. The latter is an inter-group phenomenon, and is aimed at those most vulnerable to crime.

(c) *Moral Panic*: We have attempted to separate out an objective basis for distinguishing moral realism about crime from hysteria. This is based on a close examination of the rates of victimization, the focus of crime, and the notion of the unequal vulnerability of victims.

(d) *Mass Media* and (e) *Self-Fulfilment*: We will examine these two final parts of the marginal crime thesis in the next chapter. Suffice it to say, at this point, that we are beginning to unravel the rational kernel of the mass-media imagery of crime from the layers of mystification which surround it. This is congruent with present tendencies in radical media research which have moved away from simply arguing that the media are influential because they blatantly lie to the population, towards a position which argues that they are effective because they take real problems of everyday life and recontextualize them in a framework which is supportive to the status quo (see Cohen and Young).

## 2  Crime: The Tip of the Iceberg

Up till now we have talked about the impact of crime on people; in this chapter we will ask two further questions about how the impact of what is conventionally thought of as crime compares to other social problems.

### 4 EVEN IF CRIME IS A PROBLEM, IS IT MUCH OF A PROBLEM COMPARED WITH ALL THE OTHER 'BIG' PROBLEMS OF CAPITALISM?

We live in a world beset by social problems: unemployment, bad education, deaths at work, accidents on the road, alcoholism, the medical problems engendered by pollution, the threat of nuclear war – the list is grisly and almost endless. Why should we worry about crime? Isn't this the least of our problems?

Let us note, at the outset, that even if crime were a *comparatively* minor problem, this would be no argument for ignoring it. But we are not satisfied with this: we wish to argue that, on both a real and a symbolic level, crime is a central problem for substantial sections of the population. There are several related points that must be made in arguing that crime is indeed a problem of the first order: its *real* impact; its *symbolic* impact; its *related* impact; and its *growing* impact. We will deal with these in turn.

## The Real Impact of Crime

Table 2.1.  *Deaths by certain non-natural causes*
*England and Wales 1979*

| | |
|---|---|
| Road accidents | 5,892 |
| Railway accidents | 115 |
| Accidents at home | 5,379 |
| Accidents at work | 487 |
| Homicide | 629 |

*Source: Social Trends* 12 (1982), Table 7.20.

In England and Wales in 1979 over nine times as many people died of road accidents as of homicide; a similar number died of accidents in the home. Thus crime does not overall cause death to the extent which occurs in the process of travelling or being at home, although the extent to which one might conceivably expect it to should be borne in mind when making such comparisons. Even so, surprisingly, more people are killed through homicide than die from accidents at work, although this does not encompass the vast number of people whose deaths originate in the workplace (from carcinogens, asbestosis, silicosis, etc.).

Homicide, therefore, is comparatively rare. But this does not preclude our concern about it. For although motor accidents, in gross terms, exceed every other social problem in their violent impact, this does not mean we should downgrade our concern. Let us look at a most dramatic example. F. Whitlock, in his book *Death on the Road*, makes the following comparison:

Compared with road-traffic accidents, war and war casualties affect us far more intensely. During the First World War the United States of America lost 126,000 dead and 234,300 wounded. In the Second World War casualties amounted to 291,557 killed and 670,846 wounded. On the basis of the 1964 figures for road casualties in the United States of America, the number of deaths in World War I would be exceeded

in less than three years and the number of injured in just over one and
a half calendar months of normal peacetime driving. In the Vietnam
War, by 30 December 1967, United States military forces had suffered
9,353 deaths and 32,355 seriously wounded. These figures, incurred
over a period of five years, understandably arouse concern because of
their tragic and irrevocable nature. Yet an almost equal number of
persons – men, women and children – were killed on the roads of the
United States in just over two months in 1966. (p. 9)

Moving nearer home, even in Northern Ireland – although there
have been years, such as 1972, where deaths connected with the
troubles exceeded those from motoring offences – in most years
deaths from road accidents are three or four times as many (for
example 1979 and 1978 respectively; see *Social Trends* 12, Tables
7.20 and 12.37, London: HMSO, 1981).

By pointing to such carnage on the road, are we for the
moment suggesting that we should turn a blind eye to the
bloodshed or war? Far from it: whatever one's political persuasions, one quite rightly deplores its occurrence. So be it with
homicide. Even if we skip, for a moment, the particular nature
of homicide in comparison with that of motor accidents, there
is much that still remains concealed by the figures as we have
seen them. They are gross figures, and if we make a point of
breaking down comparative death rates by social category, in the
method of analysis we have developed earlier, some startling
results become apparent. For although in all capitalist countries
motoring offences, in gross terms, have a far greater toll than
homicide, this is not true for all groups of people – or at least
in the case of one Western country. On examining the mortality
figures for the United States in 1978 (shown in Table 2.2), the
first thing to notice is the high rate of deaths by motor-car
accidents of both white and black men, compared to women (the
slightly higher rate of white males probably being explicable as
a result of the higher rate of car ownership). If we turn to all other
accidents – largely, in this instance, accidents at work – black
males have a significantly higher rate of death.

Table 2.2. *Rates of death per 100,000*

| Cause | White men | White women | Black men | Black women |
|---|---|---|---|---|
| Motor-vehicle accidents | 36.2 | 13.1 | 34.1 | 10.6 |
| All other accidents | 32.1 | 15.4 | 44.1 | 16.3 |
| Homicide | 9.2 | 2.9 | 52.6 | 11.8 |

*Source: Statistical Abstract of the United States, 1980,* Washington: US Department of Commerce, 1980; Table 120, p. 81.

Black men, then, have a higher risk of death by accident than white men and a considerably greater risk than either white or black women. Risks of death by accident, as we might suppose, focus to a greater extent on underprivileged groups. But what is extraordinary is the extremely high rate of death by homicide of black males. For whereas in any Western country it is a commonplace that more people die of motor-car accidents than by homicide, this is far from the case in terms of black males. Not only do they have an above-average death rate from accidents, they have a considerably greater victimization rate from homicide.

This conclusion involves three principles. Firstly, that the global figures often hide the *focusing* of criminal victimization; secondly, that criminal victimization often *adds* to the high victimization from other social problems. The third principle is that of *compounding.* For, as we have seen in our discussion of the unequal victim, the impact of crime on a person depends on his social predicament. Those who are already suffering from social problems are more victimized by the impact of crime than those who are well protected and secure. The *focusing* of criminal victimization very frequently *adds* to the impact of social problems in other spheres; its effect is then *compounded* on unequal and vulnerable individuals.

A clear example of such compounding is the following diary notes of a London housewife:

Set out from a Council flat to deliver the kids to school, calling in at the doctor's on the way home to pick up a prescription. Catch a bus back to find the postman delivered final demand on the gas bill. Also a dole cheque. Once again it's the wrong amount so down to the Social Security Office, there to wait three hours to see someone. Then home to find the flat had been broken into again. Tried to find a phone kiosk that's not vandalized. Eventually get through to the housing department to ask for emergency repairs. Get passed from bureaucrat to bureaucrat. Nobody wants to know. Called the police but they're not interested. 'Happens all the time,' they tell me. (Hain, p. 36)

## The Symbolic Impact of Crime

Crime ... is both a realistic threat and a symbol of breakdown of the social order. (John Conklin, p. 25)

Dislike of inter-personal violence and theft is based not merely on the injury done or the amount of money stolen. Such crime involves another individual purposely and directly violating your property or self. This is not like car accidents which are most frequently unintentional, or like an accident in the home or at work, where injury is sustained through one's own misjudgement or faulty machinery. It may be argued that in all these instances there is – at least to some extent – a culprit. Examples are the car manufacturers whom Ralph Nader investigates for lack of care for safety, and factory owners who do not thoroughly research the likely dangers associated with the domestic appliances they manufacture.

One might go further than this and point to the motor car being a direct product of the capitalist system. Thus, by underspending on public transport and encouraging the form of individualistic consumerism associated with the private motor car, the system leads directly and inevitably to a high death rate. All of this is surely true, but immediate human intention is not there. Each agent of capital pursues his or her interest in maximizing the profit on cars; each car owner pursues his

or her personal interest in easy mobility. As a result we have
the *unintentional* consequence of clogged roads, severe pollution,
and a high death rate from motor-vehicle accidents. Now, it
is not merely that the causes of such a problem are less *transparent* than, say, an incident of street crime. They surely are;
but of greater relevance and of qualitatively different moral
impact is the naked intention of theft and crimes against the
person.

Here is an answer to Whitlock's difficulty about what he
sees as the 'irrational' nature of concern about different social
problems: street crime is much more like war, where clear malice
is intended, than it is like accidents on the road. In fact, malice
is even more intentional in street crime than in war, because
its individualism produces a collapse of human solidarity; it
represents the palpable breakdown of the social order, or the
rampant individualism of a Hobbesian war of all against all.
Crime is a potent symbol of the antisocial egoism which permeates the totality of behaviour and values within capitalism.

Crime is the end-point of a continuum of disorder. It is not
separate from other forms of aggravation and breakdown. It
is the run-down council estate where music blares out of windows
early in the morning; it is the graffiti on the walls; it is aggression
in the shops; it is bins that are never emptied; oil stains across
the streets; it is kids that show no respect; it is large trucks
racing through your roads; it is streets you do not dare walk
down at night; it is always being careful; it is a symbol of a
world falling apart. It is lack of respect for humanity and for
fundamental human decency.

Crime is the tip of the iceberg. It is a real problem in itself
but it is also a symbol of a far greater problem; and the weak
suffer most. Let us take racial harassment as an instance:

Today Mrs Bashir ventured out with her eldest child, Nusrat, aged
five, and took her to school for the first time in over a fortnight – a
distance of about 200 yards. Fearful of an attack, she made her way back

to her home on the Priory Court estate, Walthamstow, via a detour to avoid the launderette by the entrance to the estate, where the white youths – mods and a few skinheads – gather. But someone saw her coming and, having dodged between the pillars and alleys of the estate, he ambushed her at the entrance to her own building. He kicked her twice in the thigh, almost knocking her down. Running off, he shouted over his shoulder ... In her broken English, Mrs Bashir expresses her feelings about the attack: 'They're very, very naughty. I'm fed up.' Her eyes, red from crying, say more: alternately, resignation and despair.

Today's attack was only the latest in a long line. Mrs Bashir stopped taking her daughter to school after a stone – the size of a small fist – fired from a catapult flew over Nusrat's head and struck her at the bottom of her ribcage. Mrs Bashir produces the rock with an air of disbelief: 'Can you tell me why they do these things?' There have been other stonings, and on several occasions both Mrs Bashir and her husband have been forced to run a gauntlet of jeering youths barring the entrance to their block. Now, when Mr Bashir comes home late from the nearby laundry where he works – as he does twice or three times a week – he is forced to spend a badly needed £1 from his take-home pay of £60 a week to get another employee to drive him home.

Yet compared to some other families of Priory Court, the Bashirs are lucky. Mrs Mahmood, two floors below, has not been out for six weeks. A frail, beautiful woman in her early twenties, she still ritually takes the housekeeping from her husband, Ford-worker Tariq, each payday. But when the family needs food, she returns it to him. Last time she went out to do the shopping, she was surrounded by a group of eight teenagers who spat in her face and abused her, forcing her back to the refuge of her flat. Now she feels insecure even there. Two weeks ago, at half-past three in the afternoon, someone bashed a crowbar through the glass pane of Mrs Mahmood's front door. Her three-year-old son ran to see what was happening, and cut his hand badly on the shattered glass. The bloodstains are still visible on the paintwork. The attacker ran off, leaving his weapon behind.

But even this case, in the grey, racist world of Waltham Forest, is far from extreme. In the same borough, earlier in the year, the Saddique family withstood an attack in their shop by a gang of armed skinheads, who smashed their plate glass window and poured a bucket of excrement inside. At the end of April, Mr Maqbool, a prosperous Punjabi businessman, was out walking with his 12-year-old son when he was clubbed unconscious by five youths in a busy main road outside a pub, suffering concussion. Finally there is the Kahn family case. Last July, all the children and the mother burned alive as they slept, when petrol was squirted through their letterbox and ignited. The father survived, but was seriously injured when he jumped from a first-floor window to escape the flames. The police at first denied that the fire was a racist attack, and those responsible have never been found.

The Kahn case exerts a powerful grip on the minds of the Asians of Priory Court. 'Always we wonder if what we suffer will lead to this,' says Tariq Mahmood. 'Will someone have to be killed here too before something is done?' If the violence against Asians of Priory Court has, until now, been sporadic and low-level, the Kahn case adds enormously to its psychological impact, while the very fact that it has not resulted in serious injury makes it paradoxically harder to contain. Mahmood says: 'Always the wife is asking me why I can't get the police to do something. Believe me I have tried. But they always say it is just kids, and they can't do anything even if we know who it is.' (Rose)

We have quoted this study of a Walthamstow housing estate at length because it frighteningly illustrates a catalogue of racial harassment which ranges from clearly criminal offences to just plain nuisance. But they cannot be separated out: the nuisance boils over into criminal violence. The crime sticks in our mind as the most blatant example of such antisocial behaviour, but it is only the tip of the iceberg. A lot of the more frequent, everyday offences are scarcely criminal – they are 'just' kids fooling around – but they are part and parcel of the same appalling aggression towards defenceless people. It is items like this that rebuff those commentators who maintain that because most crime is 'minor', it is unimportant.

A parallel phenomenon to such racist aggression is the sexual harassment of women. Women have to take a considerable amount of sexual harassment at work and in the streets, which severely restricts their ability to move in public spaces, particularly at night. Rape is the end-point of the continuum of aggressive sexual behaviour. Its comparative rarity does not indicate the absence of antisocial behaviour towards women. On the contrary, it is a real threat which also symbolizes a massive undercurrent of harassment.

We noted in the introduction to the book how a political and subjective element must of necessity enter into the definition of what is deemed criminal. Both criminal behaviour and the antisocial undercurrent are constantly redefined by public opinion – itself a product of political struggle. Race Relations Acts define behaviour as criminal which was not previously defined as such; legislation aimed at controlling sexual harassment would extend present definitions of the criminal. Similarly, the current definitions of what is antisocial change over time: inter-personal violence becomes less and less tolerated; pollution is defined in more stringent terms. Not only is crime a symbol of antisocial behaviour in general, but the boundaries between the criminal and the antisocial are constantly in flux.

## The Related Impact of Crime

It would be a cardinal error to imagine that street crime is somehow unrelated to the other types of crime and social problems so prevalent in capitalist societies. We are not faced with a competing parade of isolated problems against which crime has to be weighed: it relates closely to, and is ultimately inseparable from, the other malaises generated by capitalism.

Many radicals, however, would readily admit the related nature of crime but would still view it as a separable problem of little immediate significance. That is, they would agree that crime is an indicator of the malaise of capitalism, but argue that it is both logically and strategically unimportant, and that its most relevant feature is that it is an epiphenomenon – a product of other, more fundamental problems. For example, they would argue that poverty, unemployment and even pollution lead to crime. From this perspective, not only is the problem not at all as large as is suggested, but its cure lies in changing those basic structural problems which determine crime: if unemployment leads to crime with such determined ineluctability, then let us direct our attention to the root causes or else we will always be doomed to failure. If our political philosophy is that of reform, we must whittle away the social conditions which have led to crime; if it is that of revolution, then we must wait until after that fateful hour before we can turn to the problem of crime itself.

Closely related to this perspective is the lack of blame assigned to the criminal. For if the offender is so determined by the massive structural problems facing him or her, then it is morally incorrect to punish the criminal. Indeed, it is not only morally incorrect, it is a proven failure in terms of rehabilitation. For penal sanctions add further to the determination and brutalization of a person already beset by brutalizing circumstances. Thus, grouped together are the conceptions of crime as an epiphenomenon, of the criminal as determined and blameless, and of punishment as inappropriate and exacerbating. Crime, on this view, *is* a phenomenon related to other social problems, but in a strictly relegated and minor place.

All this, of course, is the reverse of the conservative position on crime, in which crime is a central problem: not one created *by* capitalism, but a major problem *for* capitalism. Eliminate crime and a major blemish will disappear from a structurally unchanged capitalism. It is not an epiphenomenon – a problem related to the major problems. It is not a product of poverty – for are not the vast majority of the poor honest? If crime occurs it is a wilful act – the action of a person unwilling to restrain himself. And to have justice, so that the honest person knows that his or her honesty is not to be sneered at, punishment must occur. The balance of justice must be maintained.

In our view, crime is indeed an epiphenomenon: it is a result of the fundamental structural problems of capitalism. It relates to all these problems; it is not separate from them. But it contributes greatly to these problems, both in real cost and in human experience of injustice. It is inseparable from the fundamental problems because it is one of the modes by which these problems are experienced. That is, it is through the epiphenomenon that the phenomenon of social collapse is experienced.

The conservatives stress that crime is a product of the individual separate from the social structure, whereas the radicals point to the paramount effect of structure bearing down upon the individual. Both of these positions are wrong: it is individuals who make meaning of the world, but it is the structures that make available a world of which to make meaning. Absolute deprivation, as we will stress throughout this book, may be a very real, objective phenomenon, but it moves human beings only when it is experienced and when it is perceived as relative deprivation. To be unemployed is not in essence a fact which dismays people. It is the experienced injustice of unemployment that creates discontent.

From where does such an experience of injustice emanate? From the experience of injustice in the labour market and in the streets. First of all it is from knowing that one is, for no sound reason, excluded from the possibility of earning a living wage. Then it is the knowledge that the world around one in the community is based on principles which are unfair and predatory. As a matter of fact, as far as the long-term structurally unemployed are concerned, as the first factor dims in the collective memory, the second becomes all the more important. On the street, in the community, unfairness is experienced at the hands of two sorts of people: firstly the antisocial, and secondly the agencies of the state. By the antisocial we refer to criminals, crooks, hustlers, adolescent tearaways, hooligans, vandals – everyone from the professional criminal to the kid who daubs the council-flat walls. By agencies of the state, we imply everything from the flagrant illegalities, perjury and impertinences committed by the police to the degrading behaviour of a section of social-security officials and social workers. All of this represents perceived and real injustice, and is the way in which inequality and unfairness contrast people. Crime is an important element of this: it may well be an epiphenomenon, but it is the epiphenomenon which makes one aware of the phenomenon itself!

## The Growing Problem of Crime

On the subjective level, crime is a way in which unfairness is experienced in the world, and as such it has a quality not shared by many other social problems: it propagates itself. That is, just as the harshness of crime is a survival mechanism in an unjust world, crime continues and develops this experience of harshness among the poor. As we have argued previously, it further brutalizes an environment already brutalized – it feeds upon itself. Paramount in this context is a feeling of political and social impotence. If crime is a rare event, then it is possible to write it off as an aberration, a piece of bad luck; if it occurs frequently in your area and the police seem incapable and/or unwilling to do anything about it, then it becomes an obvious and blatant injustice. If the police themselves act criminally, then it is, of course, all the more an evident sign of your own political impotence and social stigmatization.

The extent to which bad policing leads to an increase in crime cannot be overemphasized. Illegalities by the police of a blatantly prejudiced character such as in racist attacks serve to break the bond with legality. In the case of black youths, for instance, not only are they economically discarded, but then their political marginalization and lack of muscle is brought home to them by illegal treatment at the hands of the police.

Thus crime feeds the circumstances which create it. But this is only one half of the story. Street crime is caused by the experience of injustice in brutal circumstances, but antisocial behaviour is also a function of the degree of social control. It is a major theme of this book that it is the public rather than the police who are the major focus of the control. That is, in no way is society held together by the 'thin blue line' of one policeman for every 418 members of the public of England and Wales. Antisocial behaviour is controlled, first and foremost, by public disapproval. Secondly, it is important to realize that when the police are needed it is generally the public that informs them. Effective policing depends on receiving a high amount of information from the community. This usually involves the public informing the police about a crime (either as victims or as bystanders) and the police acting upon this. The public are needed as alarm systems, as providers of information, and as witnesses in court. In Mawby's study of policing in Britain, 89 per cent of crimes were reported by the public and only 6 per cent directly detected by the police. Investigative policing, like investigative journalism, is a rare phenomenon whose prominence in the public mind is more a product of television series than it is a reality.

In a situation where the police become marginalized from a community, not only do they commit more illegalities and thus generate discontent with the law, and hence crime, but they receive less information, thus facilitating the successful commission of crime. The following process occurs, which we will develop later in the book (Chapter 5).

So police marginalization contributes greatly to the feelings of deprivation which cause crime and the circumstances which make crime all the more possible. All of this produces a rational kernel to the fears of crime which grow up within the community and this itself has certain self-fulfilling consequences. Fear of crime results in the following interrelated events. It causes those who can to move away from what are seen as crime-prone areas: it increases social segregation. Secondly, it makes people retreat into their homes away from the community. It decreases the quality of life in that it keeps people off the streets: it undermines the public sphere and increases privatization. Thus, in terms of crime, it decreases public information and reduces direct informal social control. When this is combined with increased alienation from the police in the high-crime-rate areas (see Chapter 5), we have a situation where the community not only is distant from the police and loath to provide information but, more significantly, begins to break down and has, in fact, very little information to provide.

Now, all of this is part of, and contributes heavily to, much wider processes of population movement. The prime characteristic of large urban societies is the extreme social segregation that occurs within them. It was during the rapid growth of the towns in the Industrial Revolution that large-scale segregation in terms of class and ethnic groups occurred. Frank Musgrove notes what he calls 'Gresham's Law of Population Movement' within towns in which the 'bad' population (in the sense of those deemed socially inferior) drives out the 'good'. This residential segregation is further reflected in terms of segregated schools, churches, clubs and leisure activities. He writes of modern society (p. 111):

The suburban bureaucrat may live year in and year out without any but the most fleeting contact with anyone of a different level of occupation, education or civilization from himself. His work is at the administrative headquarters remote from the factory operatives whose destinies he helps to shape; there he associates with others of like kind; he travels home, insulated by his motor car from contact with any other order of being, to an area of social equals; his leisure is spent in a club with others of the same social standing. We have unthinkingly evolved, or deliberately fashioned, social concentration camps: places in which one social class is concentrated to the exclusion of others.

Class is segregated from class, young from old, rich from poor, criminal from non-criminal, black from white. This is precisely what Michael Harrington was referring to when he called the massive hidden poverty of America 'the invisible land'.

It is in situations of mass ignorance such as these that the images portrayed by the mass media become of prime importance. Not only is direct information about crime lowered, but public fears fuel the interest in mass-media series on crime and policing. It is in precisely this type of society that one would expect the media to provide a large proportion of one's social knowledge. The type of information, however, which the mass media portray is what is 'newsworthy'. In brief, it selects events which are *atypical*, presents them in a *stereotypical* fashion, and contrasts them against a backcloth of normality which is *over-typical*. Gross caricatures of criminality are portrayed which, among other things, greatly overemphasize the threat of crime, the commitment of the criminal, the

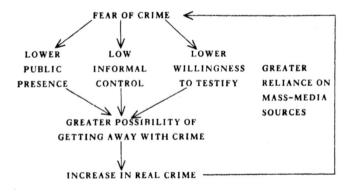

organization of criminality ('the gang', 'the Mafia', etc.), and the ability – or willingness – of the police to deal with the problem.

In this context it is possible to deal with the two latter parts of our model of crime (see pp. 48–9): the role of the mass media, and self-fulfilment.

The result of population movements engendered by fear of crime and all the related signs of urban decay and deprivation is to divide the city increasingly into 'respectable' and 'non-respectable' parts. Around this polarization grow two types of policing; one in the inner city based on force and coercion, the other in the suburbs and the smart parts of town based on consensus. Meanwhile, whereas the panic about crime has a rational kernel within and around the margins – however distorted by the media – it has little real impact within the safe suburbs replete with burglar alarms, hefty insurance policies *and*, in actuality, low crime rates.

5 GRANTED THAT STREET CRIME IS A PROBLEM, ISN'T THE SORT OF CRIME THAT THE OFFICIAL STATISTICS REFLECT AND THE POLICE FOCUS ON RELATIVELY MINOR?

Or as Angela Davis put it: 'The real criminals in this society are not all the people who populate the prisons across the State, but those people who have stolen the wealth of the world from the people.'

The stereotype of crime in our society is that of the lower-class criminal; it is within this part of the social structure that the official statistics point to an unusual concentration of criminality. Further, it is here that the cost of crime is seen to be greatest: as R. Cloward and L. Ohlin in their influential analysis of delinquency argued (p. 10):

In this study, we focus on [lower-class] delinquent subcultures because in our opinion those forms of delinquent activity that are rooted in the prescriptions of a delinquent subculture represent the most costly and difficult problem in the field of delinquency control and prevention.

It has become apparent, however, since the pioneering work of Edwin Sutherland on white-collar crime in the 1940s, that infractions of the law are prevalent throughout the class structure and, furthermore, that in cost terms the illegalities of corporations far exceed those of lower-class criminals. Thus Ferdinand Lundberg notes in his investigation of the contention that the Mafia has taken over legitimate business in the United States that, although there is little truth in it, the corporations in their own right make 'crime syndicates look like pushcart operations'.

Frank Pearce, commenting on such comparisons, notes that while the cost of organized crime in the United States has been estimated at $7 billion per year, the cost *only* of tax evasion by the wealthiest 1 per cent of the population is conservatively estimated as at least $9 billion per year. It is an irony that those powerful groups in society most influential in creating legislation are also precisely those groups most adept at breaking such rules. In the United States, the President's Commission on Law Enforcement produced the figures displayed in Table 2.3, which well illustrates the point. E. H. Johnson comments on this phenomenon of the 'subordinate position of traditional crime':

> Crimes of violence and 'traditional' property crimes get most prominent notice in the mass media, consistent with a popular belief that transgressions by 'disreputable' elements in the population are the crime problem. Yet these crimes represent only 8.6 per cent of the cost of crime.
>
> White-collar offences, usually committed by persons of high repute and prestige in the course of their occupation, took up 14.5 per cent. As individuals, employers, or organizational leaders, these offenders engage in medical frauds, fee-splitting, income tax cheating, consumer rip-offs, political corruption, violations of anti-trust laws, and so on. In contrast, only 4.7 per cent of the crime bill was represented by

Table 2.3. *Estimated economic impact of crime and related expenditures*

| Category of economic impact | Amount (in $ millions) | Percentage |
|---|---|---|
| Crimes against persons: homicide, assault, other | 815 | 3.9 |
| 'Traditional' crimes against property: robbery, burglary, larceny, car theft, forgery, property destroyed by arson and vandalism | 982 | 4.7 |
| White-collar crimes against property: unreported commercial theft, embezzlement, fraud and tax fraud | 3,050 | 14.5 |
| Driving under influence of alcohol | 1,816 | 8.6 |
| Illegal goods and services: narcotics, loan-sharking, prostitution, alcohol, abortion and gambling | 8,195 | 39.1 |
| Public law-enforcement and criminal justice: police, corrections, prosecution and defence, courts | 4,212 | 20.1 |
| Private costs related to crime: prevention services and equipment, insurance, private counsel, bail and witness expenses | 1,910 | 9.1 |
| Totals | $20,980 | 100.0 |

the 'traditional' crimes against property, which received 30 per cent of the arrests reported. Embezzlement was involved in less than 0.2 per cent of total arrests, and corporate and white-collar offenses eluded the law-enforcement net. Yet the economic impact of white-collar crimes was set at 14.5 per cent of the total cost of crime – more than three times the estimate for 'traditional' crime against property. Since the arrest statistics grossly underestimate this greater impact, they are prejudicial in this regard to lower-status groups whose members are more likely to be arrested for the 'traditional' property crimes. (E. H. Johnson, pp. 18–19)

Such a focus on 'street crime' rather than 'suite crime', as Gilbert Geis has called it, has an important impact on theories of crime. When discussing working-class delinquents, it is commonplace to talk of 'the gang', the problems of 'social organization', 'weak superego', 'under-socialization', 'hyper-activity', 'low impulse-control', etc. A battery of tests are mobilized to diagnose the condition. Depending on the theory, knee-reflexes are tested, psychological test schedules are filled out, or relationships with both mother and father in the first five years of life are ascertained, cross-tabulated and chi-squared. Yet it is amusing to note how the principles of these procedures are generally only applied to working-class delinquents. Thus if one takes the 'Ferranti Affair' of 1963, where the company overcharged the Ministry of Aviation to such an extent that they eventually agreed, after a wrangle, to return £4,250,000 – still leaving themselves with 21 per cent profit – this was a near-criminal coup which made the activities of the Great Train Robbers seem a little amateurish. Yet, to our knowledge, only one criminologist, Dennis Chapman (and he with his tongue in his cheek), has suggested that the Board of Directors should be psychiatrically examined to see if they exhibited signs of weak superegos, under-socialization, immature personality or evidence of broken homes, etc. Nor has any subcultural theorist so far produced any account of the activities of the 'notorious Ferranti gang'.

Why is there such an overwhelming focus on street crime and so little on crimes of the powerful? The most common explanations are the opaqueness of upper-class crime, the diversion of public attention towards the lower working class as scapegoats, and the way in which the individuals involved do not view themselves as criminal because their activities are seen as part of normal business or professional practices. There is a certain truth in the insolubility theories of white-collar crime. Often the crimes are hidden behind intricate organizational structures or obfuscated by expensive accountants. In addition, they often occur in a very gradual fashion. Gilbert Geis brings this point out very well (p. 282):

> That the injuries caused by most corporate violations are highly diffused, falling almost imperceptibly upon each of a great number of highly scattered victims, is undoubtedly the greatest barrier to arousing public concern over white-collar crime. 'It is better, so the image runs,' C. Wright Mills once wrote, 'to take one dime from each of ten million people at the point of a corporation than $100,000 from each of ten banks at the point of a gun.' Then Mills added, with wisdom: 'It is also safer.' Pollution cripples in a slow, incremental fashion; automobile deaths are difficult to trace to any single malfunctioning of inadequately designed machinery; anti-trust offences deprive many consumers of small amounts rather than larger sums apt to be stolen from fewer people by the burglar. It is somehow less infuriating and less fear-producing to be victimized a little every day over a long period of time than to have it happen all at once. That many very small losses can add up to a devastating sum constitutes impressive mathematical evidence, but the situation lacks real kick in an age benumbed by fiscal jumboism.

He gives as an example the case of the Coltec Citrus Company:

> The Food and Drug Administration staked out the Company's warehouse, finding sugar, vitamin C, and other substances not permitted in pure orange juice being brought into the plant. Estimates were that the adulteration practices of the Company cost consumers one million dollars in lost value, thereby 'earning' the Company an extra one million dollars in profits. For the average customer, the idea of having possibly paid an extra nickel or dime for misrepresented orange juice is not the stuff from which deep outrage springs – at least not in this country at this time.

And it is, of course, true that street crime is more transparent than the crimes of other sections of the population. Similarly, inter-personal violence is more apparent than the violence accruing from 'bending' the rules of factory safety legislation, and 'mugging' is a more obvious theft than alteration of accounts or the secret fixing of prices between oligopolies.

However, there are many working-class crimes which are difficult to detect, yet to which much greater public attention is directed. Fiddling social security, for example, despite involving much smaller sums of money than corporate crime, has much greater energy put into its eradication. The notion of focusing on street crime as a scapegoat is widespread among radical criminologists. For instance Jeffery Reiman (p. 86) writes:

> The criminal justice system does not protect us against the gravest threats of life, limb, or possessions. Its definitions of crime are not simply a reflection of the objective dangers that threaten us. The workplace, the medical profession, the air we breathe, and the poverty we refuse to rectify lead to far more human suffering, far more death and disability, and take far more [money] from our pockets than the murders, aggravated assaults, and thefts reported annually by the [police]. And what is more, this human suffering is preventable. A government really intent on protecting our well-being could enforce work safety regulations, police the medical profession, require that clear air standards be met, and funnel sufficient money to the poor to alleviate the major disabilities of poverty. But it does not. Instead we hear a lot of cant about law and order and a lot of rant about crime in the streets. It is as if our leaders were not only refusing to protect us from the major threats to our well-being but trying to cover up this refusal by diverting our attention to ['conventional'] crime – as if that were the real threat.

There is indeed a remarkable contrast between countries such as the Soviet Union where the mass media focus continually on white-collar crime and bureaucratic corruption and Western countries where public attention is focused on the street. However, where this Western myopia is presented as a product of conspiratorial activity on the part of the ruling class, we would draw the line. Such functionalist theories of control have very little currency. It is quite correct to point to the way in which powerful people both inside and outside the media are capable of shielding themselves by libel laws and mutual class sympathies. It is another matter altogether to believe that such a strategy has been worked out in a rational conspiracy, as the word 'scapegoat' would suggest.

The last argument in this area is that of the respectable nature of the crimes of the powerful. For example, Mapes notes:

> Last year in Federal court in Manhattan ... a partner in a stock brokerage firm pleaded guilty to an indictment charging him with $20 million in illegal trading with Swiss banks. He hired himself a prestigious lawyer, who described the offense in court as comparable to breaking a traffic law. Judge Irving Cooper gave the stockbroker a tongue lashing, a $30,000 fine and a suspended sentence.
>
> A few days later the same judge heard the case of an unemployed Negro shipping clerk who pleaded guilty to stealing a television set worth $100 from an interstate shipment in a bus terminal. Judge Cooper sentenced him to one year in jail.
>
> In fact, some judges don't think of white-collar criminals as criminals, legal experts say.

However, this invocation of respectability is largely tautological. After all, if crimes are not prosecuted, they are not regarded as crimes by the offenders; and the initial period after a law is passed often involves a change in attitude to the new offence as people accommodate to the existence of a fresh crime on the statute book.

What is correct is that the criminal statistics are a product of class struggle. Laws are passed, themselves a result of struggle, which aim to control, for example, price-fixing, pilfering at work, industrial relations, supplying goods to Her Majesty's enemies, etc. The existence of such laws allows sociologists to talk of 'undetected-crime rates', but the actual degree to which they are implemented is dependent on the balance of class forces at a particular time and place. It is of paramount importance that socialists mount a campaign against the illegalities of the rich. The struggles against pollution, for better factory safety regulations, and against income tax fiddling are important areas in which gains *can* be made and the community united around common concerns. They will also, as a spin-off, put street crime in its proper perspective. But, for several important reasons, it does not obviate concern about street crime.

First, let us examine the commonplace left-wing assertion that we should focus on crimes of the powerful rather than those of the poor. This is wrong, simply because the two are not alternatives. However correct it may be to deplore the lack of vigilance and interest on the part of law and order in the crimes of the powerful, this does not mean that attention should be directed *away* from street crime, not least because the poor are *themselves* victims of street crime. For street crime tends to be intra-class and intra-racial. Thus the poor have crime directed at them from two directions: from those richer than them and from within their own ranks. They are simultaneously more vulnerable to corporate and organized crime and more likely to be victims of lower-working-class crime than those higher in the class structure.

Secondly, street crime is not merely a symbol; it is, as we have argued, a symbol with a very rational kernel. Street crime is the only form of serious crime where the victim is overwhelmingly in the same social category as the offender. It is lower working class against lower working class, black against black, neighbour against neighbour. Much of it represents the ultimate in antisocial behaviour. It is a palpable proof of the harshness of our system and the political impotence of the poor. It is ideologically significant and it has, as we have argued throughout this chapter, a considerable material effect on working-class people.

And lastly, street crime displays the same values as suite crime. As Veblen put it (p. 237):

The ideal pecuniary man is like the ideal delinquent in his unscrupulous conversion of goods and persons to his own ends, and in a callous disregard for the feelings and wishes of others and of the remoter effects of his actions, but he is unlike him in possessing a keener sense of status and in working more far-sightedly to a remoter end.

We argue that what is necessary is a double thrust against both types of crime.

Let us summarize the arguments with regard to the problem of the respective impact of corporate crime to street crime. It is not an either–or situation, posing one sort of crime as a real problem compared to the other. The working class is a recipient of crime from all directions and the working-class poor in particular. A typical scenario is a modern housing estate which has a high rate of burglary, street robbery and inter-personal violence. But this community also has a higher rate of police attacks than other places. The services provided in the area are woefully inadequate as a result of a minority of council workers falsely filling in work chits. The faulty construction of the houses is such that there is a constant problem of heat loss and dampness – all adding to the tenants' bills and a direct result of a fradulent deal between certain councillors and the building contractors ten years ago. The heavy lorries play chicken along the major road alongside the estate, both drivers and owners ignoring the weight and speed regulations. The factory down the road pollutes the atmosphere way above the safety limits; the machines on which many of the tenants work are not adequately guarded.

This is not just a case of the addition of problems but, as we have stressed, their compounding: one problem multiplies its effects on another and they all focus on the most vulnerable. To this series of illegalities which combine to impinge on the poorest part of the community we must add those events which are not actually (or yet) illegal but merely antisocial. The dustbin men do not really bother in the area – the tenants are not organized enough to retaliate. The council does not repair the

estate lighting with any regularity (which encourages crime)
– why should they bother as it is a safe Labour ward? The
police act impudently towards the tenants – for these are the
lower working class, who by cultural background and conditioning, the police have been taught to despise. The social workers
drift in and out of their lives half-caring, half-arrogant – for
they view the tenants as a modern version of the feckless
proletariat.

Thus the material situation in which the poor find themselves
is intrinsically orchestrated to fix them in an inextricable
position. For some this leads to quiescence, fatalism or, worse,
mental illness; for others this syndrome of neglect leads to discontent, and in the absence of politics, crime. Thus this predicament is not only compounded and focused upon the most
vulnerable, but it is *causally* related to the emergence of street
crime in their midst. And finally, street crime itself, far from
being different in terms of values from the crimes of the
powerful, displays precisely the same ethos of individualism,
competitiveness and machismo. To the untrained eye the Jack
the Lads in the pub are very difficult to distinguish from the
young plain-clothes detectives in the next bar; nor would the
competition and pursuit of individual gain of the young hustlers
be out of place in the Stock Exchange. Thus in terms of material
reality and of values the notion of an either–or between street
and corporate crime is nonsense, for they are inextricably linked
on many levels. What is different about street crime, however,
is its transparency and immediacy.

Street crime is an important element of deprivation because,
of all forms of injustice, it is the most palpable. To experience
relative deprivation involves comparison. But to compare oneself
with others takes an effort. As we will show, such comparisons
are both aided and obfuscated by the major institutions of our
society. Education, the mass media, the Welfare State,
employment – all point to discrepancies in the equation of merit
and reward, as they also, at times, obscure any rational assess-

ment of the equation. Basically, people judge themselves and the world, and calculate their relative success and the justice of their rewards in the light of cultural tradition and day-to-day comparisons. None of this is simple; mystifications abound, injustices are often unseen and unsuspected. White-collar injustices, both legal and illegal, are of this nature. But street crime is another matter. It is blatant; it involves the direct appropriation of one's worldly goods, or an only too palpable violence against one's person.

Street crime is the most transparent of all injustices. It is a starting-point for a double thrust against crime on all levels. If we concentrate on it alone, as the political right would wish, we are actively engaged in a process of diversion from the crimes of the powerful. If we concentrate solely on the latter, as many on the left would have us do, we omit what are real and pressing problems for working-class people, and lose the ability to move from the immediate to encompass the more hidden, and thus demonstrate the intrinsic similarity of crime at all levels of our society.

# 3   The Causes of Crime

The three key concepts which we utilize throughout this book are subculture, relative deprivation and marginalization. In this chapter we will focus on the first two, directing attention to political marginalization later in the book.

Culture is seen as the ways people have evolved to tackle the problems which face them in everyday life. It includes language, ways of dressing, moral standards, political institutions, art forms, work norms, modes of sexuality – in sum, all human behaviour. People find themselves in particular structural positions in the world – their age, class, gender or race, for instance – and in order to solve the problems posed, cultural solutions are evolved to attempt to tackle them: that is, people in each particular structural position evolve their own *subculture*. Subcultures, of course, overlap and are not distinct normative ghettos: the subculture of young, black, working-class men will overlap a great deal with their female counterparts. But there will also be distinct differences stemming from the predicaments of gender. And, of course, people in the same structural position can evolve different subcultures and these will change over time. Becoming mods, rockers, teds or punks may all be ways for working-class youth to deal with similar problems. For subcultures are human creations and can vary as widely as the imagination of the participants involved.

All human beings create their own subcultural forms, and although we tend to use the term for the young and the deviant, it is important to note how this is just a matter of focus. Policemen and army officers, for example, form their own subcultures which are in their way as developed and exotic as those that exist in the underworld. But in this book we are focusing largely on subcultures of discontent, so in order to see clearly how this perspective differs from more conventional approaches to human deviance, we will look at four contrasts. Closely associated with these contrasts are the four dichotomies which the theory of subcultures attempts to transcend.

## 1 The Meaning of Discontent: The Subjective and the Objective

In subcultural theory deviant subcultures, whether juvenile vandalism or the latest teenage style, are viewed not as pathological groupings of maladjusted individuals who lack culture, but rather as meaningful attempts to solve problems faced by the individuals concerned. A whole series of terms have been evolved which, rather than explain deviant behaviour, in fact attempt to *explain it away*. Terms like mob, psychopath, undersocialized, hyperactive, primitive, animal, mindless (as in 'mindless violence'), immature, mad, all serve one purpose: they take the observers' values as obvious and 'normal' and castigate other people's values as not offering meaningful alternatives but as lacking value, meaning and rationality. In contrast, subcultural theory would argue that human behaviour is fundamentally meaningful, and that differences in behaviour represent solutions which particular subcultures have evolved for different problems. A riot, for instance, is not a situation where a mob of people have taken leave of their senses, but a response understandable in terms of the subculture concerned. This is not to say that it is necessarily the most effective method of achieving the aims of the individuals, but rather that it makes sense given their limitations and their understanding of the situation. It is, in fact, a common method of voicing protest by relatively powerless groups. As the social historian Eric Hobsbawm commented (p. 379):

No other European country has so strong a tradition of rioting as

Britain; and one which persisted well past the middle of the nineteenth century. The riot, as a normal part of collective bargaining, was well-established in the eighteenth century.

Or take a different type of behaviour. An outstanding study of classroom misbehaviour by Paul Willis dismisses all pathological interpretations such as 'hyperactivity', but analyses how the lower stream of the class realize that they are destined for low-skilled jobs where academic achievement is irrelevant. Their structural problem is that they are being asked to compete against middle-class standards for which their own background ill prepares them, in order to achieve academic qualifications irrelevant to their future jobs. They culturally 'solve' the problem by playing up in the classroom, rejecting the teacher's discipline, despising 'swots', and at the same time evolving a subculture which gives high status to manliness and physical toughness. That is, they begin to evolve a culture which rejects standards which threaten their self-esteem and more relevantly fits their future work as labourers. They turn their misfortune into a virtue. Similarly Ken Pryce in his study of young blacks in Bristol notes how a proportion reject 'shit work'; they evolve a leisure culture which helps them survive unemployment, racism and the few menial jobs available to them.

In this way, explanations of classroom behaviour which reduce the activities of kids to the defects and failings of individuals are rejected. These can be, and of course often are, phrased in a quasi-scientific language (for instance, 'hyperactivity', 'underachievement', 'low IQ'), and they can be at times associated with progressive, caring views (such as recognizing the dangers of lead poisoning in the inner cities). None of this makes them, from a subcultural point of view, any the less suspect.

In all these instances subcultural theorists, instead of viewing deviant behaviour as pathological, irrational or lacking in meaning, are interpreting it as a socially evolved activity with a definite, meaningful rationality. To start with, the theorist is seeing the problem through the eyes of the people in the sub-culture. That is, he or she is granting the group being analysed a subjectivity instead of invoking spurious 'objective' notions of pathology or sickness unrelated to their interpretations of the situation. But this is not to reject objective assessments of the situation, but rather to disagree with many of what pass as objective accounts: they are, in fact, most often attempts to belittle subcultures of discontent. By denying them meaning and reason they are unable to encompass the vital component of human subjectivity necessary in the explanation of human behaviour as distinct from animal behaviour or inanimate move-ment.

But to take the opposite viewpoint and elevate the particular agents' subjective interpretations of a situation without objectivity also poses enormous problems. Are we to say, for instance, that a Pentecostalist, a Rastafarian *and* a Primitive Methodist have in fact grasped the nature of the world they live in in a correct fashion? This is the road to relativism; how-ever 'democratic' it might seem to put the agents' interpretation on a par with that of the theorist, it has obvious pitfalls. At the very least, for instance, the three groups above would conflict about the same social predicament. It is important, therefore, not to take subcultures at face value; one must start from these values, but put them in a more objective context. One must never lose the values; for unlike animal behaviour or inanimate movement, it is impossible to explain humans' actions without retaining their values. But these values have to be interpreted or 'read' from a wider objectivity.

Therefore, to understand present-day Rastafarianism or nineteenth-century Methodism one must understand the con-cepts that the devotees of both religions use, but it would be wrong to limit a study of them to these terms alone. And riots, for instance, represent a collective response to particular predica-ments facing groups of individuals; they must be understood in terms of the alternative ranges of responses available to them, but they are not understood merely by interviewing rioters about their own assessments of their motives at the time. You cannot understand the evolution of a riot without subjectivity, but equally you cannot make a shibboleth about the views of the participants. Subcultural theory, then, attempts to bridge the problem of subjectivity and objectivity: it grants its actors meaning within a world of choice and probability which can be objectively assessed.

## 2  *The Shape of Discontent: The Present and the Past*

Discontent can take on a myriad of shapes, which may change during the lives of individuals or the social trajectories of groups. It can involve the self-debasement of the hard-drug user, the elaborate style of the deviant youth culture, the studied pose of the hustler, the other-worldliness of the religious cult, the obsessive nationalism of the fascist, the dedication of the revolutionary, or the spontaneous rebellion of the oppressed. From a subcultural perspective these responses are neither an obvious result of the present predicament of a group nor are they a simple reflex of its past cultural tradition. Subcultures constantly change under the impact of circumstances and they constantly re-interpret circumstances. Tradition brings a series of interpretations to the present but the present itself changes and, in turn, changes tradition.

Black rioting in Brixton is not an 'obvious' response to the predicament, as one writer has suggested (Widgery, in the *Socialist Worker*, 1981), nor is it part of a tradition of anti-colonial struggle carried over from the West Indies, as another commentator would maintain (Gilroy, 1983). It is a response to the present predicament from the perspective of a particular cultural tradition (which is why many other immigrant groups were less prominent at the riots). It is also the creation of a form of rioting in a specific situation with particular motives which are in no way a rerun of events in Kingston three decades ago.

Similarly, crime is not – as we shall see – a simple and obvious response to the problem of being poor, irrespective of culture, nor is it part of a working-class tradition as some writers would presume. To take the *reductio ad absurdum* of the two instances: suddenly becoming poor and facing the immediate predicament of poverty may often result in a hangover of honesty; and even being poor for six generations in certain foolhardy cultures may result in a remarkable constancy of respect for the law. What we must understand is the cultural trajectory of a group, how their material circumstances change (or remain constant) and how their understandings of their situation fluctuate (or have an air of consistency).

## 3  *The Causes of Discontent: Creativity and Determinism*

Discontent is a product of *relative*, not *absolute*, deprivation. This notion of causality is at the heart of subcultural theory. Sheer poverty, for example, does not necessarily lead to a sub-culture of discontent; it may, just as easily, lead to quiescence and fatalism. Discontent occurs when comparisons between comparable groups are made which suggest that unnecessary injustices are occurring. If the distribution of wealth is seen as natural and just – however disparate it is – it will be accepted. An objective history of exploitation, or even a history of increased exploitation, does not explain disturbances. Exploitative cultures have existed for generations without friction: it is the perception of injustice – *relative deprivation* – which counts.

The concept of relative deprivation manages to capture the creative and determined parts of the process of being human; it refuses to compromise on either side. That is, it is totally opposed to simple deterministic ideas of crime, and theories which suggest that a person is criminal because of circumstances, as if one could, with enough effort, come up with laws of human deviance like one can come up with natural laws of the physical universe. Of course, many writers, such as John Bowlby, pro-

nounce such laws. Broken homes are said, for instance, to lead
to delinquency because of the material deprivation that they
involve. But from the perspective of subcultural theory such
statements are implausible – and indeed impossible – because
they miss out the human factor. For however objective one
may be about the figures for broken homes and the statistics
of the incidence of delinquency (and many criminologists quite
rightly would dispute the 'objectivity' of both of these), a
subjective factor interposes itself in between the two facts: how
do particular individuals and groups experience, and interpret,
their broken homes?

For one child a broken home may be a bit of luck: unwitting
escape from domestic violence and tyranny. For another it may
involve the loss of the parent who would have been a civilizing
influence on their life. Each child must (and will) creatively
make something of this fact; it is not a determinant shove that
pushes a human being in an ineluctable direction. But what
of the high correlation between broken homes and delinquency?
Is this not proof of such simple determinacy? No, for two reasons:
firstly, it may be true that for a *specified* period a sizeable proportion of human beings placed in particular circumstances make
similar choices. But this is not the same as a physical law. Tables
do not choose which way to go when they are pushed: consciousness does not intervene in the process. Secondly, and more
subtly, the process of collecting criminal statistics involves
human subjectivity. We have discussed in an earlier chapter
how the whole concept of what is crime or delinquency is a
subjective decision; and undoubtedly the vandalism of lower-
working-class kids (who have a greater proportion of broken
homes) is more likely to be considered delinquent than the
vandalism of upper-middle-class youth. Thus spraying 'Sex
Pistols' on a wall may be delinquent while painting 'Ban the
Bomb' may be seen as an unfortunate but understandable lapse
due to political idealism, although both graffiti cost as much to
remove. Now, all agencies of social control – the police, social

workers and the courts – are inundated with offenders. There are too many delinquents and not enough people to cope with them or places to put them. Decisions have to be made in order to distinguish a 'real' delinquent from a kid who is merely experimenting or acting atypically. In order to make these decisions social-control agencies use theories of delinquency, a particularly potent one being Bowlby's theory of material deprivation. That is, when confronted with a kid who has committed an offence, they decide whether he or she is a 'serious' case by utilization of case-history reports in which a broken home is a crucial factor in deciding whether to proceed with the case or even incarcerate the youth. In short, if we apply subcultural theory to control agencies, we are able to see how social workers confronted with their work problems make decisions about the classification of juvenile misbehaviour, based on a theory which has become part of their culture in this period and which would self-fulfil the correlation between juvenile delinquency and broken homes. All of this, involving human subjectivity both in the commission of delinquent acts and the classification of acts as delinquent, is far removed from the formation of physical laws of inanimate objects.

## 4 *The Context of Discontent: The Macro or the Micro*

Subcultural theory attempts to place the behaviour of people in the context of the wider society. It does not explain human action in terms of the propensity of particular individuals (for example he is violent because he is a 'psychopath'; she has a large number of sexual partners because she is a 'nymphomaniac'; he is greedy because he is 'evil'). Rather, it suggests that individuals can only be understood in terms of the subcultures of which they are a part. As an instance let us look at the explanation of the relatively high level of drug addiction among physicians:

Take the example of the doctor who faces the problem of overwork combined with a painful gastro-intestinal disorder. As a member of the subculture of medicine he has a considerable knowledge of drugs, both in terms of their effects and also in terms of their required prescription. He also has high accessibility to a multitude of drugs. Secretly, therefore, he prescribes himself daily shots of morphine. He does not see himself as likely to become addicted, as his expertise in medicine equips him with the belief that he can control its use. He will take the opiate in order to pursue ends compatible with his profession (i.e. to continue working) rather than for pleasure as with the lower-class addict. If he becomes, eventually, dependent on morphine, the addiction will be shaped, timed, administered and resolved in terms of his culture. All in all, therefore, the solution to his problem is understandable only in terms of the subculture of medicine to which he belongs. (Young, 1971, p. 92)

And, of course, to explain the addiction of the street addict one must turn to the particular lower-working-class culture to which he or she belongs. It is only in this way that the extremely contrasting lifestyles of two groups who are both heavily addicted to opiates (the doctor usually much more so than the street addict, incidentally) can be explained.

Thus subcultural theory focuses on the group rather than the individual; but it then places the group in the context of the total society. The delinquent gang is not to be understood in terms of the values of an isolated group somewhere in the ghetto; but it must be understood in the ghetto and the ghetto within the culture, politics and economy of an advanced capitalist society. And Punk is not just an interesting youth style evolved out of the blue in the early eighties, but relates to and is caused by the particular problems of unemployment and disillusionment in Britain today. All the three dimensions we have discussed above are given relevance by this insistence on viewing the micro-level (subculture) with the macro-level (the total society). Thus the subcultural meanings given by the agents – the subjective level – become more capable of being seen objectively from the viewpoint of the total society. The history of a subcultural group has to be viewed as the trajectory through a changing, wider, social order. And the subcultural group is creative within the compass of a surrounding and determining totality.

Subcultural theory argues that people are satisfied or dissatisfied according to the comparisons they make. The relationship between the total society and the group is crucial here. People simply do not make comparisons and say 'That is just' or 'That is unfair' on their own, as it were. Rather, the standards and comparisons are structured by forces arising at the level of the wider social order which provide universal criteria not only by which to make comparisons, but by means of which people are actually grouped together in terms of physical proximity. That is, the social order – either intentionally or, more usually, unintentionally – facilitates or obfuscates this process. And, if we turn once again to the topic of crime, a fundamental irony is that what is seen as the most basic example of antisocial behaviour is itself a product of the dominant values and economic pressures of conforming to society. Crime, then, can only be understood in the context of the wider society: it is a product of forces within the totality and, very often, it epitomizes values which stem from the most law-abiding virtues of that society.

## Does Poverty Cause Crime?

Poverty does not cause crime. We know that a large amount of crime is committed by corporate executives, the middle class and the respectable working class. Not perhaps as much, proportionally, as by the very poor, but crime certainly occurs where there is no indication of poverty. Perhaps the quantity of crime committed by the poor is a reflection of their poverty, but even here the degree of poverty does not correlate with the rate of crime.

This can be examined by comparing two ethnic groups of

roughly equal poverty. The best available comparative ethnic figures are those cited by Charles Silberman (pp. 164–5). He notes that:

> In Texas, Mexican-Americans (18.4 per cent of the population) are about as poor as blacks (12.5 per cent of the population); yet 40 per cent of the felons committed to state prison in 1973 were black, and 14.2 per cent were Chicano. Relative to population, four times as many blacks as Chicanos were committed to prison for a felony.

More detailed information is available for San Diego, a large city that is 7.6 per cent black and 12.7 per cent Mexican-American. San Diego was one of the few cities whose police departments willingly supplied arrest data broken down by ethnicity, as well as by race. Below are the arrest rates for the years 1971 to 1973; the last column shows the disparity between black and Chicano arrest rates, relative to population.

*San Diego Arrests, 1971–3*

| Offense | Percentage black | Percentage Mexican-American | Disparity, relative to population |
|---|---|---|---|
| Homicide | 46.9 | 11.6 | 7 to 1 |
| Forcible rape | 39.9 | 14.3 | 4.6 to 1 |
| Robbery | 53.4 | 11.4 | 7.8 to 1 |
| Felonious assault | 38.5 | 15.0 | 4.2 to 1 |
| Burglary | 29.2 | 13.8 | 3.5 to 1 |
| Theft (grand and petty) | 18.6 | 12.1 | 2.6 to 1 |

Similarly, in New York Puerto Ricans are poorer than blacks, the median family income being 20 per cent below the black median, and a higher proportion of Puerto Ricans hold menial jobs than blacks and they have, on average, less education. Both blacks and Hispanics have been termed cultures of poverty, yet if one looks at Table 3.1 one finds an extraordinary disparity (Silberman, p. 163). Overall, blacks are arrested for violent crime in New York three times as often as Hispanics – controlling for population size.

Table 3.1. *Black and Hispanic arrest rates*

| Crime | Percentage black | Percentage Hispanic | Disparity between black and Hispanic crime, relative to population |
|---|---|---|---|
| Homicide | 59 | 25 | 1.8 to 1 |
| Robbery | 69 | 12 | 4.4 to 1 |
| Felonious assault | 56 | 14 | 3 to 1 |
| Forcible rape | 58.5 | 16.6 | 2.7 to 1 |

Now, as Silberman stridently points out, it is impossible to explain such discrepancies in terms of police prejudice. He notes (p. 163):

Most of the usual objections to the use of arrest statistics as an index of criminal activity disappear when we compare black and Hispanic arrest rates, since members of both groups are the objects of prejudice and discrimination. It would be hard to convince a Puerto Rican New Yorker that the police treat Puerto Ricans more deferentially than they treat blacks. It would be even harder to persuade Mexican-Americans in the Southwest that they receive preferential treatment from the police; as a bitter joke among Chicanos in southern Texas has it, members of the feared and hated Texas Rangers all have Mexican blood – 'on their boots'.

Indeed, he adds, if arrest rates are distorted by discrimination they may well run the other way, since there are proportionally fewer Puerto Rican than black policemen. The answer to the differences in crime rates are the different cultural trajectories between groups. Black Americans have experienced a very different history of discrimination from that of Hispanics. Their cultures have come from different social directions; it is a gross error to attempt to explain their behaviour in terms of the catch-all 'discrimination'. Indeed, as Silberman wryly notes (p. 180):

When one reflects on the history of black people in this country, what is remarkable is not how much, but how little black violence there has always been. Certainly, it would be hard to imagine an environment better calculated to evoke violence than the one in which black Americans have lived.

Comparative poverty, then, does not seem to have a proportionate relationship to crime. This is in line with our general subcultural approach to crime. It is not absolute poverty, but poverty experienced as unfair (relative deprivation when compared to someone else) that creates discontent; and discontent where there is no *political* solution leads to crime. The equation is simple: relative deprivation equals discontent; discontent plus lack of political solution equals crime.

## The Flaw in the Equation 'Unemployment Leads to Crime'

The presumed stigma of unemployment together with its obviousness – you are either unemployed or not, whereas the border between poverty and wealth is less clear – should, on the face of it, precipitate people into feeling unfairly deprived and have, therefore, some relationship to crime. Let us start with the simple fact that people of all shades of opinion and expertise take the relationship between unemployment and crime almost for granted. Consider the following quote from the *Sunday Times Colour Magazine* of 9 January 1983: 'Juvenile delinquency is on the increase in China, mainly – as elsewhere in the world today – due to youth unemployment.' Forget for a moment that the writer's knowledge of the People's Republic of China was based on a very brief visit and that there is precious little information on crime statistics in that country. More important is the general law of unemployment and crime which is quoted here as an international law of human behaviour irrespective of time or social system. Thus when Tarleng's recent research report from the Home Office pointed to there being no clearly discernible relationship between unemployment and crime, it was met by a barrage of criticisms. For a considerable number of people, the link between unemployment and crime is conventional wisdom. Let us look at the evidence for a 'natural law' that unemployment leads to crime.

A large amount of crime is intimately related to employment, and much of this crime is, as we have argued, of considerable impact. To take the most extreme example, the Watergate scandal was intimately related to employment, as were the activities of Poulson, Profumo and Stonehouse. Corporate crime, wide-ranging in its effect on the population both in terms of economic effects and physical illness, is by definition a crime which relates to employment. On a slightly lower scale so are middle-class tax-evasion, embezzlement and fraud, and working-class pilfering from work or falsification of restaurant bills. The motor trade, for instance, whether at corporate, retail, or repair level, is scarcely a paragon of crime-free virtue! But, of course, all these crimes are comparatively under-reported in the crime statistics. The focus of official police statistics is street crime, burglary, inter-personal violence – the crimes of the lower working class who are more likely to be unemployed. We should, therefore, look in this direction: is it unemployment which leads to crime among the poor?

## Unemployment Which Does Not Lead to Crime

Throughout the present period the rich have subsisted in situations of perpetual unemployment or semi-employment without lapsing into crime. In the sixties a generation of hippies actively chose unemployment and – apart from the use of marijuana – were not exceptionally criminal. But let us look at much more substantial sections of the population: old people and women.

The notion that unemployment leads to crime is contradicted by the existence of unemployed groups with very low crime rates. The most obvious and enormous is that of old people, who have consistently lower crime rates than youth. And, however valid the point may be that discretion on the part of the police and the courts tends to depress the real figures, there is little doubt that old ladies, for example, are minimal offenders when compared to young men! The low crime rate of the old also, incidentally, confirms our contention that there is no direct relationship between poverty and crime; there is a substantial concentration of poverty amongst the elderly, and income, in general, declines substantially with retirement.

A contribution to this section must also be a remark about the majority of the population – women. Women have, of course, a comparatively low crime rate and are also generally more peripheral to the industrial sector than men. Unemployment is defined as detachment from the productive process, and, presumably because of this, women – despite the irony of domestic labour – are included in this category. Yet not only is the crime rate low for women, but it has actually tended to increase as women have moved into employment.

## Unemployment and Crime in This Century

In this century there is no simple relationship between the amount of unemployment and the amount of crime. Let us give a few examples, first comparing the height of unemployment in the 1930s and its equivalent today. The amount of unemployment in 1933 and 1981 was roughly equal (around 11.5 per cent); the rate of serious crime per 100,000 population in 1981 was over fifteen times as great. Secondly, if we compare the enormously high unemployment rate of the 1930s with the prosperous times of the early fifties, we find that the unemployment rate of 1932 was eleven times that in 1951, yet the serious crime rate was over three times greater in 1951.

These two facts can be seen by examining the accompanying graph (Figure 3.1) which traces the relationship between unemployment and crime in the two periods, 1930–37 and 1960–81. It is significant that even in the recent period the Home Office found little *direct* connection between unemployment and crime.

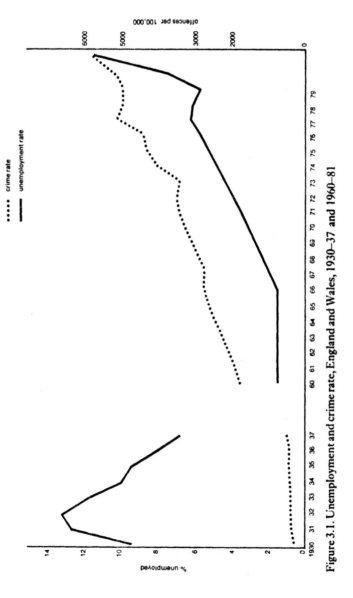

Figure 3.1. Unemployment and crime rate, England and Wales, 1930–37 and 1960–81

Nor do changes in the *rate* of unemployment relate closely
to changes in the *rate* of crime. From 1961 to 1966 the rate
of unemployment remained very low and unchanged (1.5 per
cent) whereas serious crime went up by 45 per cent. In a more
recent period, the five years between 1976 and 1981, the rate
of unemployment doubled but the rate of crime rose by only
30 per cent. Furthermore, the 1930s allow us to look at a period
when the rate of unemployment dropped. Thus from 1932 to
1937 unemployment halved, but serious crime actually rose by
15 per cent. We have had, over the last decade, enormous rises
in serious crime during the period of low unemployment and
post-war affluence, and a continuing rise, although slightly less,
in population during the slump. Moreover, the rise in crime
in both recent periods is considerably greater than in the 1930s.
In the years 1929 to 1937 it was 3 per cent per year; in the
years 1950 to 1960, 6 per cent per year; in the years 1960 to
1970, 9 per cent; and in the years 1970 to 1980, 6 per cent.

## Countries, Areas and Groups

What evidence does comparing different countries, areas and
groups give us about the relationship between unemployment
and crime? The international evidence shows no significant
relationship. In 1981 the unemployment rate in the United States
was 8.3 per cent while that in the UK was 12.5 per cent, whereas
there was more serious crime committed in New York City
than in the whole of the British Isles.

The most systematic work in comparing different areas of
the country was that of Herman Mannheim. When examining
the depression period, he found completely contradictory results.
He found it (p. 138)

little short of a miracle that there should hardly have been any increase
in indictable offences in Sheffield in years like 1926 and 1931 when
unemployment nearly doubled – just as there is nothing in the unemployment conditions to explain the sudden 'crime wave' in 1928.

Meanwhile, Leeds witnessed a decline in crime during the first years of the Great Depression while other similar cities showed a sharp rise.

Our last example is between two ethnic groups. The Home Office researchers, Stevens and Willis, in their study of the relationship between race and unemployment found that there was a high relationship between white unemployment and white crime rates but there was no relationship between black unemployment and black crime rates. What surprised them was that *white* unemployment rates, however, correlated with *black* crime rates! We will examine this case in detail in the next chapter, but let us note how the facts about unemployment and crime further substantiate our argument that it is not absolute deprivation that causes crime. *Relative* deprivation, on the other hand, can occur in employed people as well as in unemployed people since it is dependent on subjectively experienced discontent. It can occur during periods of low unemployment and rising prosperity, and of high unemployment and falling living standards. It can vary between one town and another, and one ethnic group and another. It is necessary to understand the subculture of the groups involved, and their shared experience of economic and political deprivation. By posing human subjectivity between the objective factors of unemployment and crime, any notions of simple determinism are undermined.

We are now in a position to make clear our views on crime, law and the state, separating this out from conventional criminology and what we shall term left idealism. The latter is a particular view of crime and policing which is common in socialist circles. This tendency was best described by E. P. Thompson when he wrote (p. xi):

There has been around for a decade or more a general rhetoric which passes itself off as a 'Marxism'. Sometimes this is expressed in sophisticated intellectual form, sometimes as old-style Leninism,

sometimes just as an unexamined vocabulary co-existing with other
vocabularies ... Common elements in this rhetoric are some of the
following: first, there is a platonic notion of ... the ideal capitalist
state ... This state is inherently profoundly authoritarian, as a direct
organ of capitalist exploitation and control, and any inhibitions upon
its power are seen as 'masks' or disguises, or as tricks to provide it
with ideological legitimation and to enforce its hegemony. It may ...
follow that any symptoms of authoritarianism are seen as disclosing
a 'crisis of hegemony' and may even be welcomed as unmasking the
'true' (i.e. platonic) character of the state, and as signalling the 'con-
juncture' in which a final class confrontation will take place ... And
this may ... consort with a loose rhetoric in which civil rights and
democratic practices are discounted as camouflage, or the relics of
'bourgeois liberalism'. And to cut short the list, this very often goes
along with a wholesale dismissal of *all* law and *all* police and sometimes
with the sloppy notion that *all* crime is some kind of displaced revolutionary activity.

This is not the place to engage in philosophical wrangle. I will
simply say that these are all half-truths which have a continual tendency
to degenerate into rubbish. What is more to the point is that this
rhetoric can be seen to unbend the springs of action, and to discount
the importance of any struggle for civil rights. If *all* law and *all* police
are utterly abhorrent, then it cannot matter much what kind of law,
or what place the police are held within; and yet the most immediate
and consequent struggles ·to maintain liberty are exactly about kinds
and places, cases and precedents, and the bringing of power to particular
account.

Parallel to our desire to avoid both moral hysteria and moral
inertia about crime is our contention that neither of the corresponding conventional wisdoms, of the right or of the left,
accurately reflect the problem of crime in this country today.
To make this clear we will examine in turn how each position
views the causes of crime, the nature of crime and criminal
values, the nature of criminal statistics and the role of the state
and its agencies.

## 1 *The Causes of Crime*

For orthodox criminology crime occurs because of a lack of conditioning into values: the criminal, whether because of evil (in the conventional model) or lack of parental training (in the welfare model), lacks the virtues which keep us all honest and upright. In left idealism, crime occurs not because of lack of value but simply because of lack of material goods: economic deprivation drives people into crime. In the conventional viewpoint on crime, the criminal is flawed; he or she lacks human values and cognition. In the radical interpretation of this, the very opposite is true. The criminal, not the honest person, has the superior consciousness: he or she has seen through the foolishness of the straight world. To be well conditioned is to be well deceived. The criminal then enters into a new world of value – a subculture, relieved in part of the mystifications of the conventional world.

We reject both these positions. The radical version smacks of theories of absolute deprivation; we would rather put at the centre of our theory notions of relative deprivation. And a major source of one's making comparisons – or indeed the feeling that one should, in the first place, 'naturally' compete and compare oneself with others – is capitalism itself.

We are taught that life is like a racetrack: that merit will find its own reward. This is the central way our system legitimates itself and motivates people to compete. But what a strange racetrack! In reality some people seem to start half-way along the track (the rich), while others are forced to run with a millstone around their necks (for example, women with both domestic and non-domestic employment), while others are not even allowed on to the track at all (the unemployed, the members of the most deprived ethnic groups). The values of an equal or meritocratic society which capitalism inculcates into people are constantly at loggerheads with the actual material inequalities in the world. And, contrary to the conservatives, it is the *well-*

socialized person who is the most liable to crime. Crime is endemic to capitalism because it produces both egalitarian ideals and material shortages. It provides precisely the values which engender criticism of the material shortages which the radicals pinpoint.

A high crime rate occurs in precise conditions: where a group has learnt through its past that it is being dealt with invidiously; where it is possible for it easily to pick up the contradictions just referred to and where there is no political channel for these feelings of discontent to be realized. There must be economic and political discontent and there must be an absence of economic and political opportunities.

## 2  *The Nature of Crime and Criminal Values*

For conventional criminology, as we have seen, crime is simply antisocial behaviour involving people who lack values. For left idealists it is the reverse: it is proto-revolutionary activity, primitive and individualistic, perhaps, but praiseworthy all the same. It involves, if it is a theft, a redistribution of income, or if it is part of youth culture, symbolic and stylistic awareness of, say, the loss of traditional working-class community or the repressive nature of the system. In either case it involves alternative values.

We would argue that both of these interpretations of crime are superficial. It is true that crime is antisocial – indeed the majority of working-class crime, far from being a prefigurative revolt, is directed against other members of the working class. But it is not antisocial because of lack of conventional values but precisely because of it. For the values of most working-class criminals are overwhelmingly conventional. They involve individualism, competition, desire for material goods and, often, machismo. Such crime could, without exaggeration, be characterized as the behaviour of those suitably motivated people who are too poor to have access to the Stock Exchange. Crime reflects the fact that our own worlds and our own lives are materially and ideologically riddled with the capitalist order within which we live. Street crime is an activity of marginals but its image is that of those right in the centre of convention and of concern. As Jeremy Seabrook (p. 64) puts it:

> What we cannot bear, rich and liberals alike, is to see our own image in actions that are ugly and more stark reflections of trans-actions in which we are all implicated in our social and economic relationships: the universal marketing, the superstitious faith in money, the instant profit, the rip-off, the easy money, the backhander, the quick fiddle, the comforting illusion that we can all get richer without hurting anyone, the way in which individual salvation through money has become a secularized and man-made substitute for divine grace.

The radicals are correct when they see crime as a reaction to an unjust society. But they make a crucial mistake: they assume that the reaction to a just cause is necessarily a just one. On the contrary: it is often exactly the opposite. The reaction to poverty among poor whites, for example, may be to parade around waving Union Jacks: it may be the tawdry nationalism of the National Front. The reaction to relative deprivation may, as Paul Willis has so ably shown, be sexism, racism and anti-intellectualism. Crime is one form of egoistic response to deprivation. Its roots are in justice but its growth often perpetuates injustice.

## 3 *The Nature of the Crime Statistics*

If we look at the official crime statistics in any Western capitalist country we see a remarkable similarity: the young are consistently seen to offend more than the old, the working class more than the middle class, black more than white, and men more than women. In Figure 3.2. we have constructed a series of Aztec pyramids each representing the likelihood of going to prison dependent on class, age, race and gender. We have

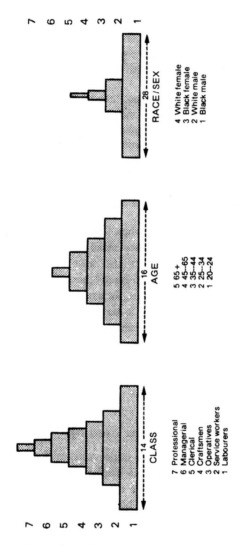

Figure 3.2. Likelihood of going to prison

used American statistics rather than British, as they are more complete. The British figures, particularly in terms of class and race, are kept much more closely guarded. The shape of these pyramids is, however, constant across cultures and there are close parallels; for example, one British study showed that the chances of going to prison by class were exactly the same as in America.

As can be seen, a labourer is fourteen times more likely to go to prison than a professional; someone aged between twenty and twenty-four is sixteen times more likely than a sixty-five-year-old; a black male is twenty-eight times more likely than a white female. If one compounds these figures, of course, one achieves much higher ratios, the most extreme being the contrast between the chances of going to prison of an elderly, white professional woman compared to a young, black, lower-working-class man. This has some very dramatic results; for example, on an average day in the United States one in 450 Americans is in prison, but one black man in twenty-six between the ages of twenty-five and thirty-four. Offenders, like victims, are sharply focused in terms of social category; in fact, the same social attributes which tend towards high victimization rates tend also towards high offender rates. We have talked about this so-called moral symmetry between the victim and the offender in Chapter 1. Serious crime, according to the official statistics, is a minority phenomenon within which certain social categories most marginal to society are vastly over-represented. The prisoner is thus on the fringe of the economy (unemployed or a casual labourer), has missed out on the educational system, and belongs to a minority group.

Now, these pyramids illustrate the major empirical problem for understanding crime. For conventional criminology it is scarcely a problem: the lower orders are much more likely to be badly socialized than the middle and upper echelons of society – hence the pyramid. For left idealists, however, this fact poses a considerable quandary. For, on the one hand, gross economic

deprivation will surely lead to crime; but on the other, is it
not true that the police pick on the poor, ignoring the crimes
of the rich? Our response to this contradiction is simply to
ask why either–or is a realistic analysis. There is no doubt that
different social categories of people behave differently both in
their degree of orderliness and criminality and that this relates
to their position in the world; but there is also no doubt that
the police react differently to different categories of people.
If both these points are true, then the official statistics are
a product of differences in the 'real' rates of crime between
groups and differences in the police predisposition to arrest
them. Thus the crime rate of old ladies is no doubt actually
very low, but it probably appears *even* lower in the official
statistics because of the police disinclination to suspect or arrest
elderly persons. And as far as lower-working-class youths are
concerned, the exact opposite is true: they commit more crimes
and they are excessively harassed, the result being an augmented
crime statistic. Moreover, different types of people commit
different types of crimes. This point is put particularly well
by Reiman (pp. 7–8). He writes:

> There is evidence suggesting that the particular pressure of poverty
> leads poor people to commit a higher proportion of the crimes that
> people fear (such as homicide, burglary, and assault) than their number
> in the population. There is no contradiction between this and the
> recognition that those who are well off commit many more crimes
> than is generally acknowledged both of the widely feared and of the
> sort not widely feared (such as 'white-collar' crimes). There is no
> contradiction here, because, as will be shown, the poor are arrested
> far more frequently than those who are well off when they have com-
> mitted the same crimes – and the well-to-do are almost never arrested
> for white-collar crimes. Thus, if arrest records were brought in line
> with the real incidence of crime, it is likely that those who are well
> off would appear in the records far more than they do at present,
> even though the poor would still probably figure disproportionately
> in arrests for the crimes people fear. In addition to this ... those

who are well off commit acts that are not defined as crimes and yet that are as harmful or more so than the crimes people fear. Thus, if we had an accurate picture of who is really dangerous to society, there is reason to believe that those who are well off would receive still greater representation.

In other words, (a) the pyramids we have constructed with regards to class and crime (and the same is true of race, gender and age) are quantitatively too dramatic: if middle-class people were equally subject to arrest and conviction the contrasts between each level could not be as steep. (b) Qualitatively, given the above provision, they are reasonably correct if one does *not* include white-collar crime and focuses, as Reiman outlines, on the 'normal' crimes which people fear. If people were arrested and imprisoned for white-collar crimes, then the pyramid would remain in shape but its gradient would be lessened even more. (c) To admit to a pyramid of crime by class is not, of course, to believe in a pyramid of impact. That is, the fact that lower-working-class males commit more crime than their upper-class counterparts does not mean that the overall impact of such crimes is necessarily greater. As we have seen, it is probably less, although none of this suggests that we should concentrate on either one or the other, as criminologists, both radical and conventional, have done in the past. Both types of crime create considerable problems for the population.

## 4 *The Role of the State and Its Agencies*

For conventional criminology the state is a neutral institution that protects the universal interests of all against problems such as crime. In parliamentary democracies it is an eminently reformable institution where popular demand can be translated into legislative practice. For the left idealists, the state is the direct instrument of the ruling class. The various institutions – whether ideological (like education and the mass media) or directly repressive (such as the police and the judicial system)

– exist in order to maintain capitalism. They mesh together in a seamless web of interrelating institutions which are explained by the function in which they contribute to the status quo. Reform in a progressive direction is an impossibility. The most that will happen is neutralization – like punching into a beanbag; the worst, and more usual, the reform will be turned against the working class. Thus part of the explanatory task of such theoreticians is to explain how 'anomalies' such as Intermediate Treatment or Community Service Orders are, in fact, in the interests of the ruling class despite the fact that they look, on the face of it, eminently progressive.

As regards the explanation of the behaviour of the agents of social control, such as the police, there are parallel differences between the two positions. In the conventional model the police are seen as attempting to solve the problem of crime. They are faced with a problem and they do their best to deal with it within the limits of the law, and with a choice of action based on the pragmatic possibilities of resources and the science of detection of crime. For the radicals, the behaviour of the police is, at base, materially determined: it follows the logic of capital. The policing initiatives which Police Commissioners take and the notions of the rank-and-file police officers are in the end determined by the imperatives of maintaining a disciplined work-force and subdued population. Such policies follow a drift towards an increasingly strong state which is seen as inevitable and itself a product of the declining fortunes of world capitalism. Events which look like having a reasonably progressive content, such as the publication of the Scarman Report or the shift from McNee to Newman as head of the Metropolitan Police Force are seen as cosmetic touches in what is an inevitably worsening situation.

This sheds light on the left idealist position on crime. The problem of crime – or, more correctly, working-class crime – is very largely an illusion, orchestrated by the ruling class in order to engender moral panic which distracts the population from the real problems which assail them. The fear of crime is a potent symbol in the armoury of mystification. For, by mobilization of this fear, the powerful can literally replace the class war by the war against crime. The preponderance of crime-reporting in the mass media is no accident, for the spectre of crime is a central component of the mystification which besets us.

We reject the notion of conventional criminology that the state is a neutral institution acting in the universal interests of the population against, in this instance, 'the crime problem'. At the present moment the British state represents very largely ruling-class interests, but gains can be wrung out of it; reforms, however difficult to achieve, are possible and, in fact, relate to the state as in essence a site of contradicting interests.

The basis for the political support of bourgeois society among the mass of the population is closely entwined with their fears of crime and disorder. For the ruling class takes real working-class demands for justice and attempts to enmesh them in the support of a class-ridden society. The existence of a class society leads to desperation, demoralization and a war of all against all, and the working-class community suffers immensely from the criminals in its midst. Law gains its support not just through mystification of the working class, an ability to render people spellbound by its paraphernalia of pomp and authority. Legal institutions partially represent, it is true, the interests of the ruling class but they are also much more than just this. As Herbert Marcuse put it (p. 101):

In Marxian theory, the state belongs to the superstructure in as much as it is *not* simply the direct political expression of the basic relationships of production but contains elements which, as it were, 'compensate' for the class relationships of production. The state, being and remaining the state of the ruling class, sustains *universal* law and order and thereby guarantees at least a modicum of equality and security for the whole society. Only by virtue of these elements can the class state fulfil the function of 'moderating' and keeping within the bounds of 'order' the class conflicts generated by the production relations. It is this 'mediation' which gives the state the appearance of a universal interest over and above the conflicting particular interests.

The class society which creates social disorganization also creates its partial palliative. Law not only involves ruling-class domination: it has a legitimate component to it, in terms of the protection of working-class interests. It is not, therefore, just a mystification disguising the naked one-to-one interests of the powerful, as left idealists would maintain. Laws against vandalism do to some extent protect working-class property, those against rape are intended to protect women, however sexist the manner in which they are employed, and those against income-tax fiddling are there often to aid income redistribution, however tardily they may be invoked in practice. It is in the interests of working-class people that crime is controlled, and it is in their interest that the agencies of the state deal with crime in a just and effective fashion. The struggle for justice in the area of crime is a central part of a socialist strategy.

# 4 The Race and Crime Debate

The repeated issue by the Metropolitan Police of crime statistics involving ethnic distinctions for a particular type of street crime, commonly called mugging, has once again raised the question of race and crime. The overwhelming response from the left has been, correctly, to deplore the one-sided, political nature of these statistics and to see them as consistent with an attempt to fuel an atmosphere of moral panic in which the issues raised by the Scarman Report and the Greater London Council's campaign for a democratic police authority can be safely ignored. It has given rise to an extreme reaction in the gutter press; for instance, the *Sun* ran a headline BLACK CRIME SHOCK and carried *without* inverted commas the statement: 'Blacks carried out twice as many muggings as whites in London last year' (23 March 1983). Let us state now the extremely strong objective reasons for being highly sceptical about statements such as that out of 19,258 cases of robbery and violent theft in London, 10,960 were carried out by blacks.

(1) They focus on only one type of crime out of a whole catalogue of serious offences. Robbery and violent theft only account for about 3 per cent of all serious crime. They ignore the fact that whites are more likely to commit the vast majority of serious crimes and present us with the image of the 'black criminal'.

(2) Many of these crimes are of an amateurish and minor nature, but the phrase 'robbery and violent theft' suggests something of a more extreme nature. In a Home Office Research Study of mugging, for example, it was found that 54 per cent of those mugged suffered minor injuries such as cuts and

bruises, and only 3 per cent needed to stay in hospital for longer than twelve hours (*New Society*, 25 March 1983).

(3) The category 'robbery and violent theft' is a very flexible one and blends with other offence categories such as 'theft of personal property'. By allocating crimes from the latter to the former, inflated figures can easily occur. The exercise of police discretion can quite easily alter the amount of a particular crime by changes in recording practices. A recent study, for example, suggests that precisely such a manipulation occurred in the claim that there was a dramatic rise in street crime in Brixton in 1981 (Blom-Cooper and Drabble).

(4) They ignore the fact that mugging is a very indistinct category and that only about one third of all robbery and violent theft fit the conventional notion of it. This was put well in a Runnymede Trust Bulletin:

> Mugging is not, however, an offence known in law and the term is not normally used by police. To the public it usually means a theft, in the street, which is accompanied by violence. But the Metropolitan Police category of robbery and other violent thefts includes 'snatches' where the victim is neither threatened nor injured (7,330), robberies from business premises open to the public (2,684), and 'other robberies' which are not street robberies (2,860). This leaves 5,889 robberies which would fit in with the popular meaning of 'mugging', only 31 per cent of the figure bandied about in the press, and only 0.9 per cent of the total recorded serious offences. (No. 143, p. 8)

(5) It does not present us with the ethnic origins of the victims of crime, thus serving to feed the illusion that black crime is predatory upon white. Of course, most crime is intra-racial and intra-class.

(6) It does not allow for the fact that police statistics are *in part* a function of police prejudices. It presents the figures on ethnic divisions as objective reflections of reality.

All in all, we have an extremely slanted portrayal of the crime problem which, no doubt, contributes considerably to the build-up of racial fears in the non-black community. It is a blatant example of the type of moral hysteria about crime which has occurred throughout the century. The main preoccupation during the fifties and sixties was the crime of lower-working-class youth, and now attention has been shifted on to young blacks.

Even if the figures were totally accurate – and we have seen that this is an impossibility – it is a priority that they be presented in context, to allow the audience to understand their true significance. Figures do not speak for themselves and there are plenty of racist 'contexts' into which they will inevitably be slotted if the presenters of the statistics 'naively' inform us that they are only giving the public 'the facts'. It is vital, therefore, that we debunk this strategy and provide accurate interpretations to counter the moral panic over crime which serves to fuel racism.

But a common reaction on the left and among liberal commentators has been significantly different from this. Instead of scrutinizing the figures impartially and providing a context in which they can be understood, they have engaged in a wholesale dismissal of the evidence, often in a very contradictory fashion. They have either questioned the validity of any connection at all between race and crime (e.g. Bridges and Gilroy), or argued that the problem is irrelevant as such crime is insignificant by comparison with the 'crimes of the powerful' (e.g. Harman). Bridges and Gilroy suggest that any link between crime rates and ethnic background is purely a function of police prejudice and that any discussion to the contrary gives 'intellectual support to racist stereotypes of the black community as socially and politically disorganized' (p. 35). Such a position, quite apart from the vacuous definition of racism involved, appears to associate critical discussion with silence. As if silence can eliminate the fear of crime, or blank denial rid us of racial prejudice! It is precisely such silences that have placed the left continually on the defensive and guaranteed the hegemony of the right over the terrain of law and order. A challenge to this long established domination by the right must begin with the simple recognition that crime is a pressing problem for the poor and for the black community, and that the control of crime is a vital issue for socialists.

As we have argued, in all industrial societies a small minority of the oppressed sections of society are brutalized into criminality. But because crime is produced by the system, it does not follow that crime is some sort of crypto-political struggle against the system. Bridges and Gilroy refer evasively to the 'social and political character' of working-class black crime (p. 35). One might as well argue that dying of asbestos poisoning, undoubtedly a disease produced by industrial capitalism, is some sort of political activity. The notion of crime as a kind of politics rests on a few myths that need to be dispelled. Working-class crimes are predominantly intra-class and intra-racial. A poor person is more likely to rob a poor person than a rich person, a black is more likely to assault another black than a white, and a white more likely to attack a white than a black. Eighty per cent of crimes of violence involving serious injury and 62 per cent of those causing slight injury are intra-racial (see Stevens and Willis).

The high crime rate of certain minority segments of the black community is directed to that community. Street culture is, on the one hand, expressive and liberative, and on the other, individualistic, macho and predatory. Hustling is not a pursuit of angels; only the most unmitigated romantic would believe this. 'Hyenas and wolves of the street' was how Malcolm X referred to street criminals, and George Jackson in his prison letters wrote to his mother about intra-racial crime in his community:

The men can think of nothing more effective than pimping, gambling and petty theft. I've heard men brag about being pimps of black women and taking money from black women who are on relief. Things like that I find odious, disgusting.

And as a matter of fact, socialists ever since Engels have consistently viewed the vast majority of crime as serving to destroy the community, as something that has to be resisted. Yet these idealists tend merely to invert the imagery of the mass media. If the mass media say that crime is a danger then it obviously is not!

Both the mass media and the left share one thing: they overwhelmingly concentrate on inter-racial crime. Inter-racial crime is a minor, albeit very serious, phenomenon; within this category a substantial proportion occurs because of overtly racist reasons. Thus a recent Home Office study attributes one quarter of all inter-racial crimes to racist motives. In absolute terms these represent only a 0.25 per cent of recorded crime, but what is of significance is the victimization rate for minority groups. The rate for Asians was fifty times that for white people, and that for blacks thirty-six times (see *Racial Attacks*, Home Office, 1981). We have no doubt that this is a gross underestimation and that the police response to racial persecution is severely inadequate. What we must note, however, is that the criminal victimization rates *as a whole* are considerably greater. Furthermore, the left, although correctly focusing on racist incidents, seems, quite incorrectly, unable to see the existence of crime outside this category.

A startling illustration of this shortsightedness is the following quote from *Policing London*, commenting on the Metropolitan figures and the study we have just mentioned:

Though they possess the information, the Met did not publish at the same time figures which show what proportion of the victims of these crimes are also black. The Home Office report on *Racial Attacks* (November 1981) indicated that, with regard to offences such as violence against the person and robbery: 'The incidence of victimization has been much higher for the ethnic minority populations, particularly the Asians, than for white people. Indeed the rate for Asians was 50 times that for white people and the rate for blacks was over 36 times that for white people.' (*Policing London*, No. 1, July–August 1982, p. 3)

Now, to any reader this remark could only be read as suggesting that serious criminal victimization was fifty times greater for Asians, and thirty-six times greater for blacks, than for whites. This is precisely what has been repeated in several other articles. Of course, these figures do not refer to the total extent of criminal victimization by ethnic groups. They do not even refer to inter-racial attacks. What they do refer to, as we have already noted, is inter-racial attacks where there is 'strong evidence or some indication' of a racist motive. As a matter of fact, the criminal victimization of blacks in the very restricted category of robbery and violent theft alone (about 3 per cent of all serious crime) is over ten times greater than for *all* serious crime against blacks of an overtly racist nature; for Asians the figure is fourteen times. This is not to deny the problem of racist attacks. *On the contrary*, police inactivity with regard to such outrages is a scandal. Our point here is simply that the left, while quite rightly pressing for police involvement in combating such crime, turns a blind eye towards the existence of a massive amount of crime against blacks and the working class.

Inter-racial crime, involving blacks against whites, is a minor phenomenon. Mugging is far from being an exclusively black crime – yet it is also one of the *few* crimes where there is some evidence of a substantial, if still minor, racial component (Pratt). The mass media have picked upon an atypical black crime and portrayed it as the *typical* crime, while at the same time grossly overestimating its seriousness. It is, in fact, largely without serious violence, involves small sums of money and it is the amateurish crime of young boys and adolescents. But its impact should not be underplayed. £5 stolen from an old age pensioner is of far greater significance than £500 stolen from Woolworths, which is why the former, rightly, creates more alarm and disgust than the latter. Mugging, regardless of whether the perpetrator or victim is white or black, is a despicable crime but one which must be seen in perspective. It must neither be exaggerated, in an alarmist fashion, nor ignored as a matter of petty importance.

Intra-racial crime and intra-class crimes are of massive proportions, but because much of the left is locked in a debate with the mass media they are simply not seen. Thus, for ideological reasons, real problems facing the community are quite simply ignored and a ground-swell of anxiety allowed to build up. Both intra-racial and inter-racial crime are demoralizing and divisive within the black community and the working class. The fact that most working-class crime and black crime is directed against the working-class and black communities, coupled with the situation where such communities are less likely to receive adequate police protection than the rich, should be the starting-point for the left. The need is surely for more efficient police protection responsive to the needs of the working class and the groups within it.

If unemployment and deprivation brutalized into criminality a minority of the poor in certain cultural and political circumstances, why is there such a problem for writers on the left to accept the proposition that the accentuation of such deprivation through the additional mechanisms of racial discrimination results in higher crime rates? The claim that the higher recorded rate for certain types of crime for young blacks is purely and simply a product of police prejudice is open to a number of objections. We will examine these in detail later in the chapter but the following four points form an incontestable basis:

(1) Such a claim makes the assumption that the 'real' crime rate for all social groups is the same. This is tantamount to the suggestion that the black community does not in reality suffer any additional ill-effects from racial discrimination.

(2) The recorded rate for a range of Asian crimes is consistently lower than the white rate (Stevens and Willis). Police racism would have to manifest very strangely indeed to be entirely responsible for such results.

(3) The crime rate for the first generation of West Indian immigrants recorded in the 1960s was lower than the general rate (Lambert). Either real changes in the crime rate within the black community have occurred or the police were exercising positive discrimination for over a decade in favour of the black community!

(4) The argument for higher crime rates for black youth is only made for certain types of crime. The police do not claim, for example, that blacks have a higher rate for burglary than whites, or for bank robbery. The issue centres around street crime (see Scarman Inquiry Minutes, Day Two).

## *Shadow Boxing and the Debate about Race and Crime*

In 1982 we referred in an article to the fact that there seemed to be real differences in the crime rate between different ethnic groups. We argued that of all the groups on the receiving end of social deprivation – black, Asian and white – blacks most acutely experience the combination of social deprivation and lack of political power, within the established framework, to change their situation as a group. We argued that this combination of economic and political marginalization lay behind the high crime rate within and around the black community, which affected a minority of the community and only sporadically. Crime was a negative manifestation of this discontent, whereas the uprisings of 1981 were an extremely positive response to deprivation. Moreover, we argued that the degree of deprivation experienced by black youngsters in British society was not a product of their being 'aliens' within Britain. On the contrary, it was the very cultural assimilation of these black Britons that made their deprivation all the more acute. Because they had assimilated so well – both in terms of aspirations and expectations – they felt the impact of discrimination and prejudice all the more acutely.

Our work has received an extremely hostile response from certain quarters. Thus Paul Gilroy commented:

> Various factions of the left movement, increasingly marginal to popular concerns, have recently glimpsed, in the intensity of feeling around questions of law and order, a means to gain proximity to the working class. (1982, p. 50)

We were accused of being 'ready allies of the police' (Bridges and Gilroy, p. 35); of giving 'intellectual support ... to racist stereotypes of the black community' (ibid.); of capitulating to 'the weight of racist logic' (Gilroy, 1982, p. 52); of reproducing 'pathology ... in polite social democratic rhetoric' (ibid., p. 53) and of being 'a couple of trendy sociologists who advocate harassment and mugging by the racist police force' (J. Crutchley, in a letter to *Marxism Today*, September 1982, p. 47).

Our astonishment was increased by our awareness of the contrast with the situation in America. For instance, here is a comment from two prominent American liberals writing on race relations:

> If a careful, detached scholar knew nothing about crime rates but was aware of the social, economic and political disparities between whites and negroes in the United States, and if this diligent researcher had prior knowledge of the historical status of the American negro, what would be the most plausible hypothesis our scholar could make about the crime rate of negroes? Even this small amount of knowledge would justify the expectation that negroes would be found to have a higher rate of crime than whites. And the data at hand would confirm this hypothesis. (Wolfgang and Cohen, pp. 30–31)

Even American radicals would not deny the greater crime rate of blacks compared to whites. Nor would they deny the dire problem of intra-racial crime in the black community. It is difficult to stand in black Harlem and not deplore the way the community destroys itself. It is almost impossible to be romantic about the extent of crime and believe it is part of the colonial struggle against White America. Rather, as all black activists are ready to point out, it is a product of oppression.

In Britain our critics seem to fall into two categories: liberal and orthodox left on the one hand, and on the other, those people, highly critical of the labour movement, who see the black struggle as special and pioneering. The first position is in essence defensive: it argues that the imputation of a high crime rate to certain immigrants is racism and that everything must be done to debunk such a 'myth'. At the same time it tends to hold the contradictory notion that because of poverty and racism immigrant groups are driven into crime. One could sum the stance up as: 'Of course there isn't a higher black crime rate and even if there is it would scarcely be surprising!' In every sense this position is ideological in that its role is totally propagandist and inflexible. It could, in fact, never admit that there was a higher rate; its role is to defuse arguments that are 'racist' enough to suggest it. And, more importantly, it has never worked its way through the contradictory nature of its suppositions because it sees any critical position as being, at the very least, closet racism. The second position, which superimposes itself on the first, is more sophisticated and much more on the offensive. It does not work its way through the contradiction, but as an ideology it scarcely worries about being contradictory. It is this version that has made most of the running and which we will tackle first.

Despite the level of unthinking abuse levelled at us, it became apparent that there was an implicit coherence in the patterns of criticism. Strangely, we encountered a peculiar *déjà vu* in the sense that the position on crime taken up by our critics – and reflecting a largely untheorized position prevalent on the left – was that of the radical criminology of the late 1960s and early 1970s. During the last ten years a considerable amount of work has been done to reconstruct the original but sometimes naive left idealism of the original formulations of radical criminology and to remove its more obvious theoretical in-adequacies. It was thus something of a surprise that these ghosts should choose to resurrect themselves and return, in the guise of a debate on race and crime, claiming to be a new, updated version of a critique of radical criminology! Let us briefly reiterate the main features of the new criminology of the 1968–1972 period:

1 *Crime as proto-revolutionary:* Crime was viewed as a misconstrued but proto-revolutionary activity. Radical criminology played down the extent of crime within the working class and focused on crime between the social classes.

2 *Crime statistics as a result of police prejudice:* Radical criminology maintained an extremely critical stance towards the official crime statistics. The high proportion of working-class and black crime within the figures was seen more as the result of police prejudice than of actual behavioural differences between the social classes.

3 *Panic over crime as a fabrication:* Left idealism saw the official crime rate as used – intentionally or otherwise – by powerful groups such as the police and the media to create a 'moral panic', to mislead the public as to the real social problems they faced, and to divert attention away from the crimes of the powerful – including the police – towards seeing the poor as the main threat. This served as part of a conspiracy to blame the poor for poverty and to portray the rich and powerful as the protectors of society against crime. The war against crime was seen, largely, as an ideological smokescreen behind which the police could siphon off resources in their mobilization against the working class.

In this type of criminology there was a contradiction – which has now revealed itself anew in the writings of our critics – between poverty as an obvious cause of crime, and the crime statistics as constructed by and reflecting simply the activities of a prejudiced police force. There was little attention in such thinking to the simple fact that both could be true: that crime could be a product of poverty *and* that the poor, as a group, could be more susceptible to arrest. Such simple additions were anathema to the either–or dichotomies so characteristic of such theorizing. Over the more recent period, radical criminologists have realized that it is impossible to have it both ways. If crime is one of the consequences of social oppression and deprivation of the poor, then the higher crime rate for the poor cannot simply be a function of police prejudice. Furthermore, criminologists have come to realize the essentially contradictory nature of crime, economically, socially and politically. Thus, in 1975, one of the present authors noted that:

> Crime and deviancy, from a socialist perspective, are terms which encompass an uneven array of activities and behaviours – at times behaviours which are quite inimicable to socialism; at other times rebellions against property and repression which are as justifiable in their consequences as they are primitive in their conception. Forms of illogicality exist within the working class which are adaptive, collective in their accomplishment and progressive in their function: objects 'fall off the back of lorries', factory property metamorphoses as property within the home. Forms of deviancy occur as attempts to create unhampered and liveable space; the tyranny of the workplace and conventional sexuality being left momentarily behind. Marihuana and booze, pub life and gay bars, black music and white rhythm-and-blues – a tenderloin of the city where a sense of 'the possible' breaks through the facticity of what is. But just as one must discriminate actively between crimes which are cultural adaptions of the people, and crimes which derive from the brutalization of criminal and community alike, so we must clearly distinguish between the contradictory nature of many of these adaptive manifestations. Deviance will contain both positive and negative moments; the breakthrough from repression is distorted and beguiled by the reality from which it springs. (Young, 1975, pp. 90–91)

At the same time the American criminologist Tony Platt wrote:

> The political solution to 'street' crime does not lie in *mystifying* its reality by reactionary allusions to 'banditry' nor in *reducing* it to a manifestation of 'lumpen' viciousness. The former is utopian and

dangerous because it defends practices that undermine the safety and solidarity of the working class (and glorifies spontaneity and putchism); the latter objectively legitimates the bourgeoisie's attack on super-exploited workers especially black and brown workers ... Pimping, gambling rackets, illegal drug operations, etc., are just as damaging to working-class communities as any 'legal' business which profits from people's misery and desperation.

But we must be careful to distinguish organized criminality from 'street' crime, and the 'lumpen' from the superexploited sections of the working class. Most 'street' crime is not organized and not very profitable ... The conditions of life in the superexploited sections create both high levels of 'street' crime *and* political militancy. The urban black community, for example, is hit the hardest by 'street' crime, but it is also the locus of tremendous resistance and struggle – as witnessed by the civil rights movements, the ghetto revolts of the 1960s and the anti-repression struggles of today. (p. 26)

Thus, in very pronounced terms, radical criminology has made clear its position on the problem of working-class crime. It explicitly eschews *both* romanticism *and* the law-and-order campaigns of the conservative variety. But it notes quite urgently that there is a substantial element in street crime which is merely the poor taking up the individualistic, competitive ethos of capitalism itself and that its consequences are anathema to the standpoint of socialist concerns.

Now, it would be incorrect to suggest that such strictures cleared the debate on the left of such romanticism about crime. There have always been people unwilling to confront these problems except through rose-coloured spectacles, and this tendency is perhaps stronger in Britain than elsewhere. But the key to the re-emergence of this position in such a strident form was race. The debate over the nature of lower-working-class crime has been transposed to a debate over black crime. Accusations of a high black crime rate were seen as racist and the denial of such an occurrence as a defence of the black community. From this standpoint the duty of all anti-racists was

to show how the crime statistics were exaggerated and constituted a smokescreen while on another, more combative level,
the image of an illicit colony growing up within the host country
was evoked in which crime was seen as a form of resistance
or anti-colonial struggle. This is well captured by two left-wing
writers, Friend and Metcalf, who write:

> The establishment of these black neighbourhoods opened up for
> some the possibility of surviving by alternative means, by a process
> of hustling involving activities such as gambling, undeclared part-time
> work, ganja selling, shoplifting, street crime, housebreaking and dis-
> tributing stolen goods. Sections of the white working class have long
> chosen to survive through similar strategies, demonstrating in their
> communities a collective contempt for work discipline, concern for
> and dependence on the goodwill of an employer or outside authority.
> (p. 156)

They go on explicitly to identify the crimes of young people
as a direct challenge to capitalism with black youth being in
the forefront of such a struggle:

> During the seventies the challenge to property relations and the
> smooth reproduction of capitalist social relations increasingly came
> from working-class youth in general. The decade began with a fairly
> narrow set of youth singled out for attention – skinheads, hippies,
> student militants and blacks. There followed constant rumblings about
> vandalism, hooliganism and truancy and from 1976 onwards both media
> and state were glancing anxiously at the militancy and self-organization
> of Asian youth. By the end of the decade politicians, media and the
> state functionaries were talking of youth as a whole as being a 'problem'.
> The number of crimes recorded as committed by young people rose
> throughout the period ...
> This progression has not, of course, been unconnected to the
> structural unemployment which was hitting black youth at the
> beginning of the period and is now bearing down on all working-class
> youth. Loss of income through unemployment debars youth from
> almost all recreational and cultural activities which have to be bought
> in the marketplace and inevitably leads to problems of social control.
> As vandalism has become a routine recreational activity for younger

kids and teenagers alike, thefts have risen and truancy has reached a level where one London borough estimates between 450 and 600 kids skip school every day. (ibid., pp. 161–2)

We wish to argue that such an approach commits a cardinal error. The challenge to property which such young people evinced was directed not so much at capitalism as at the working class – both white and black. And the social relations which were threatened were, very often, not those of capitalism but of the working-class community around them.

## The 'Anti-Colonial Struggle' in the Inner City

The image of crime as a proto-revolutionary struggle is made to fit a particular view of race and immigration: a view of the alien colony within the imperialist city. This is well summed up in the title of a book recently produced by the Race and Politics group of the Centre for Contemporary Cultural Studies: *The Empire Strikes Back*. The image is that of a colonial culture, steeped in resistance, existing in the heart of the Empire. The traditions of anti-colonialism dormant in the first generation of immigrants are resuscitated in the youth of the second generation. Thus such areas as Railton Road in Brixton or Saint Paul's in Bristol represent the toehold of a colonial people fighting back against imperialism. The frontline is a colony *within* the host country. The culture that has grown up there is the vanguard of Afro-Caribbean culture – it is the culture of survival which every now and then breaks out into the open as resistance. Crime, from this perspective, is *part of* the continuing fightback of a downtrodden people against their colonial oppressors.

From this perspective the police are not merely 'an intrusion into that society, but a threat, a foreign force, an army of occupation – the thin end of the authoritarian wedge, and in themselves so authoritarian as to make no difference between wedge and state.' (Sivanandan, 1981, p. 150.)

Not only the culture but the form of policing itself originated in the colonies. As Courtney Griffiths put it (p. 10): 'Police practices and attitudes towards black people in the UK have a history originating in the conditions of imperialism'.

The 'white left' fail to understand the nature of such resistance. Paul Gilroy, for instance, is 'unable to accept ... the assertion that all sections of the population are united in their opposition to street crime' (1983, p. 150). He presumably believes that a substantial minority of the black population support such activities. As to the *genuine* fightback, such as during the riots of summer 1981, the belief that these occur because of a lack of political organization is seen as incorrect. The 'black communities' response [is not one] of "alienation" or "political marginalization" but of organized resistance, albeit in terms drawing on traditions of anti-colonial struggle which do not necessarily fit with the Left's perceptions of politics' (Bridges and Gilroy, p. 35). Furthermore,

> We must also realize that forms of political action and organization developed in previous struggles offer no guarantees of efficacy in new circumstances and relations of force. The ahistorical fetishism of organizational forms which have outlived their adequacy in the dogmatic prescriptions of omniscient bureaucrats and party officers is both a fetter on progress and a set of blinkers preventing useful analysis of the present. (Gilroy, 1981, p. 220)

Lastly, concomitant with this position is a belief that all the various immigrant groups – but Asians and West Indians in particular – share common responses to their situation in Britain. This is because of their postulated common anti-colonial heritage and their uniform experience of discrimination in this country.

An attempt can be made to sum up at this point the main principles of the colony-within-the-imperialist-city approach to race:

1  A *minimization* of the differences between the various immigrant groups' cultures.
2  A *maximization* of the differences between immigrant groups

and the native culture: in the case of West Indians this involves an attack on notions of acculturation – a minimization of the impact of British culture in the Caribbean and a maximization of the importance of its African roots.

3 A *minimization* of the social problems occurring within immigrant cultures *despite* the recognition of the deleterious impact of colonial oppression. As a consequence a degree of relativism enters into the discussion of family structures, relationships between the sexes, inter-generational disputes, etc. All of these, of course, are highly controversial areas.

This represents a perspective on race within which discussion about crime is only one aspect of a much wider debate. However, because of the moral panic in the mass media concerning race and crime, the problem of immigrant criminality has become a central cockpit for both right and left. Furthermore, as Paul Gilroy says:

Because of their capacity to symbolize other relations and conflicts, images of crime and law-breaking have had a special ideological importance since the dawn of capitalism. If the potential for organized political struggle towards social transformation offered by criminality has often been low, images of particular crimes and criminal classes have frequently borne symbolic meanings and even signified powerful threats to the social order. This means that 'crime' can have political implications which extend beyond the political consciousness of criminals. The boundaries of what is considered criminal or illegal are elastic and the limits of the law have been repeatedly altered by intense class conflict. It is often forgotten that the political formation of the working-class movement in this country is saturated with illegality. The relation of politics to 'crime' is therefore complex. These points should be borne in mind if socialists are not to rush into the arms of the right in their bid to 'take crime seriously'. (1982, p. 47)

## The Political Context of the Debate

Let us briefly outline our political differences with authors such as Gilroy and Bridges. The most clear exposition of their politics is Lee Bridges' diatribe against the Labour Movement in the recent *Sage Relations Abstract*. Bridges' political position can, we believe, be summarized in four propositions:

(1) The state and all its institutions, but notably the police and the media, are monolithically racist. This racism is an aspect of the functional relationship between state policy and the 'logic' of capital.

(2) Current concerns with crime, rather than reflecting real social problems, are part of a moral panic orchestrated by the state in the interests of capital accumulation. There is no real rise in black crime – there is merely an increased victimization by the police of blacks as scapegoats.

(3) The only real resistance to this process comes from the black movement, which is not concerned with the problem of crime as it affects the black community but is oriented towards the employment of essentially anti-colonialist techniques of defensive struggle against the racist state.

(4) The 'white left' is marginalized from this struggle although it makes periodic attempts to co-opt black politics and issues.

The position that we represent, which has come to be labelled the 'new left realism about crime' and against which Bridges directs his polemic, starts from a different set of propositions concerning the state and the nature of the problem of crime. The practical political orientation of this tendency is towards the left of the Labour Party. The main ingredients of the position can be summarized as follows:

(1) The state as an institution does not start simply from the 'logic' of capital. The state is concerned above all with the reproduction of social relations. This involves *both* securing a stable framework for the process of capital accumulation *and* attempting to minimize some of the more destructive results of the latter. Thus, during the 1970s state policy on race relations was contradictory, involving attempts both to secure immigrants as a low-wage labour-force *and* to

achieve a degree of integration sufficient to forestall a repetition in Britain of the American riots of the late sixties (Lea).

(2) Integration policies were thrown into disarray by the onset of economic recession. Massive unemployment and the attempts by capital to alter the composition of the working class have resulted in such phenomena as the weakening of the working-class community, and a growing alienation from the Welfare State and the social democratic politics that sustained it. An increase in political racism within the working class has been one response to this situation.

(3) Another response has been increased crime. Increases in crime rates are one manifestation of the destructive effects of recession upon working people. Moral panics concerning crime have a resonance precisely because they accord with the perceptions and fears of ordinary working-class people. There is an increase in black crime as a consequence of economic deprivation and police harassment. As Stuart Hall and his colleagues put it (p. 390):

The position of black labour, subordinated by the processes of capital, is deteriorating and will deteriorate more rapidly, according to its own specific logic. Crime is one perfectly predictable and quite comprehensible consequence of this process – as certain a consequence of how the structures work, however 'unintended', as the fact that night follows day.

(4) Likewise, recent changes in policing policy cannot be seen simply as orchestrated from above. The move to what we term 'military' policing has to be seen as a response to real social problems, a complex interaction between the structure of state organs such as the police and the forms of response institutionally available to them, and the changes in the structure of the working class resulting from de-industrialization. Consequently, struggles to change state policy in the direction of democratic control of social policy must also be aimed at re-strengthening forms of local

community rather than taking the latter for granted. As was
made clear in Cowell (ed.), *Policing the Riots* (p. 152):

The whole point about democratic accountability of the police to
properly elected and constituted police authorities ... is that it can
be part of a process whereby a political culture is established in the
communities and extended into new areas.

## *A Subcultural Approach to Race and Crime*

In contrast to the 'colonial' approach, we would argue for an
approach which stresses the fact that human beings continually
*create* solutions at the level of culture and subculture to the
material experiences with which they are confronted. Men and
women make their own cultural history, but they do so out
of the cultural traditions they carry with them and in historical
situations and environments not of their own choosing. What
characterizes the view of our critics is its misunderstanding of
the process whereby peasants and workers from the colonies
and former colonies find themselves in the labour markets of
the imperialist metropolis. The notion that some sort of cultural
*Geist* accompanies immigrants from the colonies to the imperialist city and is directly available to the second-generation
sons and daughters of immigrants born in the city is profoundly
idealist. The continuity of imperialism consists in the transition
from the status of ex-slaves, peasants, etc., in the colonies or
ex-colonies, to that of an exploited 'ethnic minority' condemned
to low wages and long and unsocial hours of work in the
metropolis in occupations vacated by native labour. This process
is accompanied by a high degree of racial hostility and discrimination from all social classes in the imperialist city, and
in today's economic circumstances very high rates of unemployment for the minority communities. The means whereby the
immigrant communities and especially the second-generation
children of immigrants *adapt* culturally and emotionally to this
process is complex and contradictory involving elements both

of assimilation to the culture of the 'host' country and of rediscovery or reconstruction of elements of the culture and political experience of the countries from which the first generation of immigrants came. The main ingredient of the response of the second-generation descendants of immigrants to the social and economic deprivations which they face in metropolitan society is certainly not describable as the simple transfer of 'traditions of anti-colonial struggle'.

The history of an immigrant group is, of course, important. But immigrant communities must be understood in terms of their real histories, not ones imposed upon them to fit in with some political preconceptions. The conflation, for instance, of the West Indian and Asian experiences under the general rubric of anti-colonial struggle and a common experience of prejudice scarcely does justice to the very different traditions, experiences and actual outcomes involved. Subcultures constantly evolve; they do not merely propagate a cultural essence such as 'the anti-colonial experience' from generation to generation. This is particularly important to understand when such extraordinary transitions and upheavals as migration are concerned. At a minimum, therefore, we must distinguish between (a) the culture of the country from which migration takes place, within which there are often diverse subcultures, (b) the particular subculture of those who migrate, and (c) the subcultures which grow up as part of the process of adaption to the country of immigration. The link from (a) to (c) is tenuous. To believe, for example, that the activities of second-generation West Indian youth are simply the enactment of a resuscitated home culture of the West Indies denies the extremely different conditions in Britain compared to those of the West Indies. It also blatantly denies creativity and innovation to the youth. It denies the way in which immigrant groups are heterogeneous, not only inter-generationally but also intra-generationally. The same predicament may produce a diversity of solutions: witness Pentecostalism, Rastafarianism, hustling, and respectability, among

blacks (see Pryce). To take one's favourite subcultural solution
as indicative of the vanguard or even of the whole group just
because it fits certain political preconceptions is a common
problem which we must constantly be aware of.

Subcultures emerge as adaptions to problems faced by individuals and groups, but such adaptions do not necessarily bring
a solution to the problem which is either tenable or in the
interests of the group as a whole. Often the response to injustice
is itself individualistic and competitive and may bring harm
to the people involved. To believe that the reaction against
injustice is of necessity just and effective is a common mistake
of the optimist. The relation between politics and subculture
is itself complex. History is rich with examples – and the anti-
colonial struggle is one of them – of how groups with profoundly differing cultural practices can unite around common
political aims (for example, the unity between blacks and Asians
in the struggle for colonial independence in the West Indies).
The problem is not, therefore, to deny politics in favour of
'mere' cultural habits, but to avoid the reverse: the ossification
of subcultural *adaptions* to injustice into the status of political
*struggles* against it. Nowhere is this problem clearer than in
the case of criminality.

Crime is one aspect, though generally a small one, of the
process of cultural adaption to oppression. While a fetish is
not to be made out of legality – class struggle may involve
the violation of laws whose only purpose is to defend the
particular interests of ruling élites and to criminalize anyone
who challenges their power – neither must it be thought that
all criminal acts by oppressed groups advance the struggle for
emancipation. In reality the issue is not criminality *per se* but
responses to suffering which further debilitate and brutalize
the sufferers, as opposed to those which advance the struggle
for justice.

There is no reason whatsoever to assume that unintegrated
ethnic cultures are more likely to generate instability and dis-

content than a situation of cultural homogeneity. In fact, the reverse is probably true. The first generation of immigrants entering this country in the 1950s and 1960s more often than not had lower expectations of living standards than the indigenous population because comparisons were still predominantly being made with conditions in the country of emigration. Under these circumstances cultural diversity is a factor working against instability and discontent. It is the second generation, born in this country of immigrant parents, educated to have equal job expectations by the school, and consumer demands by the mass media, that begins to see itself, when compared with the native population of the same age, as manifestly unequal. If discrimination remains entrenched in the practices and attitudes of the majority of the population, then it is not the separateness of cultures but the process of their homogenization, through the school and the mass media, that gives rise to discontent.

Secondly, it is a mistake to see the culture of many black youths in Britain today as derived from their parents. Take 'West Indians' as an example. What we are witnessing among 'West Indian' black youth is the development of a culture of discontent resulting precisely from the visibility of deprivation, a visibility highlighted by the very process of integration into British standards and expectations of life. The street culture of black youth of West Indian parentage is *not* a hand-down from the previous generation of immigrant parents as the conservative thesis of 'alien cultures' would suggest. Rather, it is an improvised culture based on the import of elements from the West Indies by kids most of whom either have never been there or left when they were very young. Indeed, such culture is widely disapproved of by the older generation of West Indian immigrants and it is, furthermore, a minority and deviant subculture within the West Indies itself.

So the conservative thesis has got it badly wrong: the 'alien' culture feared by conservatives grew not out of the values of the previous generation of immigrants but out of the process of cultural assimilation itself, a process in which a new generation of young people have assimilated the expectations of the majority culture, only to be denied them in reality. The question arises at this point of the differences between Asian and West Indian youth. As a result of discrimination, the unemployment rate for ethnic minority youth in general has risen at a much faster rate than for their white counterparts. But between youth of West Indian and Asian parentage there are two differences which have the effect of comparatively insulating the latter from the process of relative deprivation. Firstly, by comparison with West Indian youth, Asians have a more substantive opportunity structure within their own community. This is due to the larger size of the professional and business class in the Asian community. Secondly, the distance between Asian culture and indigenous British culture is greater than that between the latter and West Indian culture. Assimilation to indigenous British standards and aspirations has thus probably been a more rapid process for youth of West Indian parentage, and hence relative deprivation is felt more acutely, with the consequent fostering of a deviant counter-culture. There are other factors at work here which will be mentioned later.

Actually, the most 'alien' or way-out cultures are, in fact, often the most innocuous. For example, the Hasidic Jews among the ethnic groups, or hippies among youth cultures, are, probably, the most distant from mainstream conventions. It is subcultures involving crime and delinquency which, because they are closest to our wider values, have the greatest criminal impact on our lives. And this includes not only lower-working-class delinquents, but also criminals, whose lives are so conventional that they would heartily deny that their illegalities were really criminal.

Part of the wrath which Paul Gilroy and his associates vented on us stemmed from this analysis of the predicament of second-generation West Indian youth in Britain. We argued that their disquiet stemmed from their similarity to native white youth. The culture of West Indian youth, unlike that of various Asian immigrant communities, was close to that of the British, and their socialization through British schools made it even more so. It was the degree of *assimilation* which made them – quite rightly – discontented when they compared themselves, in terms of opportunities, with their white school-mates, and not their alienation from British culture. Bridges, Gilroy, and a large part of the Race and Class Collective argued the opposite: that West Indian kids had carried with them cultural notions of the anti-colonial struggle. Like conservatives, but for the opposite reasons, they conceived of black youth as exhibiting an alien culture. However much their parents, as immigrants, had been quiescent, the youth had revived the tradition. For us, however, the 'frontline' was a creation of those black youths who had assimilated, yet at the same time seen themselves rejected by British society through racial discrimination and deprivation. These kids have created their own cultural means of surviving that rejection, by reviving half-warm memories of the Caribbean, and this culture has to be understood both in terms of its creativity and of its disorganization, in terms of its being a black British rather than an undiluted Caribbean culture carried genetically from a widely differing society. Like all poor and marginalized groups throughout history, black youth has developed a contradictory subculture, part collective resistance and part criminality and disorganization. The contradictory nature of such subcultures – and the same goes for those in white youth cultures, such as punks or skinheads – must always be kept in mind. They can be both progressive and divisive, both rebellious and reactionary. Hence the one-sided readings that occur either by radicals who, through rose-tinted glasses, see only positives, and the conservatives, whose jaded glance notes merely the negative.

By pointing to the differences in crime rate between Asians and Afro-Caribbeans we were seen to be 'driving a wedge' between the two communities, despite the fact that the vast majority of authorities are in agreement on this issue. Most recently, Mawby and Batta, in their painstaking study of crime published by the National Association for Asian Youth, came to this conclusion, as does every single research study that we can trace. This is not to make insidious comparisons at all, it is merely to record the differences that culture makes to experienced deprivation. As Jefferson and Clarke (pp. 37–8) put it:

We wish to distinguish firmly between West Indian and Asian communities in Britain, in terms of their differing cultures. Asian teenagers do not experience the worst effects of structural and racial inequalities since they remain within the strong, self-contained Asian culture, primarily contained in family and religion.

The shaky nature of evidence to the contrary is summed up by Gilroy's rather desperate remark (1982, p. 177):

Of course, since police rely heavily on intelligence from outside their own ranks to catch criminals or even to detect their crimes, and Asian people have every reason to steer clear of a force which assumes them to be illegally resident rather than take their grievances seriously, there may be some much simpler reason for the low rates of reported crime.

The fact that Asians have a very high rate of criminal victimization which is reported to the police (over four times that of blacks or whites in certain categories of offence) belies this point, however true it may be that they have a totally justifiable suspicion of the police.

## Subcultural Theory and Racism

Accusations of racism have, as we have noted, been made against our argument. It is therefore necessary to demonstrate that subcultural theory is quite innocent of such accusations. Moreover, subcultural theory enables us to locate embarrassing similarities between genetic theories of crime and the notions of cultural continuity such as those exhibited in the 'colonial-struggle-in-the-metropolis' approach discussed above.

For subcultural theory the behaviour of a particular group relates to its specific history and the opportunities and constraints which that brings. Subcultural theory is opposed to any notion of 'natural' criminal tendencies of a particular group whether this be established in a genetic, racist fashion or by means of a cultural essence transmitted relatively unaltered over time. Nowadays the belief in a pre-written genetic script determining the behavioural characteristics of a group has little audience. Culturalist theories have a more pervasive influence, however. From the latter standpoint the essential characteristics of a group are seen to be determined by cultural traditions whose 'essence' can be discovered by the discerning analyst. Thus a Jewish propensity for finance is discovered, or an African propensity for rhythm identifiable in contemporary black America. Such theories abound in the discussion of ethnic groups and their history, and stretch from music (jazz as the direct expression of an African culture in America) to politics (Jews as innately quiescent in the face of adversity), and embrace all those writers, of the right or left in politics, who see the behaviour of second-generation immigrants as a cultural replay of their ancestry.

The point is not to deny cultural legacies and traditions but to emphasize that they are constantly changed, reinterpreted and reworked in the face of changing circumstances. The immense variations of human behaviour cannot be accounted for in terms of the genetic script or the cultural essence. Those who a generation ago were talking of Jewish quiescence in response to persecution presumably now speak of the innate aggressiveness of Jewish culture. The relationship between one generation and the next is a process of *reworking* rather than a process of *transmission*. A group in a new set of circumstances or environment reconstructs, adapts, and innovates, culturally as in other aspects of existence. Aspects of the new environment are combined with the appropriation of often contradictory elements of the past in the process of the creation of a new subcultural adaption to a new environment. A New York Jew is both a Jew and a New Yorker.

As far as crime is concerned it is very useful to look at the work of the Chicago School of Urban Sociology, which charted the progress of immigrant groups through the city of Chicago. They started from the observation that certain areas of the city invariably had high crime rates, and that these areas were close to the city centre, in the poorer neighbourhoods. Delinquency rates progressively decreased as one moved from the urban centre out towards the suburbs.

As each immigrant group arrived they moved into this cheap inner-city area – the zone of transition – while the group already there began the trek to the suburbs. Irish, Germans, Jews – each moved through this zone of migration, adapted to the high delinquency rate of the area and began to lose its delinquency as it moved 'over the tracks' towards the suburbs. What the Chicago School demonstrated was that delinquency was not the perquisite of any one ethnic group alone, but that of any group placed in certain predicaments. It is not common, for example, in Britain today to think of Jews or Italians as having high crime rates. Indeed, the opposite is true. Yet at the beginning of the century in London this was the case. Witness this extract from Arthur Harding's description of Whitechapel:

Edward Emmanuel had a group of Jewish terrors. There was Jackie Berman. He told a pack of lies against me in the vendetta case – he had me put away ... Bobby Levy – he lived down Chingford way – and his brother Moey. Bobby Nark – he was a good fighting chap. In later years all the Jewish terrors worked with the Italian mob on the race course ... The Narks were a famous Jewish family from out of Aldgate. Bobby was a fine big fellow though he wasn't very brainy. His team used to hang out in a pub at Aldgate on the corner of Petticoat Lane. I've seen him smash a bloke's hat over his face and knock his beer over. He belonged to the Darby Sabini gang – that was made up of Jewish chaps and Italian chaps. He married an English lady – stone rich – they said she was worth thousands and thousands of pounds. He's dead and gone now. (Samuel, pp. 133–4)

A proportion of poor people everywhere have turned to crime. But not to the same extent. The Chicago School was too mechanical in its linking of constant adversity with a constant rate of crime. Different ethnic groups react differently to deprivation, whether it be, for example, unemployment, poor education or bad housing. As Terrence Morris commented on the Chicago School:

> Although Chicago's immigrant groups were concentrated in the deteriorating interstitial areas of the city, and delinquency and deterioration correlate positively and highly, it remains that the Negroes and Italians produced delinquency out of proportion to their numbers when compared with other ethnic ... groups. (pp. 86–7)

This is not to say that blacks and Italians, due to a cultural essence or to genetic predisposition, inevitably have higher crime rates. The crime rate is *neither* wholly a function of the material conditions – the areas with their unemployment, bad housing, etc. – *nor* of a particular culture, but a complex interaction between the two. Subcultures arise out of material conditions, but at the same time the culture a group carries with it into a new situation will influence how the new material conditions will be experienced, enjoyed, tolerated, suffered, or actively fought. The existing culture will provide a major *part* of the raw material out of which a new cultural adaptation will be worked.

In concluding this stage in the discussion we wish to underline three of the points we have tried to make above. Firstly, as regards crime, one cannot have it both ways. Street crime cannot be seen as having a 'social and political nature' which links it to the tradition of anti-colonial struggle if at the same time it is maintained that the crime statistics are purely a function of police prejudice. Secondly, the culture of second-generation black youth in Britain today is not simply a transmitted culture embodying an unbroken tradition of anti-colonial struggle. It is, rather, a complex entity involving assimilation to native British culture, the received cultural adaptions of the first generation of immigrants, and a process of innovation and cultural construction attempting to make sense of, and survive in, the harsh conditions of racist Britain. For some the political rediscovery of the anti-colonial struggle has been a way of trying to make sense of their position in Britain. For many, shifting in and out of criminality and hustling have become forms of adaption to the same problems. Finally, the fact that criminality will be used as an ideology by ruling élites in attempts to legitimize the repression of groups meeting their displeasure does not entail that street crime is some form of politics. Those who refer to the 'social and political nature' of the criminality of a minority of black youth have yet to demonstrate its contribution to the struggle for social justice as opposed to the demoralization and weakening of that struggle. We can only echo the words of Stuart Hall and his colleagues

> The fact is that there is, as yet, no active politics, no form of organized struggle, and no strategy which is able adequately and decisively to *intervene* in the quasi-rebellion of the black wageless such as would be capable of bringing about that *break* in the current false appropriations of oppression through crime – that critical transformation of the criminalized consciousness into something more sustained and thoroughgoing in a political sense. (pp. 396–7)

## The Colonial Model in the United States

It should be noted as an aside that even if one accepted the colonial-struggle model in its entirety, the political deduction of ignoring crime simply would not follow. This becomes apparent if one looks at the American black leaders who have embraced the colonial model. It is in the United States where writers such as Sivanandan (1981) see the colonial model of blacks assuming its most characteristic form. It is paradoxical that it is black nationalist leaders, who are precisely those who see their struggle in colonial terms, who are adamant about the need to eliminate criminal, and indeed a wide range of deviant behaviour from their communities. They do not deny the existence of crime or antisocial behaviour; they see it as a prime source of weakness. From the Muslims who worked strenuously against crime, hard drug use, gambling and prostitution, to the revolutionaries like George Jackson who attempted to 'transform the black criminal mentality into a black revolutionary mentality', there was scarcely a denial of crime or the problems that crime created.

## Race and the Crime Statistics

Turning now to the actual debate on race and crime which has proceeded on and off over the last decade, we find that some of the themes featured in the positions of Gilroy and his associates are in fact shared by a much wider circle of liberal commentators. In particular, the debate has been heavily characterized by what we call the 'either–or' approach, in which the questions whether young blacks living in deprived areas have higher rates of street crime, and whether the crime levels for young blacks are a reflection of police prejudice in arrest procedures and the allocation of resources to certain areas of the city, have been seen as mutually exclusive. While not all the contributors to the debate have explicitly held such positions, the whole tenor of the debate, as we shall see, has been couched in terms of ascertaining which of these two hypotheses is true. *Either* young inner-city blacks really do have a higher rate of street crime, *or* the difference is a result of police activity. After reviewing the major contributions to this debate we shall return to this question.

### The 1972 Select Committee Report

If the problem of the crime rate of young blacks is simply a result of police activity and prejudice then we have the following problem: how is it that as late as 1971 the police themselves were of the opinion that there was no special problem as regards black crime? In their evidence to the 1971–2 session of the House of Commons Select Committee on Race Relations and Immigration the police denied that black crime rates were any different from those of any other sections of the population. The Committee concluded:

> Of all the police forces from whom we took evidence, not óne had found that crime committed by coloured people was proportionately greater than that by the rest of the population. Indeed in many places it was somewhat less. Both the Police Federation, which represents all policemen up to and including the rank of Inspector, and the Metropolitan Police confirm this ... The conclusions remain beyond doubt: coloured immigrants are no more involved in crime than others; nor are they generally more concerned in violence, prostitution and drugs. The West Indian crime rate is much the same as that of the indigenous population. The Asian crime rate is very much lower. (House of Commons 471–I, pp. 240–42, session 1971–2)

The conclusions of the Select Committee were based on the submissions of several police forces and the Police Federation. In what from the standpoint of today's mentality might seem like a left-wing outburst, the Police Federation argued:

> It is urgently necessary that the government pays extra attention to ... special efforts to minimize discrimination in the employment field for young people. If this is not done then it will no longer be possible to criticize the vociferous militants as being unrepresentative. On the contrary, they will be the leaders of the Black and Coloured peoples in Britain. (House of Commons 471–II, p. 24, session 1971–2)

Of the Metropolitan Police divisions giving separate submissions to the committee, all argued that black people presented no special problems as regards crime:

> The proportion of coloured to white people in Notting Hill is about 1:8. The following figures which cover the year 1971 show that in arrests etc., this proportion is roughly maintained. ('B' Division)

Islington has a high concentration (11.6 per cent) of coloured people ... it is recognized by the police that there is no evidence that the coloured community are less law-abiding than the indigenous population. ('N' Division)

'W' Division (Wandsworth) was the only division to give a hint of things to come:

There is, however, one area where we are concerned over the number of coloured youths who are involved. This relates to 'Theft from the Person' which ... usually involves the snatching of property, generally handbags, from a person without the use of violence ... In 1971 there were 135 cases reported and from the facts given by the victims 84 or 62 per cent of the total were committed by coloured youths ... On the other hand when violence was used on the victim in the course of such an offence (which changes the classification of the offence to robbery) there is no evidence that coloured youths are involved to any great degree.

This qualification was, however, not mentioned in the report of the Select Committee itself. The government commented in its official response to the report:

The government have noted with interest the evidence from several police sources given to the Select Committee that crime rates in the immigrant community are no higher than, and in some cases significantly lower than, those for the indigenous population and will draw it to the attention of chief officers of police. (1973 Cmnd 5438, p. 6)

The whole tenor of this passage, of course, makes it clear that attitudes within the police force towards black crime were certainly not free of race prejudice. But that only makes it harder to explain the change in the official police attitude to black crime only in terms of race prejudice. For by the time of the 1976–7 session of the same House of Commons committee, the opinion of the Metropolitan Police concerning the figures given to the committee in 1971 was that 'so far as West Indians in London are concerned, this no longer holds good.' A disproportionately high rate of black crime among young West Indians in London was now the official police argument. What had happened in the mean time?

If black crime rates, or rather however much crime among young black people in the inner cities is above average, are simply the product of police prejudice, then to explain the change in the police position between 1971 and 1976 we have to engage in some rather dubious hypothesizing. Either the police were almost entirely free of prejudice prior to 1971 and rapidly became prejudiced during the 1970s, which is rather unlikely, or their prejudice led them, in some strange way, to engage in a form of positive discrimination prior to 1971, consciously under-representing black crime and Asian crime in particular. Such a way of thinking also inevitably involves the assumption that in the absence of police prejudice the crime rate for all social groups would be the same. To argue this in the face of our knowledge of the relation between crime, particularly street crime, and unemployment, poverty and deprivation has an air of fantasy to it.

A more plausible explanation might be to suggest that what was happening during the 1970s, and which was marginally reflected in police evidence to the Select Committee in 1971, was the failure of the Race Relations legislation of the 1960s to lay the basis for racial integration. In this context, the growth of the second generation of young black British, coming through the school system and facing, as we have argued above, the dual process of assimilation and rejection, resulted in a growth in street crime.

### The 1977 Select Committee Report

The burden of the evidence of the Metropolitan Police to the 1976–7 session of the Select Committee on Race Relations and Immigration was:

An examination of Metropolitan Police statistics relating to persons arrested for indictable crime during 1975 reveals that of the 103,252 people arrested, 12,640 (i.e. 12 per cent) were classified as being apparently of West Indian or African origin. Comparing this figure with the estimated black population (4.3 per cent), a disproportionate involvement is indicated. In fact the involvement of black people in the arrest figures is disproportionate for every major category of crime. (para. 99)

The police were well aware that 'the use of arrest figures as a yardstick is, of course, a two-edged weapon. For it opens the door to the charge that the police discriminate against black people when enforcing the law. The implication is that if the police did not discriminate, black people would not be disproportionately involved in the arrest figures' (para. 15). The police were, in other words, aware of the problem of crime statistics being a product of police activity itself rather than any indication of the 'real' rate of crime. Accordingly, they made some effort to provide alternative evidence, by including a compilation of crimes reported to the police by victims: 'Evaluation of the extent of the involvement of black people in street crime from crime reports relies on the evidence of the victim. It therefore avoids the charge of discrimination by police which could be raised in the use of arrest figures. It also provides a yardstick for testing the validity of the discrimination charge.' The evidence that the police provided for the descriptive identity of alleged attackers for the offences of robbery and violent theft showed a disproportionate representation of black people in victim-reported crime relating to these offences. The police concluded that 'Accepting that arrest figures for robbery and other violent thefts reasonably reflect the extent of black involvement as perceived by victims, it is not unrealistic to assume that arrest figures for other crimes also provide some guide to the actual degree of black involvement in these crimes' (para. 40). What the claim by the police amounted

to can be seen in Table 4.1, which is constructed from the
statistics for robbery and violent theft given by them to the
Select Committee.

Table 4.1

|  | Arrests | Victim-reported crimes (Includes both detected and undetected crime) |
| --- | --- | --- |
|  | per cent | per cent |
| White | 65 | 25 |
| Coloured | 35 | 36 |
| Mixed race groups | — | 5 |
| Not known | — | 34 |

*Note:* The figures are constructed from the police data on p. 181 of volume I I
of the Report. The category 'coloured', while a single category in the figures
for victim-reported crime, corresponds in the arrest figures to five different
race codes. However, within this breakdown in the arrest figures, categories
besides 'Black West Indian/African' only amount to 4 per cent. Thus, while
not strictly comparable because mixed-race groups of attackers, and those whose
identity was not known, do not feature as a category in arrest statistics, the
figures illustrate the police's general argument that in both arrests and victim-
reported offences blacks were over-represented, without in any way implying
that the two columns of figures could be translated into each other.

Finally, in the presentation of their evidence to the committee
the police specifically underlined that: 'It is no part of our
position that there is a causal link between ethnic origin and
crime. What our records do suggest is that London's black
citizens, among whom those of West Indian origin predominate,
are disproportionately involved in many forms of crime. But
in view of their heavy concentration in areas of urban stress,
which are themselves high crime areas, and in view of the disproportionate numbers of young people in the West Indian
population, this pattern is not surprising' (para. 25).

Apart from the irregularities in the presentation of data, there
were other main criticisms made of the police evidence by indi-

viduals or organizations submitting evidence to the committee. The first issue raised was that of controlling for geographical and age distribution of the black population. The Community Relations Commission (CRC), now the Commission for Racial Equality, noted this as a weakness, and a similar point was raised by the Home Office in its own comment upon the police evidence: 'The Home Office knows of no reliable, up-to-date statistics of the age and sex distribution of minority groups within London or parts of London. Nor does it know of any reliable, up-to-date figures showing the geographical distribution of particular groups in London. The Home Office does not therefore feel that the evidence presented to the Committee, or any other material now available provides a basis from which conclusions can safely be drawn about the relative involvement in crime of particular groups within the community in London' (para. 5).

There is, however, a curious ambiguity in this aspect of the debate. If the police were attempting to establish a *causal* connection between ethnic difference and criminality – a racist theory of criminal types – then at the very least they would have to attempt a control for age, sex, geographical position, economic position, etc. Likewise, if it was being argued that the particular subculture which black youth had created in response to the experience of racial discrimination and deprivation of itself contained proclivities to crime, then again a control for age, sex, economic and geographical position would have been an essential stage of the argument. But it does not appear that the police were reasoning on this level at all. Indeed, they explicitly avoided it in the passage quoted above where they not only assert that it is 'no part of our position that there is a causal link between ethnic origin and crime', but go on to make the explicit point that given the disproportionate concentration of young blacks in areas of stress their over-representation in the crime statistics is 'not surprising'. The police, it appears, simply wished to draw the Select Committee's

attention to what they considered to be the 'fact' of the increasing
involvement of young blacks in crime. The CRC criticism on
this point appears, therefore, to have been wide of the mark
and to attack the police for something that they were not arguing.
That this misunderstanding occurred can be seen, however,
as a reflection of the changing political atmosphere concerning
race, and no doubt what was at the bottom of the CRC's thinking was the understanding of how these figures would be used
– as they indeed were – by the extreme right in subsequent
debate in the media to establish what the police had gone out
of their way to deny: a direct connection between ethnicity and
crime.

The second main point made against the police evidence was
that police arrest figures for young blacks could easily have
been artificially boosted by the police devoting more resources
or using different tactics in black areas. The CRC argued that:
'It is certainly possible that the presence or absence of the Special
Patrol Group has an important effect on the level of arrests
and the relationship between young black people and the police.'
Professor Terrence Morris, the criminologist, in his own submission to the committee added: 'One can only speculate, but
in the absence of data to the contrary, one must continue to
examine the possibility that the arrest rates of black persons
are in some part – though not of course wholly – determined
by the concentration of police presence in areas in which large
numbers of black persons live and work.'

The police had an opportunity to reply to the CRC submission, though not that of Professor Morris. Their response
to this point consisted simply of the assertion that 'The organization and employment of specialist squads is simply a response
to the existing patterns of crime.' The police had also attempted
to protect themselves from the charge that higher black crime
figures were a product of police activity rather than anything
else by the inclusion of figures on victim-reported crime and
we shall consider this aspect of the question presently. In the

mean time, what is the response to be to the assertion, entirely plausible, that arrest rates for young blacks were determined largely by the presence of large numbers of SPG officers in the area where they lived, and on the other hand to the equally plausible assertion that the decision to deploy the SPG in certain black areas in the first place was a result of the rising crime rates of those areas? There is a strong 'either–or' flavour to the debate about the evidence to the Select Committee, as if *either* the police explanation (the SPG was a response to rising crime rates) *or* the CRC–Morris line (high arrest rates were a result of heavy police presence in the area) must be true and by implication the other false.

In our opinion it is far more plausible to see *both* positions as true in the sense that they focus upon different moments of a continuous and related process. Such a process is describable as a vicious circle (this concept will be elaborated in the next chapter) and, briefly, can be seen to involve the following elements:

(a) There has been a real rise in the types of crime in which young black people are disproportionately involved due to rising unemployment and its over-representation among young blacks due to racial discrimination.

(b) In these circumstances, against the background of a high level of racial prejudice in British society, the police come to employ stereotypes of criminality among the black community as a whole and to employ saturation policing in such areas, the type of strategy which in the early eighties constituted the 'Swamp' operations in Brixton.

(c) This leads to a progressive deterioration in relations between the police and all sections of the black community – despite the increased police resources being put into 'community relations' during the seventies – and results in a marked fall in the supply of information from the community to the police.

(d) The result is that crime detection, because of less information

and a rising rate of real crime, becomes increasingly harder
and leads to a further incentive for the deployment of the
SPG in stop-and-search operations in an attempt to catch
offenders.

In a vicious circle like this, the crucial factor is the breakdown
in the supply of information flowing from the public to the
police. This brings us to the third type of criticism made of
the police evidence to the Select Committee, concerning the
connection between arrests and crimes. The CRC pointed out
that 'an arrest is merely an arrest on suspicion of crime; it
is not the same as a recorded crime ... In the well known
Carib Club case forty people were taken to the police station;
twelve were charged; two were convicted but subsequently
released because of inadequate evidence of identification and
their conviction quashed.' It is quite consistent, however, with
the 'vicious circle' hypothesis outlined above that saturation
police operations designed to gather information not otherwise
forthcoming from the public and to apprehend offenders by
catching them in the net will lead to a higher rate of arrests
not corresponding to crimes actually committed.

The fourth question mark placed against the police evidence
concerned victim-reported crime. As we have seen, the police
had presented their data on victim-reported crime in an attempt
to corroborate the general conclusions from their arrest figures.
The statistics for victim-reported crime, though not constructed
in the same ethnic categories as the arrest figures, nevertheless
share with them an over-representation of black people. The
police saw this as adding weight to the conclusions drawn from
the arrest figures. Professor Morris questioned the reliability
of victim-reported crime statistics even in cases where the victim
claimed to have seen the attacker:

Problems of identification are well known and ... in an area in which
it is the subject of public comment that 'young blacks are knocking
people down' it would be consistent with everything we know from

experiments in perception and memory for a person to perceive his or her assailant as 'black' or 'coloured' if there were any ambiguity and if the stereotype of the robber or thief is one of black youth.

There is, however, an additional problem which both the CRC and Professor Morris in his submission pointed to: the level of undetected crime. The police seemed to be totally un-critical of the fact that their statistics on victim-reported crime, drawn from an area with a high concentration of black persons showed that 'of the victims of the robberies, 84 per cent were white, 5 per cent were apparently of Asian origin, 5 per cent apparently of West Indian or African origin, 3 per cent apparently of Chinese origin, and in 3 per cent of the cases data was not available'. These figures were drawn from a smaller survey done by the police of the Brixton subdivision for the crime category 'robbery'. They do not correspond, therefore, to the figures mentioned above on victim-reported crime for the Metropolitan Police District (MDP) as a whole for the offence 'robbery and violent theft'. Professor Morris made a number of methodological criticisms of this sub-survey con-ducted by the community relations branch of the Metropolitan Police, the most important of which was the problem of basing such a survey on an area which was very likely to attract offenders from elsewhere.

However, even if we ignore this point, a set of figures drawn from Brixton in which the majority of the victims are white seems quite incredible. It seems very unlikely that Brixton should be an exception to the fact that the vast bulk of the victims of black crime are themselves black. This point is complicated by the fact that the police statistics on this question were constructed for a category 'robbery'. *Certain* categories of robbery, which have come to be named by the media as 'mugging', may have a high inter-racial component. This might account for the high percentage of white victims. However, other types of robbery committed by black persons find their victims within the black community and it is entirely plausible that the high percentage of white victims in figures for *victim-reported* crime reflects the fact that black victims are less forthcoming in reporting offences committed against them. If this is so, then of course black crime rates are higher than either the police arrest statistics or the victimization statistics indicate. But such a situation would certainly be consistent with a break-down in police relations with the black community and would be one consequence of the vicious circle process described above.

Some independent evidence of relevance to this argument might appear to come from the Home Office sponsored study by Tuck and Southgate in 1981. The study involved the comparison of crime reporting rates between whites and West Indians in an area of Manchester. The study does not bear out the drift of our argument, concluding that 'the overall frequency of reporting was similar for each group' for all categories of crime. However, this study was based upon a particularly small sample. It would be interesting to see a similar study done in Brixton. Police–black relations in Manchester may not be the same as those in areas such as Brixton. An indication of the difference between Manchester and Brixton may be the statistics for the use of 'sus' (arrest under the Vagrancy Act – now repealed – for suspicion of criminal intent). According to Demuth's study, in 1976, the Metropolitan Police District accounted for 55 per cent of all charges brought under the Vagrancy Act, whereas Manchester accounted for only 7 per cent. Again, any firm conclusions would require a thorough comparison of policing methods in each area together with precise figures for the distribution of the black community in the two areas.

The Select Committee concluded that, in the light of the problems surrounding the evidence of the Metropolitan Police, 'there is no evidence available to justify any firm conclusions about the relative involvement of West Indians in crime' (para. 103). The Committee also noted that the police had given the

Home Office access to its data and that research might further clarify the relationship between ethnicity and crime.

## Race Crime and Arrests

One result of Home Office research was the most detailed study yet published of the relation between ethnicity and crime in Britain. *Race Crime and Arrests*, written by Philip Stevens and Carole Willis and published by HMSO in 1979, is divided into two parts. The first is a study of the relationship between recorded serious crimes and ethnic minority populations in the major conurbations, and the second part is a study of the arrest data of the Metropolitan Police District for the year 1975.

Of the two parts of the survey the conurbation study is by far the least sophisticated. It shows that for the major conurbations and for police divisions within them there is no tendency for areas with a high West Indian or Asian population to have a high rate of recorded crime. Thus, for example, the recorded rate for indictable crime in Lambeth with a population about 10 per cent West Indian is 5,821 per 100,000 of the population, whereas that for Newcastle upon Tyne 'F' division with only around 0.10 per cent West Indian is 6,081 per 100,000. Indeed, a simple correlation between West Indian and Asian proportions of the population and the recorded rate of indictable crime is *negative* in both instances, although only in the case of Asians is this statistically significant.

Because the size of the conurbations might swamp any effect attributable to ethnic minorities, the researchers carried out further studies *within* police divisions and, again, no significant relationship was found between the size of the ethnic minority population as a proportion of the total population and the recorded rate of indictable crime. Areas such as the City of London and Liverpool city centre have extremely high crime rates and very low ethnic minority populations. London was found to be no exception to the general conclusion.

But what conclusions about the relationship between ethnic minorities and crime can be drawn from such a study? The authors conclude this section of their investigation by stating that 'there is no tendency for areas with high West Indian or Asian proportions to have high recorded indictable crime rates', and that 'the existence of a high rate of recorded indictable crime in an area does not mean that there is likely to be a high proportion of West Indians or Asians in the population of that area'. However, no conclusions can be drawn from such evidence as to the relative involvement of ethnic minorities in crime. The problems with this aspect of the study centre around varieties of the 'ecological fallacy' – the fallacy of moving from the characteristics of the population of a city or area to the characteristics of particular groups, such as ethnic minorities, within it. The fact that areas with high crime rates do not necessarily have high ethnic minority populations and areas with high ethnic minority populations do not necessarily have high crime rates does not enable us to draw conclusions about the crime rates of ethnic minorities contrasted with other sections of the population. A high crime rate by one group or minority may be cancelled out by an exceptionally low rate on the part of some other group. While the authors recognize that their conclusions might 'merely reflect the size of ethnic minority populations which are too small to influence significantly area-recorded crime rates', they do not entertain the possibility that this cancelling process might be present. For example, within an ethnic minority, an 'acquiescent' older generation with a very low crime rate may live together with an 'alienated' second generation of young people with a very high crime rate. Such a distribution would be masked in the aggregate figures as the two groups will balance each other out. Or a number of different immigrant groups with different crime rates may inhabit the same area. A very low crime rate for one could balance out the high crime rate for the other and produce the statistical result that the presence of ethnic minorities has no significant relationship with the crime rate for the area. Similar factors may operate on the level of the class composition of an area. For example, an area like Tyneside with a large poor population and a high rate of unemployment could be expected to have a high crime rate quite irrespective of the presence or absence of ethnic minorities. No one would find this surprising. But it may also be true that some inner-city areas with a high working-class West Indian population may also have a high proportion of middle-class white professionals with a low crime rate. The presence of these professional, middle-class, low-crime-rate groups may relate directly to the presence of high crime rates among problem populations: for example, social workers may live in the same areas as their clients. Again, such phenomena would reduce the general rate of recorded indictable crime for an area and so reduce any correlation between high crime rates and ethnic minorities suffering high rates of inner-city deprivation. Finally, a significant proportion of crime occurs outside the areas of residence of the offenders. Thus high crime rates in the city centres of London and Westminster with their low immigrant and ethnic minority populations – or indeed resident populations of any description – does not prove or disprove either way a relationship between ethnic minorities and crime.

In view of these problems with the first part of the Race Crime and Arrests study, it is not possible to agree with the authors that the 'findings are important in the context of some current beliefs that there is a positive relationship between the presence of ethnic minorities and the level of crime in an area' (p. 12). Only the most rabid racist would believe that all crime is attributable to ethnic minorities and it is this preposterous proposition *alone* that is being tested in the first part of the study.

The second part of the study is of much greater significance and sophistication. The starting-point for the study is the arrest rates of whites, blacks, and Asians for indictable crime in the MPD in 1975. These figures are summarized in Figure 4.1.

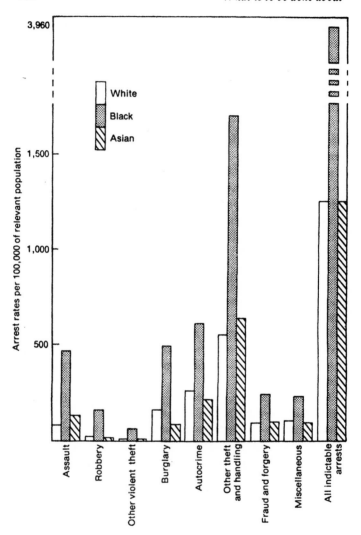

Figure 4.1. Arrest rates of whites, blacks and Asians for indictable crime
MPD, 1975
*Source*: Stevens and Willis, p. 16.

The object of the study is to look at the relationship between what the authors term 'intrinsic' and 'extrinsic' factors which might be held to explain the large concentration of blacks in certain categories of crime. Intrinsic factors refer to characteristics such as the youthfulness or the low income of the black population – both of which are factors known to be associated with the types of crime listed in the figure opposite. Or, on the other hand, intrinsic factors may concern actual differences in involvement in crime even when such factors as age and poverty are allowed for. Extrinsic factors are those which might account for a high representation in the crime statistics but which have nothing to do with the actual properties of the group concerned. Examples would be a greater propensity for the police to arrest black people, or the greater visibility of black people in a predominantly white population.

Stevens and Willis set out to analyse the relationship between extrinsic and intrinsic factors in the explanation of the black crime rate. First, they turn to the intrinisic factors of age and socio–economic situation. Youthful populations are more crime-prone than elderly ones. It could, therefore, be the case that the crime rates of blacks and Asians is simply a reflection of their age composition as a community. It is possible to calculate what black and Asian crime rates would be if there was no

Table 4.2. *Expected and actual indictable arrests per 100,000 of the population (MPD 1975)*

|  | White | Black | | Asian | |
| --- | Actual | Expected | Actual | Expected | Actual |
| --- | --- | --- | --- | --- | --- |
| Assault | 77 | 85 | 466 | 95 | 124 |
| Robbery | 18 | 22 | 160 | 24 | 13 |
| Other violent theft | 4 | 6 | 60 | 7 | 4 |
| Other indictable arrests | 1,149 | 1,403 | 3,275 | 1,516 | 1,112 |
| Total indictable arrests | 1,248 | 1,516 | 3,961 | 1,642 | 1,253 |

difference between the compositions of these communities and that of the white population *apart* from age. But this exercise, the results of which are reprinted in Table 4.2, shows that age alone was not able to account for the difference between the white crime rate and that of the Asian and black populations. The authors comment:

> From this it can be seen that a small part of the excess black arrest rates can be accounted for by age. Some of the excess Asian assault rate can be accounted for in the same way, while in the case of Asian rates for robbery, other violent theft and all other indictable arrests, allowance for age would actually lead one to expect a rate higher than that observed. It is perhaps surprising that, these exceptions apart, age does not account for more of the difference between the different groups, since ethnic minority communities are known to be young and the young are known to be more prone to arrest. One reason for this is perhaps that the most arrest-prone age group is the 15–24 year olds, and ethnic minorities in 1975 did not have particularly large proportions of their populations in this age group. There were, however, large proportions of the ethnic minorities aged 0–14 (about 40 per cent of the black and Asian communities were aged under 15 in 1975 compared with 20 per cent of the whites); this age group, not surprisingly, has an arrest rate lower than the average for all ages.
>
> The direct comparison of arrest rates by age groups leads, therefore, to the conclusion that age differences account for a small part of the excess black arrest rates and some of the excess Asian assault arrest rate, and, in the case of other Asian arrests, leads one to expect higher rates than are actually observed. (Stevens and Willis, pp. 18–19)

It should be noted, first of all, that the comment on the very youthful age structure of the sample population, while most probably correct, points to the distinct possibility of a sharp increase in crime in the years following 1975, the year to which the statistics relate – in other words, *at the present time*. Also to be noted is the variation in the findings for different ethnic groups. Apart from the rate for assault, for which the actual rate is a little above what would have been expected, Asians have a lower crime rate when age is taken into consideration and blacks a considerably higher one. The black rate for assault was five times the expected rate and for robbery seven times.

As regards socio-economic situation, for the twenty-two Metropolitan Police districts it was possible to compare crime rates and ethnic groups against such factors as unemployment, membership of socio-economic groups, and household tenure. The main findings of the investigation can be summarized as follows. Firstly, black, white and Asian arrest rates were all associated with common measures of deprivation. Secondly, however, better explanation was achieved when the effects of these variables were allowed to differ for each ethnic group: that is, the effects of each variable were mediated by the ethnic group involved. Thirdly, the strongest indicator of arrest rates was

for whites ... related to the white unemployment rate. Unemployment rates for blacks and Asians, however, although generally much higher than the white rates, were not strongly related, statistically, to arrest rates. For both the black and Asian arrest rates no single indicator emerged as strong as white unemployment for white arrests; but the best indicator of high ... arrest rates for blacks [for violent crime] appeared to be a low rate of home ownership whilst that for Asian arrest rates appeared to be a high proportion of Asians in the lowest socio-economic group. (ibid., p. 41)

Two comments can be made about these findings at this point. Firstly, the discovery of an ethnic factor which mediates the effect of 'objective' factors such as unemployment and housing tenure could be an effect of something intrinsic to each ethnic group or it might simply be the effect of an extrinsic factor such as police prejudice and stereotyping. Secondly, the 'objective' factors do not always link up in a natural causal fashion. Thus, for example, the *black* crime rate is most clearly linked, statistically, to the *white* unemployment rate.

None of the above should really come as a surprise to anyone approaching the problem from the standpoint of subcultural theory. We will explore this issue later, but for the moment let us note that it is something of a surprise to Stevens and Willis (that, for example, black crime rates should relate to white unemployment rates), and why this should be so is not at all obvious from conventional views, whether of the right or the left, which tend to assume an automatic link between deprivation and crime.

The study next turns to the 'extrinsic' factors, to examine the hypothesis that the crime rate is to some extent a product of differential law enforcement. It is important to note the process, well documented by criminologists, whereby a crime becomes a part of the official statistics. This process involves a series of stages, each of which might well explain the differential in official crime rates between different ethnic groups.

Different rates of actual crime
↓
Different rates of crime reported to the police
↓
Different rates of crime recorded by the police
↓
Different rates of crime cleared up by the police
↓
Different rates of crime recorded in the official crime statistics

Bias can, of course, creep in at every stage in this process. The question is, to what extent do such extrinsic factors explain differences in the official crime rate compared to the intrinsic factors mentioned above? Let us follow Stevens and Willis in their attempt to analyse each stage. Where the different rates of crime reported to the police are concerned, it is important to make clear how it is that the police become aware of crime. As Mawby has shown, 92 per cent of crime known to the police is a result of public reporting and only 8 per cent a result of direct policing. It is this fact that undermines the contention that the crime statistics are, in a quite direct way, a product of racial prejudice on the part of the police at the point of apprehension of offenders. As Susan Smith notes:

> With the memory of 'sus' still vivid in people's minds . . . it is tempting to attribute the arrest figures to racial bias on the part of the arresting officers. However, most academic opinion is now that with the exception of a few specific types of arrest (sus was one of them) the police have very little control on specifically which offenders come to light.

The police have some measure of control after crimes have come to light, but it is extremely important to recognize that to apprehend and convict an offender successfully, public involvement at every stage from reporting to the police to providing witness in court is vital. Stevens and Willis do not spell out this crucial point although, quite correctly, they focus on the *process* by which the statistics are created. They do not employ the mistakenly simple dichotomy of 'Are the police biased or not?' common to commentators of all political persuasions. As regards the reporting of offences the authors note: 'Most crime, as would be expected on statistical grounds alone, is intra-racial (e.g. white against white, black against black) and there is no evidence relating to the comparative likelihoods of white and black intra-racial crime to be reported to the police' (ibid., p. 29). We have already noted other Home Office sponsored research that could find no difference in the amount of crime reported by blacks and whites to the police, and some reasons for doubting whether it can be generalized to areas like Brixton or Toxteth. However, what is important here is the stress on two factors, the public initiation of crime proceedings, and the largely intra-racial nature of crime. The implications of this seem to be as follows: firstly, as most crime is reported by the public, the crime rates of ethnic groups are initiated, since most crime is intra-racial, by members of the ethnic groups concerned. Secondly, if public racism occurs it would exaggerate the *inter*-racial element in crime (mostly of

blacks against whites). Thirdly, one would expect a reaction to
police racism among minority groups to involve a suspicion of
the police. This would almost certainly involve a reduction in the
likelihood of reporting crimes by fellow members of an ethnic
minority to the police, and perhaps, in certain areas, an overall
lower rate of crime reporting to the police.

Such processes as these would tend to *under-represent* crime
committed by ethnic minorities known to the police. Stevens
and Willis do not go as far as this assertion but it is, in fact,
one possibility at this first stage in the process of offence to
statistic. The next stage in the process concerns police recording
of crime reported by the public. Here the authors note two
factors which could contribute to a possible imbalance in the
statistics. Firstly, a higher clear-up rate for black offences and/
or proportionally more mistaken arrests of blacks. On the first
factor Stevens and Willis conclude (p. 34):

> To explain the 1975 arrest figures in terms of differential success
> in clearing up black and white crime it would have been necessary
> for police to arrest 66 per cent of all black offenders but only 21
> per cent of white offenders ... Such an imbalance is implausible given
> that the ethnic identity of most offenders is unknown at the outset.

As far as the second strand of argument is concerned, an equally
implausible assumption would have to be made. That is, 76
per cent of all black arrests and only 19 per cent of white arrests
would have to be mistaken ones. This *reductio ad absurdum*
used by Stevens and Willis does not, of course, rule out discriminatory behaviour by the police. Rather (pp. 34–5)

> the previous calculations have shown how large the element of black
> offender visibility or discriminatory police activity would have had
> to be for such elements to account alone for the difference between
> the black and the white arrest rates. Nonetheless, it is possible that
> some of the difference between the two rates could be accounted for
> by differential clear-up rates or differential mistaken arrest rates or
> by a combination of the two.

Given that much crime is intra-racial, there is most probably a degree of neglect by the police of crimes reported to them by ethnic minorities. In other words, racism operates in two directions: it leads to prejudice in the arrest process, with a resultant over-representation of blacks in the arrest figures, but also to an opposite, albeit less powerful result, of an under-representation because crimes within the ethnic minority communities do not count as much as among whites. Whatever the impact of police prejudice and stereotyping it does not serve as a sufficient explanation of the actual, observed differential arrest rates.

Having dealt with these 'intrinsic' and 'extrinsic' factors, Stevens and Willis turn to the actual crime rate itself. Here they rely on victim reports, comparing them with the racial differentials in the official statistics. A similar comparison, it will be recalled, was part of the Metropolitan Police argument to the 1977 Select Committee. Stevens and Willis draw up the table, reproduced as Table 4.3, which shows the results based

Table 4.3. *Numbers and rates of attacks by ethnic group(s) of attacker(s) – victims' reports (MPD 1975)*

| Attackers | Number of attacks | Rates per 100,000 |
|-----------|-------------------|-------------------|
| White | 7,164 | 102 |
| Coloured | 4,553 | 841 |
| Mixed gang | 870 | |
| Not known | 6,527 | |

*Source:* Stevens and Willis, p. 35.

on the police data which involved the asking of the victim to classify his/her attacker within rough categories of ethnic identity. The figures, on the face of it, are a striking confirmation of the arrest statistics. However, the following points should be made. Firstly, the category 'coloured' probably includes an even higher black crime rate, given the generally lower rates for Asian crime. Secondly, there is a very big 'not known' category. Thirdly, there may be a tendency, arising from the widespread existence of racial prejudice, for attackers to be classified as coloured when the victim is, in fact, unsure. Professor Morris stressed this factor in his submission to the 1977 Select Committee. Fourthly, these figures represent an analysis of crimes of violence where the victim is likely to know the offender. Such figures would not necessarily bear any relationship to those for burglary where the characteristics of the offender are usually unknown to the victim. Fifthly, the factor mentioned before of the possible under-reporting of crime by ethnic minorities would distort the figures, although no estimate can be made of the extent to which this might be the case. Finally, none of these qualifications are sufficient to lead to a rejection of the notion that blacks are disproportionately involved in at least this type of crime. On the contrary, the evidence of a high black crime rate is patiently assembled by Stevens and Willis.

The authors make a major contribution to a most intriguing and, for socialists, important issue: the extent of intra-racial crime. Using the MPD victim data, they draw up the table of intra-racial and inter-racial attacks reproduced as Table 4.4,

Table 4.4. *Inter-racial and intra-racial attacks: expected rates and actual rates (MPD 1975)*

| Attacker(s) | Victim | Expected | | Actual | |
|---|---|---|---|---|---|
| | | No. | % | No. | % |
| White | White | 6,663 | 93 | 6,521 | 91 |
| | Coloured | 501 | 7 | 643 | 9 |
| | Total | 7,164 | 100 | 7,164 | 100 |
| Coloured | White | 4,235 | 93 | 3,616 | 79 |
| | Coloured | 318 | 7 | 937 | 21 |
| | Total | 4,553 | 100 | 4,553 | 100 |

*Source:* Stevens and Willis, p. 37.

comparing the expected rates (those that would have been expected considering the proportion of black people in the population) with the actual rates drawn from the crime figures. These figures constitute startling evidence not only of the intra-racial nature of such crimes, but also that the high crime rate of blacks is reflected in their extremely high victimization rates. As the authors put it (p. 36):

It can be shown that the proportion of white attacks on whites is about what would be expected, but that the proportion of coloured attacks on coloured victims is much higher.

We have spent some time on this study, because it is by far the most exhaustive British study on the issue of the relationship between race and crime. We will conclude by summarizing the main findings of Stevens and Willis, adding some of our own observations.

(1) The study considers the relationship between what it terms 'extrinsic' and 'intrinsic' factors in accounting for the higher recorded rates of black crime.

(2) In terms of the intrinsic factors the study concludes that age explains little variance, although it points to the youthfulness of the ethnic minority sample. A higher rate of crime is normally associated with the 15–24-year-old age group and this was not well represented in the sample – though it is now.

(3) In looking at the intrinsic factor of socio-economic deprivation the study found that much of the variance could be explained by unemployment, housing tenure, etc. However, these factors were considerably more potent when linked to an 'ethnicity' factor: in other words, they were mediated in their effect by factors peculiar to the ethnic group concerned. None of this is at all surprising to anyone taking a subcultural approach to the issue which emphasizes that objective indices of deprivation are always experienced through the group's subculture in order to become factors actually affecting behaviour, be it lawful or criminal. Though

a considerable amount of the variance in crime rates between whites, Asians and blacks can be explained by reference to differences in socio-economic status, there remains a degree of difference which points to the effect of an 'ethnic factor' intrinsic to the ethnic minorities themselves.

(4) As regards 'extrinsic' factors, the study considers how far the 'ethnic factor' might turn out to be differences in police behaviour with regard to different ethnic groups. The public initiation of crime reporting to the police and the intra-racial nature of crime scarcely provide the basis for the hypothesis that the differentials are simply a function of police behaviour.

(5) The study finds it 'surprising' that although the white crime rate related closely to the white unemployment rate the black crime rate did not relate to the black unemployment rate but in fact related *likewise* to the white unemployment rate. As we have argued throughout, there are no *direct* relationships between objective factors and behaviour. The experience of blacks in areas of high white unemployment may well be that of racial discrimination and being made scapegoats. Such an alienated subculture would have a con-siderable reason to break its lawful bonds with the wider society; it might also experience the demoralization which is the basis of much criminality. In areas of massive black unemployment, there may be less basis for a comparison with whites and thus a relative lack of the frustration that leads to criminality. The lack, however, can only be relative in a society dominated by mass media and the expectations derived from the education system.

(6) There is, then, a mechanistic flavour to the study, an expectation that there will be simple causal links between objective circumstances and behaviour. This imprisons the study, in the last analysis, within the 'either–or' view of things. In this respect, it takes us no further than the analysis and debate of 1977. The authors put themselves in

the dilemma that *either* high black crime rates are due to deprivation, the socio-economic structure of the ethnic minority communities, and the way deprivation is experienced by them, *or* they are due to police behaviour, and after carefully surveying both sets of factors, they can only conclude that there is insufficient evidence to 'place exclusive emphasis on one or the other of the two possible explanations of high black arrest rates. It cannot be emphasized too strongly that with the data available currently it is not possible to say how much weight should be given to any of them' (ibid., p. 41). However, there is one subtle change between the 1977 Select Committee report and *Race Crime and Arrests*, which concerns the notion of the 'ethnic factor'. As we have seen, there was an element of confusion in the 1977 debate in that the police were careful to dissociate themselves from any notion of a direct connection between ethnicity and crime. They were quite happy with the notion that higher black crime rates were the product of age composition and deprivation. All they were concerned with was, as they put it, the 'fact' of higher black crime rates. *Race Crime and Arrests* tested for indices of deprivation and found that they could not explain black crime rates. There is a residual 'ethnic factor'. The discussion in *Race Crime and Arrests* is no longer, therefore, about higher black crime rates being the product of either deprivation or police behaviour. Deprivation has been eliminated as an explanation: the issue is now either a higher real participation of black people in crime, *irrespective of deprivations*, or heavy-handed police behaviour.

It is our contention that only a subcultural approach, which looks for the subjective meanings behind objective statistics and at the same time recognizes that the real world is not experienced in terms of clear-cut 'either–or' distinctions between different types of causal variables, but as a process of complex interaction, can take the debate further. What is important is to understand how the 'extrinsic factor' of heavy-handed policing, in the context of the 'intrinsic' factor of a high level of socio-economic deprivation, gives rise to an alienated subculture among young people. From the standpoint of such subcultures, over time, a break with law and order is a response both to policing and to social deprivation experienced as different aspects of the same thing. The 'vicious circle' process mentioned above then emerges as a mechanism whereby a turn to crime by young people, and the increasing use of racialist stereotypes by the police, act to reinforce one another. We shall return to a fuller discussion of these issues in subsequent chapters. Here our task is to follow through the debate.

### The Scarman Report

The next occasion on which the issue of black crime became the object of public debate was in Lord Scarman's inquiry into the causes of the riots of summer 1981. Scarman identified an essential dilemma in the policing of areas like Brixton: how to cope with a rising level of crime – and particularly of street robbery ('mugging') – while retaining the confidence of all sections of the community, especially the ethnic minority groups (Scarman Report, para. 49).

The crime situation in Brixton in 1981 was summarized for Scarman by local police commanders as follows. In 'L' District during the years 1976–80 the number of serious offences recorded by the police grew by 13 per cent compared with a 15 per cent increase for the MPD as a whole. However, the growth over that period of recorded offences of robbery and other violent theft was 38 per cent for the Metropolitan Police District as a whole, 66 per cent for 'L' District and 138 per cent for the Brixton subdivision of 'L' District. During that period robbery and violent theft constituted 2.2 per cent of all serious crimes in the MPD, 5.1 per cent in 'L' District, and 7.2 per cent of all serious offences recorded in the Brixton division. Brixton accounted for 35 per cent of all crimes in 'L' District, but 49 per cent of robbery and other violent theft.

Scarman noted that the police conclusion was 'that "L" district and Brixton in particular faced a particularly high level of street crime – indeed this was referred to in the police evidence to the Inquiry as unique – and one in which black people were disproportionately involved' (ibid., para. 49). A response to Scarman on this point appeared in the *British Journal of Criminology* for April 1982, by Louis Blom-Cooper and Richard Drabble. The article argued for three basic criticisms of the police figures. Two of them were familiar: that Brixton's high crime rates were a product of heavy-handed policing, though no particular evidence was cited; and secondly that the crime phenomenon was exaggerated by the age structure of the West Indian population in the area. Again, the use of this argument, which is undoubtedly correct, is curious if the object is to deny the actual existence of a high crime rate in the area.

This was precisely the intention of the article. The third argument concerned the actual statistics for the crime rates themselves. Taking figures provided by the police for the *percentage* distribution of various crimes for the MPD as a whole and for the Brixton subdivision, the authors argued that although there is indeed a comparatively high percentage of robbery and violent theft for Brixton, this is 'counterbalanced' by a lower rate for 'other theft and handling stolen goods'. This point appears absurd for two reasons: firstly, the whole issue of high rates of street crime surrounds the category of robbery and violent theft. The police have not been concerned to deny that other types of crime (autocrime, for instance) were similar in Brixton and the MPD as a whole or might even be lower. That is not the issue. Secondly, Blom-Cooper and Drabble's argument amounts to a tautology: if the percentage of total crimes in Brixton falling under robbery and violent theft is higher than for the MPD as a whole, then since the figures for the MPD and for Brixton must both add up to a hundred

per cent, some other category of crime *must* be lower! The
assertion in the article that if the high rate of robbery and violent
theft in Brixton, as a percentage of the total crimes for that
subdivision, is counterbalanced by its lower rate of 'other theft
and handling stolen goods', then you get 'a profile for Brixton
characteristic of the MPD as a whole', is worthless. The issue
is the *amount* of crime.

   Scarman made some criticisms of police tactics and behaviour
and called for changes particularly in the field of police–
community liaison. A discussion of these questions is not our
concern in this chapter. The period since Scarman, up to Sir
Kenneth Newman's announcement of his intention to introduce
quite far-reaching changes in the organization of the Metropolitan Police, was one in which guarded police support for
Scarman's recommendations was accompanied by a good deal
of criticism. It is in the context of something approaching a
counterattack on Scarman from within police circles that we
must see the release by the police of annual crime figures giving,
as a departure from normal procedures, a breakdown in
accordance with race codes, on 10 March 1982. Normally these
figures are collected by the Metropolitan Police but only made
available to special investigations, as, for example, was the case
with the Select Committee in 1976–7. The release to the general
public of these figures was viewed by many as an attempt to
foster an anti-Scarman atmosphere by refocusing the public's
attention upon the disproportionate involvement of black people
in certain categories of crime. As Susan Smith pointed out,
the March 1982 figures did not add to knowledge of the real
crime situation in London. This was because

The only additional information supplied by this press release is a
breakdown [of crime statistics] by district. However, this is not
particularly useful, since without knowing the population composition
of the same districts, and/or the race of the victim, no valid conclusions
can be drawn about the distribution and directedness of violent offences.
(p. 16)

The police later announced that they did not intend to make available to the public a race-code breakdown the following year. These figures would be collected but reserved for special inquiries as was previously the case.

## Conclusion

It seems to us, therefore, that the most important characteristic of the debate on the relation between ethnicity and crime which has proceeded throughout the seventies has been its polarization into a futile 'either–or' argument: either young blacks are really disproportionately involved in certain categories of crime, or the crime statistics which paint this picture are really a product of police prejudice. This conception of what the race-crime debate should be about has straddled both right and left, but on the left it has, in our opinion, been the single most important factor which has prevented the emergence of a clear socialist position on crime and policing adequate to the present situation.

It is, of course, possible to argue that both sides of the coin express elements of the truth: that *some* of the black crime rate is due to police prejudice and that *some* is a reflection of a higher real rate of crime for black people. That is not our position either, or rather it is only part of our position. What is crucial, from a socialist point of view, is to see the interconnection between the two sides of the coin, and to understand that the connection between race and crime involves the following three distinct elements.

Firstly, black people have a higher crime rate than would be expected from their numbers as a proportion of the population. During the sixties there was an increase in a type of amateurish, largely uncommitted street crime by West Indian youth. At first this rise in the real crime rate was a product more of the shifting age composition of the West Indian population than anything else. A young population will have a higher

crime rate than an old one, and in the late sixties the West
Indian population had an extremely youthful profile. But
further, an ethnic minority that is oppressed by racial discrimination and the denial of equal opportunities may, if the
cultural conditions are there – as was the case in the West
Indian much more than the Asian community – develop an
even higher crime rate. The effects of prejudice and denial of
opportunities and the consequent deprivation and sense of
frustration increased the frustrations caused by massive rates
of unemployment for young people in general, which in this
case were experienced in terms of a particular culture. But whatever the precise balance of age, discrimination, etc., there was
a real rise in crime among the West Indian population, and
the police, in responding to it, were not responding simply to
figments of their imagination.

But, in the second place, the police responded *readily*. Racial
prejudice against black people, always present among a substantial part of the police force as in other sections of British
society, was used as a *specific* explanatory hypothesis concerning
a particular type of crime ('street crime' or 'mugging'). Police
prejudice may be high but need not relate to crime. Indeed,
as in the case of Asians in Britain or Chicanos in the United
States, it may involve the belief in a below average crime rate
which is vaguely associated with 'laziness' or 'lack of guts'. What
marks off the seventies (as revealed, for example, in the change
in police evidence to the 1977 as opposed to the 1971 Select
Committee) is the association of race and crime. While, as we
have seen, those officers from the police hierarchy who prepared the evidence went out of their way to distinguish between
a high black crime rate and race as a *cause* of crime, for the
average policemen on the beat, already equipped with racist
stereotypes, the niceties of the connections between race, discrimination and deprivation, and crime rates are lost. In the
*popular* police consciousness race becomes a cause of crime.

Thirdly, it is at this stage that the two processes reinforce each other: the increased rate of black crime and police predisposition to associate blacks with crime become part of a vicious circle which criminologists have termed 'deviancy amplification'. The police begin to focus upon black youths as likely criminals, and this results in a rise in the crime statistics for blacks. Joe Sim, in a recent contribution, at first sight appears to portray something like this process (p. 59):

> The key to understanding the disproportionate number of black people in the official criminal statistics could be found in the practices of the Met both bureaucratically and on the streets ... By concentrating both manpower and resources in areas such as Brixton, the police were likely to pick up more black people, especially the black youth who spent much of their time on the streets. This group then found their way into the criminal statistics, thus leading to an even greater police and media concentration on the activities of black people. This, in turn, led again to more of them being picked up.

This argument is a totally idealist (in the methodological sense) parody of the 'deviancy amplification' process. It starts at an arbitrary point: the police decision to devote more resources to Brixton, and sees this *alone* as the cause of rising black arrest statistics. The fact that an important component of the police decision to devote more resources to areas such as Brixton is a rising crime rate for the area is completely overlooked. It is quite correct that, because of the figure of 'unrecorded crime', an increase in police resources in an area will result in a higher crime rate for the area, and that racial prejudice on the part of the police will influence what sorts of people are arrested. But this does not eliminate the fact that a real rising rate of offences caused the police decision to devote more of their resources to the area, nor that the impact of 'military' policing on black youth is to generate precisely the conditions which further increase the real rate of crime. The notion that increasing youth unemployment, coupled with a high young population in the black community, and the effects of massive, well-documented, racial discrimination and the denial of legitimate opportunity, did *not* result in a rising rate of real offences is hardly credible. If these sorts of deprivations are not crucial factors leading to increasing crime rates then what are? It is a weakness of Joe Sim and his associates to believe that they can somehow give an account of what is happening to the relationship between police and black people in the inner cities without any discussion of this factor. The process of deviancy *amplification* is precisely a process of the amplification of real, existent, deviancy. The real increase in crime is amplified as a result of police action and police prejudice. To understand this is to understand that a socialist policy must not be simply a policy about policing. It must be a policy concerned with crime and policing.

# 5 The Drift to Military Policing

The harassment of the public, or sections of it, by the police has become a major political issue. Lord Scarman characterized the Brixton riot of summer 1981 as 'a spontaneous act of defiant aggression by young men who felt themselves hunted by a hostile police force' (3.25). He went on to note that 'the weight of criticism and complaint against the police is so considerable that it alone must give grave cause for concern' (p. 65). How has such a state of affairs come to develop? In this chapter we attempt to give an explanation of what has been happening to policing in the inner-city areas and (the two largely overlap) to policing in areas with a high concentration of the ethnic minorities. In order to do this, it is necessary to begin by contrasting at a very general level two types or styles of policing. The first might be called 'consensus policing' or 'policing by consent' and the second, rather more bluntly, 'military policing'.

## Consensus Policing

As the name implies, consensus policing is policing with the support of the community. The community supports the police because it sees them as doing a socially useful job. They are protecting the community against crime and crime is something that the community recognizes as harmful to its well-being. Of course, there may be other ingredients behind the support of the community for the police. In Britain during the last century there was considerable resistance to policing on the continental model, and the establishment of police forces acceptable to the British public was very much associated with the fact that constables had no more legal powers than those of the ordinary citizen. As Patricia Hewitt remarks, the accountability of the police to the law in the same way as the ordinary citizen is often regarded as sufficient accountability. Michael Brogden has noted in his recent book on policing that the gaining of acceptance by the police in working-class areas was a slow process. Brogden, surveying historical studies of the police–public relations, concludes:

> By the Edwardian period, varying relations had been constructed between the police institution and the different social classes ... the merchant capitalists, the business proprietors, the professionals, the shop-keepers, and the new ancillary strata of clerical workers gave increasing consent, a support that was most visible at times of crisis. For the urban industrial workers and their kin – the 'respectable' strata of Victorian England – by the 1900s the relation with the police institution had assumed the features of a truce, a grudging acceptance, with occasional direct confrontations in the course of an industrial dispute. For the lower classes, the participants of the street economy ... attitudes to the police institution throughout the first century of policing remained essentially unchanged. They were subject to continuing, occasional, and apparently arbitrary 'culls'. (p. 181)

Working-class response to the police institution during the first century varied over time, by region, and by strata. In general, by the end of that period the relations that had developed were not so much ones of consent but rather a grudging acceptance, a tentative approval, that could be withdrawn instantly in the context of industrial conflict.

But whatever the ingredients of community support for the police, to the extent that this exists, a second important characteristic of consensus policing follows. We have already mentioned the crucial role played by information flowing from the public to the police in the detection of criminals. Where the community is supportive of the police, then it can be expected to maintain a reasonably high flow of information concerning crime, or at least those types about which information exists. Police requests for members of the public who saw the incident concerned, or 'saw anything suspicious', to come forward can be expected to yield results. From this high flow of information follows a third characteristic of consensus policing: what we might call the 'certainty of detection'. Most policing is preventative, concerned with public order and deterring crime, rather than the investigative pursuit of crimes that have already been committed. Under consensus policing the close relationship between police and the community as regards the sharing of information and thus the likelihood of successful detection act as a deterrent upon the potential criminal. After the event, it is that same close sharing of information that will lead investigative policing to a likely successful conclusion.

There is another characteristic of consensus policing that is worth mentioning since it will become important in our later discussion: the role of stereotypes. All policing involves the use of stereotypes. No police force can operate on the basis of suspecting all sections of the community equally when a particular crime has been committed. Some notion of what *type* of person (from what social group, however defined; what area of the city; etc.) has to be employed to enable investigation to get off the ground. What can be said, however, is that the closer the relationship between the police and the community as regards the sharing of information (that is, real information, not pseudo-information generated by the prejudices and stereotypes held by the community at large), the more the police can begin their investigations following actual leads and the less recourse to stereotypes becomes the basis for starting investigations.

Some or all of the features of this description of 'consensus policing' are often held to describe the British police system either in the past, or both in the past and at the present time. We are not making such a claim here. More particularly, we are not claiming that the ethnic minority communities in Britain have at any stage in the past enjoyed a relationship with the police which could be said to correspond to a situation such

as we have described. The description we have given of consensus policing is intended to serve two purposes. First, it
describes a situation which policing practices in the inner city
are moving away from. Second, it describes a system of policing
which we believe is the only possible one for a civilized society
compatible with freedom and the rule of law.

## Military Policing

If policing in the inner city and as regards the ethnic minorities
is moving away from consensus policing, what is it moving towards? The opposite pole to consensus policing we have termed
military policing. By this term we are not referring to the
activities of the Royal Military Police or the army generally (in
Northern Ireland, for instance), though such a situation could
certainly be taken as an example of military policing. What the
term describes is a policing style which is linked to a certain
type of relationship between the police and the community being
policed. The characteristics of military policing can be largely
specified simply by reversing the conditions of consensus policing.

Military policing is, therefore, first and foremost policing
without the consent, and with the hostility, active or otherwise,
of the community. The community do not support the police
because they see them as a socially or politically oppressive force
in no way fulfilling any protective functions. This general
alienation between the community and the police may, though
not necessarily, be reflected in a general support by the
community for the criminal. If the police are enforcing a legal
system which the community does not take to reflect its own
concepts of morality, as would be the case with an occupying
army holding down a subject population, then the 'criminal'
may be seen by the community as a symbolic rebel, to be
secretly admired, and if circumstances permit, to be offered
shelter and assistance in escaping from the police.

Under such circumstances the flow of information from the

community to the police concerning 'crime' can be expected to approach zero. If the community has this information to give and can identify those who commit what it, as opposed to the occupying forces, identifies as crime, then the emergence of some type of surrogate policing from within the community may well occur. Vigilante squads may clandestinely operate, or if there is a guerrilla force attempting to overthrow the occupying military force, then it may well take on certain policing functions on behalf of the community. On the other hand, the community may be so disorganized and demoralized by the effects of war, or simply by poverty and deprivation, that the channels whereby information could accumulate are weakened and ineffective.

Either way the police force under such circumstances will not be in a position to receive the type of information from the community which would enable its activities to be characterized by the principle of 'certainty of detection'. The crucial consequence of this situation is that an important part of police activity will come to constitute the random harassment of the community at large quite irrespective of involvement in crime. This randomness of activity is the central characteristic of military policing, and has two closely interrelated functions.

Firstly, it constitutes a method of obtaining information. Where the community will not voluntarily offer information to the police, then to the extent that the police are still determined to track down criminals, the necessary information will have to be prised out of the community, if necessary by force. A network of paid informers is, of course, indispensable, but also what might be termed 'high-profile' activities assume a crucial role: stopping people randomly in the streets, raiding premises, taking people in for questioning not on the basis of information already received, but as part of an attempt to secure information. These types of activities, aimed at forcing the community to yield up its supply of information, become central in military policing. But secondly, activities such as stopping people randomly in the streets and searching them, besides being attempts to obtain information, become in themselves forms of generalized deterrence. The certainty of detection, with its dependence upon a smooth flow of information to the police, becomes replaced by the arbitrariness or randomness of penalty as the main form of deterrence. 'Do not do anything in case you are stopped by the police at a road block or in some sudden and random street search' becomes the form of deterrence replacing the 'do not do anything because you are sure to be caught eventually' of consensus policing. Indeed, it could be said that a certain type of 'goal displacement' characterizes these random activities. That is to say, even if the strategy of 'sweeps' of the public through mass arrests, searches, etc., starts off as a device for gathering information, its effectiveness in this respect is so dubious and random that its role as a generalized deterrent inevitably comes to the fore.

Finally, under systems of military policing the investigative activities of the police are maximally dependent upon the use of stereotypes. To the extent that the police are determined to track down particular offenders for a crime under conditions of zero information, they will have to begin their investigations with a stereotype of the social group or milieu from which the offender is most likely to have come and to begin their investigations there.

As with consensus policing, what we are concerned with at this stage is capturing the essential characteristics of a style of policing rather than accurately describing any particular situation. It is, of course, easy to think of situations which our description would fit without modification: the American army in South Vietnam, the British in Northern Ireland, the policing of rebellious colonies, etc. But for our discussion of what is happening to policing in mainland Britain the description of military policing fulfils two functions. First, it describes a situation which we see, for reasons we are going to discuss, policing in the inner cities approaching. Second, it describes a type of policing which we see to be incompatible with freedom and the rule of law and as a general form of policing to be closely linked with the authoritarian state. We will return to this point later.

## Towards Military Policing

In his evidence to the Scarman Inquiry, Chief Superintendent Plowman of the Metropolitan Police claimed: 'In Brixton ... there is no information that comes from the black community to the police ... We are very short of the co-operation of the community' (Scarman Inquiry, Day 4, p. 17). There is no reason to doubt Plowman's statement. What it reflects is the seriousness of the state of affairs as regards policing Brixton and similar areas up and down the country. Consensus policing is dead, if it ever existed, in Brixton. What exists in its place? It is our argument that, firstly, over the last decade and a half the signs have been of a drift towards military policing in areas like Brixton; and, secondly, that this drift is self-reinforcing. It results in a vicious circle in which moves in the direction of military policing undermine whatever elements of consensus policing may remain, and lay the conditions for further moves in the direction of military policing. The crux of the matter is that the police come to view the population in such areas as generally criminal. Where, as in Brixton, that population is black, the assumption of criminality becomes linked to race and the racial stereotype quickly crystallizes: all blacks are potential criminals.

There have always been areas of large cities which the police have defined as crime-prone; so what is new about the situation that has been developing over the last decade and a half? It is the way in which the definition of a population as crime-prone has been the occasion for acting towards it in terms of styles of policing which have drawn progressively closer to the military model: random stopping and searching, raids on youth clubs and houses, operations often involving the more explicitly 'military' sections of the police such as the Special Patrol Group (SPG) and up until recently the massive use of the Vagrancy Act (or 'sus', as it was known) by some police forces, largely against black youngsters.

During the 1970s one set of statistics in particular illustrates the changing nature of policing. The Institute of Race Relations in its submission to the Royal Commission on Criminal Procedure compiled the table (5.1) showing the numbers of people stopped and questioned by the Special Patrol Group of the Metropolitan Police in operations involving random stopping of people in the street and at road blocks.

Table 5.1

| Year | Number stopped |
|------|----------------|
| 1972 | 41,980 |
| 1973 | 34,534 |
| 1974 | 41,304 |
| 1975 | 65,628 |
| 1976 | 60,898 |

The figures are compatible with the development of some of the characteristics of military policing. The growth in the number of people stopped and searched indicates a situation in which the police are not so much stopping people on the basis of some particular suspicion, based on information that the individual concerned is likely to have committed a crime, but as part of a generalized screening of the population of that area for information, and as a generalized deterrent. The police officers concerned in such activities acted on the basis of a stereotype, that the population of the area – young blacks – were 'very likely' to have committed crimes.

A second indication of the changing style of policing in areas like Brixton during the 1970s was the widespread and growing use of 'sus' as an offence. In 1976, for example, in the Metropolitan Police District, of 2,112 people arrested under the 1964

Vagrancy Act 42 per cent were black compared to a general arrest rate for all offences of black people of 12 per cent. The use of 'sus' against young black people can come to function as a generalized disciplinary mechanism against a whole category of the population since it needs very little evidence to secure a conviction in a particular case. The 'convenience' of sus as a component of generalized deterrence strategies against the black community was well summarized by the National Council for Civil Liberties in its evidence to the Home Office Working Party on Vagrancy and Street Offences in 1975:

> The evidence is invariably given by Police Officers only. Because by definition no substantive theft, or even sufficient proximate act to charge an attempted theft, takes place, the question for the court becomes one of interpretation of a few actions which may or may not indicate an intent ... We would suggest that convictions for this offence are largely based on probability rather than certainty.

The widespread use of 'sus' and the effective campaign against it resulted in its repeal on the recommendation of the Royal Commission on Criminal Procedure. It remains to be seen to what extent the Criminal Attempts Act will be used in a similar way, or whether other offences will fill the gap left by the repeal of 'sus'.

To return to the question of stop and search, the example now best known to the public is undoubtedly the famous 'Swamp '81' operation in which over one thousand people were stopped and searched in the central part of Brixton but fewer than one hundred were charged with criminal offences. Two features of Swamp '81 and similar types of operations stand out. Firstly, their inefficiency at catching criminals, and secondly, the effect of antagonizing a large number of people. Swamp '81 serves as a tailor-made example of how to antagonize the greatest possible number of people while at the same time achieving the minimum control of a particular type of crime, in this case footpad robbery. As it was unlikely that a snatch theft was going to take place directly in front of the eyes of police officers, the operation involved the random stopping of 'suspicious' youth. As the NCCL remarked: 'Even if police officers behaved with impeccable courtesy towards every person stopped and searched and apologized to those found not to be carrying suspect items, many people would resent being treated as suspects when innocently walking to the tube or home' (Evidence to Scarman, p. 14).

With operations like Swamp '81 as a normal aspect of policing strategy the move to military policing has taken a decisive step. Deterrence is no longer based on the certainty of detection but on the randomness of stop and search, and information provided by the community to the police is replaced by stop-and-search procedures as the basis of the detection of offences. The 'goal displacement' from catching actual offenders or gaining useful information to generalized deterrence of the population at large is illustrated by the very low number of actual arrests resulting from Swamp '81.

But why have these changes in policing been taking place? An obvious explanation would be to point to the generalized recession of the capitalist economy, the emergence of long-term structural unemployment among youth in general and black youth in particular, and the increased unwillingness of such groups peacefully to acquiesce in poverty, discrimination and lives of despair. This is especially so when they have been conditioned through the mass media and the education system to expect something different. From this point of view the move towards military policing in the inner cities is part of a general move in state policy towards the 'pole of coercion' in the control of a new generation of unemployed, and to keep down new forms of struggle against the capitalist crisis (cf. Friend and Metcalf). There is a substantial body of evidence for this analysis, but we have two disagreements. Firstly, such a view can easily lead to an exaggerated focus upon the initiatives of the centralized state apparatus, as if they were consciously formulated, even if behind closed doors. In contrast, we shall develop an argument which stresses the dynamic movement at ground level within the inner city, and the relationship between the police and the community itself which drives policing towards the military model. Often the initiatives of the central state are attempts to come to terms with and respond to what is already happening 'spontaneously' at ground level.

Secondly, this view can easily slip into the rather simplistic view that what military policing is keeping the lid on is a progressive struggle for emancipation by those suffering the consequences of economic crisis. Such a view necessitates imposing a general label of political struggle on the variety of activities in the inner city that are, in the last analysis, a response to deprivation. Precisely because, as we have already argued, the culture of deprivation includes a variety of activities including forms of crime that are genuinely antisocial, harmful and destructive to the communities within which they occur, retaining the simply dichotomy of repressive state bottling up struggles against oppression involves an inability to come to terms with the existence of crime. Once it is recognized that among the responses to deprivation are to be included antisocial activities, then both the dynamics of the drift towards military policing at ground level and the legitimacy that such a move has for the population at large can be more clearly understood.

Our disagreements, therefore, are based on the issue of analysing solely from the point of view of the total system. While we cannot simply focus on the level of day-to-day interaction between the police and the community, if we ignore the dynamic at that level, we are in danger of projecting on to the community beliefs which fit the grand theory well, but only approximate to reality.

The shift towards military policing is to be attributed to three closely related factors. Firstly, a combination of rising rates of street crime and the assimilation of the lifestyle of the petty criminal with the general lifestyle. Both of these result from unemployment and deprivation. Unemployment on a massive scale means that large numbers of young people are hanging out on the street. In other words, the younger members of the community as a whole come to take on a lifestyle which in the eyes of the police is associated with petty crime. This assists the police in stereotyping a whole community as 'crime-prone'. It is the opposite of the situation of organized crime in which criminals may constantly hide behind a respectable business life-style which is defined by the police, following the conventions of society at large, as non-criminal.

The second factor is racial prejudice within the police force. Whenever this issue is raised it is usually in terms of the 'bad-apple theory'. A rather condescending version comes from the 1977 report of the House of Commons Select Committee on Race Relations and Immigration on the West Indian community: 'Occasionally they [the police] will act wrongly, but this should be seen as a reminder that despite their inordinate burden they are after all human' (Evidence, p. 187). This scurrilous identification of racism or police law violation with 'being human' is, of course, insupportable. We do not expect our police officers to be criminals or to be racially prejudiced. Lord Scarman, in a more serious discussion of the problem, admits its existence: 'Racial prejudice does manifest itself occasionally in the behaviour of a few officers on the streets' (p. 64). Scarman continues: 'It may be only too easy for some officers faced with what they must see as the inexorably rising tide of street crime to lapse into an unthinking assumption that all young black people are potential criminals. I am satisfied, however, that such a bias is not to be found among senior police officers' (ibid.). Scarman has identified the important factor: it is not simply that individual officers may be racists but that in a situation in which a whole community is becoming defined as crime-prone, and large sections of that community are black, then a fertile breeding ground for racism is created. The sentiments of the individual officer become less important than the general form that policing takes. If black youngsters are being routinely harassed by the police, then individual officers, whatever they may feel about black people in moments of cool reflection, will in their operational duties become conditioned into a view of the black community in which racism makes a lot of sense. Thus it is difficult to square Lord Scarman's remarks about 'a few officers' and 'occasionally' with the very next page where he notes the massive weight of criticism and complaint against the police from the black community. Yet, of course, it is a fact that only a minority of the black community, as with any other section of society, are criminals. The generalized racialist sentiments which are currently so pervasive in British society undoubtedly facilitate the smooth transition in the mind of the police officer from the proposition that certain areas with a high black population also have a high crime rate to the proposition that all blacks are potential criminals. Such thinking in turn smooths the path for the transition to military policing.

A third factor has also undoubtedly assisted the transition towards military policing. The changes in policing methods following the introduction of modern technology and communications have been concisely summed up by John Alderson (p. 41):

> The impact of science and technology on the police over the thirteen years from 1966 to 1979 was very considerable ... it has had a profound effect on police methods, public image and reputation, to say nothing of police psychology. The police have been helped considerably, even crucially, by technology ... Stemming from the universal introduction of personal pocket radio ... together with the availability of cheap motor vehicles and later on expensive computerized command and control systems, what was basically a preventive foot-patrolling force has become a basically reactive patrolling force.

Alderson goes on to note how the reactive or 'fire-brigade' style of policing involving fast response to incidents minimizes a normal, day-to-day, peaceful contact with the public. This type of contact, of course, is a vital aspect of consensus policing; it is both a source of information, and a familiarization of the public with the police officer as an individual human being, and the conditions are created whereby the public willingly passes on information to the police. Alderson's 'technological cop' faces a dilemma: on the one hand, modern data recording and storage–retrieval systems are at his service; on the other hand, the weakening of the link with the public that 'fire-brigade' policing has involved means that there is less reliable information to store in the system. This paradox – rather than any deliberate policy formulated at State level – probably accounts for growing public concern at the extent to which police computers reflect what Alderson identifies as an 'innate tendency to want to record almost anything'. Where there is little useful information coming from the public to the police then inevitably a tendency arises to record almost anything on the grounds that it might conceivably be of use in the future (see Baldwin and Kinsey).

## The Vicious Circle

Once the move in the direction of military policing is established, as a result of factors we have just been discussing, a vicious circle is set in motion whereby the initial moves to military policing themselves create the conditions in which further moves in the same direction are encouraged and made more plausible. There are three broad areas in which this vicious circle can be identified.

The first and most obvious effect of military policing is that it antagonizes a large number of people; it helps to turn the community against the police. The more the stop-and-search procedures, the road blocks, the house-to-house searches, and the raids on youth clubs become a normal part of police activity in the inner city and ethnic minority areas then the more the flow of information from that section of the community dries up and the situation described by Plowman (above, p. 175) comes into existence. An example culled from the Report of the Working Party into Community Police Relations in Lambeth (p. 36) brings this out well:

> The area is patrolled regularly by plain clothes and uniformed police within a radius of 100 yards and there are frequent raids involving 50 or more police with dozens of vehicles and police dogs.
> As some of the schoolchildren were arriving from school and waiting at the gate of the playground for the leader to arrive, about six to eight of the members in school uniforms were frisked and searched by two plain clothes policemen. The young people were annoyed and so were their parents when they knew.
> The observations of young people and their parents at the time indicated that the SPG were being totally successful in keeping everyone off the streets – even to the point of preventing them coming to and from their club. The Working Party were told that the areas just outside the clubs are where 'groups of young blacks leaving [the clubs] are picked up by the police waiting at the end of the road. It's the roughness, the whole brutality, it's sickening'.

The reinforcement process lies in the fact that the easiest police response to a situation in which information from the community has dried up is *more military policing.* More road blocks, more Swamp '81s, desperately to try and catch street criminals and, of course, the easier the transition becomes from attempts to catch criminals to general harassment of the community at large. The end result is a further distancing of the community from the police, a further reduction of information (if it has not entirely dried up anyway), and if nothing is changed, a further drift towards military policing. Military policing produces the alienation of the community from the police and the alienation of the community from the police produces military policing.

The second component of the vicious circle is what might be called the 'spread effect' of alienation. The effect of military policing, though it may initially be directed against a particular section of the community (young people, and young black people in particular) is to spread out to other sections of the community in such a way that the conditions leading to military policing are reinforced. This spread effect takes the form of the undermining of other social institutions in the community which under a system of consensus policing might be expected to promote social control and integration, leading young people into non-criminal forms of behaviour and out of a form of contact with the police characterized by conflict. Three examples of this process readily come to mind.

## 1  The Effect on the Family

Lord Scarman noted that 'one of the most serious developments in recent years has been the way in which the older generation of black people in Brixton has come to share the belief of the younger generation that the police routinely harass and ill-treat black youngsters' (p. 65). On the simplest level, this is simply a question of parents observing what is going on. But the point about military policing is that, by its very nature, harassment of the young tends to spread into the harassment of the parents as well.

Consider the following example. In an environment in which information coming from the community concerning crime is low, and the police are already relying heavily on stop-and-search procedures in an attempt to contain street crime, and the community within which they are operating already has to a considerable extent become stereotyped as crime-prone, a black youngster is stopped by police officers while carrying a piece of hi-fi equipment. Given the background factors, the police suspect the youngster of having stolen the equipment with no more evidence than the simple fact that he has it in his possession. This is the first stage of the process. The next stage is familiar from countless complaints and reports of police behaviour over the last decade: the police 'know' he is guilty but, because of the general lack of information from the community about crime, they have no information to back up that assumption. So they 'prise' that evidence out of the community. Here is a harrowing account from the Lambeth Report (p. 37):

At approximately 6.45 a.m. I had just got up but had not dressed when I heard a banging on the front door.

I went downstairs not thinking that there was anything serious and with the intention of just opening the door and sticking my head round to see who was there. When I did open the door there were four police officers in plain clothes and they did not give me time to invite them in or ask them if they had a warrant. They just said 'Is X (my son) here?' brushing me aside as they were saying this. I said 'Just a minute' and got in front of them and went up the stairs.

They followed me and passed me at the top of the stairs and held me back. In fact they barred my way. Two of them went to my daughter's room and opened it. I should say that both children have their names written on the doors so it was quite obvious whose room belonged to who. I objected to two of the officers going into her room, but I was completely ignored. They banged loudly on my son's door and after a little while he opened the door. I wanted to be there but they barged in and I did not have a chance to get in. I was kept back. They shut the door in my face. Two of them were in the room and two of them were outside on the landing. They came out of his room with my son and I asked what it was all about. I said either 'What are you charging him with?' or 'What are you arresting him for?' They said 'Attempted murder of a policeman.' I did say that he would not do that but I was completely ignored and they bundled him downstairs and out of the house.

Our concern here is not simply to point out the injustices involved nor to get into an argument about the extent of such activities. Undoubtedly, some police raids on homes are justified if properly conducted, but it is equally clear that many are not: extensive complaints are testimony to that. Our point is that this type of activity on the part of the police is an inevitable component of military policing. The relationship between arrest and evidence is becoming *reversed*. Under policing by consent, information from the community enables the police to restrict their incursions into the private lives of citizens to those whom investigations and information have made suspect. In investigative policing as traditionally understood a raid on premises is a response to information already received and is carried out in the expectation that it will result in further important evidence leading to an arrest with a chance of conviction by the courts. Under military policing, however, until the raid is conducted there is no evidence, since there are no other sources of information. Where virtually everyone is under suspicion in a community stereotyped as crime-prone, it becomes an option to apprehend almost any young person found in possession of a consumer durable – given that the area suffers a high crime rate – by a raid on his/her home in the hope that further evidence, proving the item was stolen, might be obtained. In this sequence of events police racism acts not as the cause but as a facilitating factor: no doubt racist officers will more willingly crash through the homes of black families than others, but the practice is an inevitable ingredient of military policing rather than a consequence of the sentiments of police officers.

The effect on the family is severe. Parents, experiencing the same treatment at the hands of the police quite irrespective of their involvement in crime, develop the same antagonism towards the police as these children do. This, of course, is part of the process whereby military policing dries up the supply of information from the community. But more fundamentally, this parental antagonism changes the relationship between the police and the family. Under a system of consensus policing the police could be expected to see the family as an institution with which they work in concert, and the police constable undertakes a paternalistic role towards a juvenile involved in minor offences. For more serious offences the trend of juvenile justice since the 1960s has been towards a combination of detention with various forms of intermediate treatment. The latter, like all forms of community treatment, presupposes a cooperative relationship between the police, social-work agencies and the family. Pitts has argued that the simultaneous growth during the seventies of both detention and more control-oriented forms of intermediate treatment, combined with the activities of the police Juvenile Bureau, represented a spreading of the net of the juvenile justice system into areas which would previously have been left to the family and social-work agencies. Within this system the growing antagonism between black parents and the police would lead to the expectation that a higher proportion of black juvenile offenders would find themselves in detention centres with less reliance by the courts on supervision orders involving social-work agencies and the family. This is borne out by Landau. An accentuation of this trend can follow from the decision of area police commanders as to which offences by young people should be referred to the Juvenile Bureau with the automatic notification of social workers prior to court appearances, in which case a recommendation for a supervision order is less likely to be made in court and a custodial sentence becomes more likely.

This state of affairs can also create antagonism between parents and children. On the one hand, parents, scared that their kids, out in the streets, will get into trouble with the police, will put pressure on them to stay indoors, which will result in conflict:

> In October 1979 I sent my son, 15, out to get fish and chips. He was stopped in the street by two men, plain-clothes, who searched him and asked him where he got his money. They showed nothing to say they were police officers and my son was very shaken by the experience. Since then I take him to and from the youth club every week; he is very embarrassed, but I have to do it. I lock their shoes up at the weekend so they can't go out when I am sleeping in the day. (Lambeth Working Party)

## 2 The Effect upon Social-Work Agencies

We have already mentioned a tendency for social-work agencies to get excluded from sentencing processes. But far more widely than this, military policing tends to create a situation which undermines the activity of youth workers and other volunteers who would normally keep young people off the streets. The effect of police raids on clubs looking for suspects or evidence can be disastrous:

Recently one of the club members aged 15 was picked up for creating a disturbance and it was said that he was found to have drugs in his possession. This resulted in police visits to the club, which caused much unrest and so the leader told the police that these visits were causing havoc. They appeared to understand but the visits continued until at last the youth said to the leader: 'For the sake of the club members, I will not come again, so you will be left in peace.' So he left the club.

During November 1978, when the SPG were in Brixton, the activities of the Youth Project were severely affected. Our chief club night, on Thursdays, was reduced to a handful of attending members. Through January and February, it recovered to the usual 100 mark. (Lambeth Working Party)

## 3 The Effect upon Community Relations

Part of the attempt by governments in the sixties and seventies to link the ethnic minority communities to the existing political structure was the system of Community Relations Councils (CRCs) under the aegis of the Community Relations Commission (now the Commission for Racial Equality). We shall discuss the effect of these councils in the next chapter. Here our concern is with the effect of military policing upon a more specific component of community relations, that conducted by the police itself. Local CRCs were encouraged to set up police liaison committees, and during the 1970s the Metropolitan Police expanded its community relations initiative. In 1972 Humphrey and John claimed: 'The jobs in Community Relations go only to "dogsbodies" and "liberals". There is no mileage in such positions for promotion, the turnover is frightening in posts where years of experience are necessary.' Since then community relations training and what is now called 'human awareness' training has been stepped up and the number of Community Liaison Officers expanded. In 1976–7 a variable rank structure was applied to C L posts permitting promotion within such posts and enabling career-minded officers to regard community relations as more than a passing interest.

What is very clear from Scarman's report is that the development of military policing as a general strategy undermined and continues to undermine the effectiveness of police–community dialogue. Indeed, the expansion of community-relations work by the police can be seen as an attempt to recreate some of the characteristics of consensus policing in the context of a generalized drift to high-technology military policing. Scarman showed how in Brixton saturation operations like Swamp '81 'provoked the hostility of young black people who felt they were being hunted irrespective of their innocence or guilt . . . However well intentioned, these operations precipitated a crisis of confidence between the police and certain community leaders. In particular they led to the breakdown of the formal arrangements for liaison between the ethnic minority communities, the local authority, and the police.'

But Scarman failed to see the contradiction between police–community liaison schemes as at present constituted and military policing. He went on to recommend *both* that 'hard' policing (by which he meant much the same as our term 'military' policing) should necessarily continue, that this 'requires the use on the streets of stop-and-search powers and the occasional "saturation" operation' *and* a statutory requirement for police–community liaison at borough level. Scarman tries to straddle the contradiction between military policing and community liaison (p. 92):

I appreciate, of course, that secrecy is essential to the success of certain operations and that consultation will not be possible or appropriate in those cases. Neither will consultation always produce an agreed result: in the end it will be necessary for the responsible police commander to take a decision. But the object must be to enable the community to understand fully why the police regard such an operation as necessary, and there must be a willingness on the part of the police to listen to community views and to be prepared to modify their plans in the light of them.

One can understand why this sort of proposal has cut little ice with police commanders at ground level who believe both that military policing is the only solution to rising crime rates and that this, by definition, does not permit a consultation approach to the community which is going to bear the brunt of it. One can sympathize with Deputy Assistant Commander Leslie Walker of the Metropolitan Police who on the ITV London Programme in January 1981 complained: 'He [Scarman] says that a police operation of that sort will at times be essential [but] when the commander of an area having embarked on a large scale exercise is told by community leaders "I think you may be getting a disturbance this weekend" he is going to be committing professional suicide if he doesn't call off the operation.'

This inability of the police to discuss their tactics with community-liaison committees in situations where operations depend upon secrecy (the prior publication of something like Swamp '81 would simply have the result that all criminals vacate the area for the duration rendering the exercise useless) can be exacerbated by a local commander who is not oriented towards a community-relations approach. Thus, in another case of breakdown in September 1980, Hackney Council for Racial Equality ended its relationship with the local police. According to the local paper:

In Hackney it has been made clear time and again that while the HCRE can raise issues, the police reserve the right to be complete masters of their policing policy and that a liaison committee has only the function of airing issues ... Hackney CRE received a continuous stream of complaints and with a police commander who has applauded the SPG, made some very outspoken remarks in favour of 'sus', and whose attitude towards minority communities has left a strong suspicion, HCRE has felt that its role must be that of a monitoring agency which makes representations to MPs and the Home Office. (*Hackney Gazette*, 2 September 1980)

The third component of the vicious circle can be called 'the mobilization of bystanders'. The phrase originated in discussions of the consequences of massive intervention by law-enforcement agencies in the American riots of the late 1960s where it was noticed that massive and indiscriminate police response often had the effect of provoking people who otherwise would not have participated in the rioting to join in. The same sort of process can be identified as a general characteristic of military policing. As we have seen, military policing involves the blurring of the distinction between offender and non-offender. The essence of the mobilization of bystanders is that this tendency on the part of the police is reproduced within the community itself. Firstly, the attitude of the community towards the actual offender starts to change. The experience of the community as a whole becomes assimilated to the experience of the criminal: treatment at the hands of the police becomes more and more indistinguishable for both categories. Also, since both, due to unemployment and deprivation, and the declining effectiveness of other institutions of social control, lead a life fundamentally centring on the streets, then they intermix freely. As Scarman remarks: 'There he meets criminals, who appear to have no difficulty in obtaining the benefits of a materialist society.'

The result of this process is that the offender temporarily comes to be regarded as a sort of symbolic rebel by the community. At least he is hitting back, and so crime can come to be seen as a sort of quasi-political response by youngsters. Since one is equally likely to be harassed by the police whether or not one is a criminal, then actual criminality can come to be seen as defensive activity on behalf of the community against the sources of collective oppression. This is the thinking behind the remark of Stuart Hall and his colleagues in an earlier study (pp. 34–5):

> Mugging for some ... supplied the necessary bread to kill long periods of time where little can be done for nothing, and where little time is likely to be spent at home. It allows an identity of toughness and physical superiority, a channel to a dented identity ... It is perhaps a 'non-ideological politics'.

But there is a second aspect to this. The other side of the coin is that there is a loss of confidence by the community: when they witness someone being apprehended by the police, they doubt that this is anything other than a case of symbolic attack upon the community as a whole. Under conditions of consensus policing, where the police act upon solid information, if the community witnesses anyone being apprehended, there is the presumption that the police must have good reason for their action, and in any case the consequent process of clearly formulated charges, access to a solicitor, and, if necessary, trial by jury guarantee that only those guilty of crimes will be punished. Under the conditions we are describing here, the process is very different. The assumption becomes that the person being apprehended is probably innocent and, secondly, that his apprehension by the police is going to be the first step in a long process of harassment involving him and his family while the police attempt to 'construct' the information leading to a successful conviction. This, of course, puts the police in a difficult position, since once this type of atmosphere becomes generally established in the community, then, even if reasonably responsible local commanders take care to ensure that arrests only occur where there really is evidence -- a difficult enough state of affairs to achieve under general conditions of military policing, as we have already seen -- it will, in the short term at least, be regarded in exactly the same light by other members of the community who happen to be bystanders at the event.

The end result of this process, and something that had been

noticed long before the riots, was the tendency for collective resistance to arrest to develop among black youths. In its evidence to the House of Commons Report on the West Indian Community, the Metropolitan Police noted that:

> Recently there has been a growth in the tendency for members of London's West Indian communities to combine against police officers who are effecting the arrest of a black person or who are in some other way enforcing the law in situations which involve black people. (Evidence, p. 178)

The most large-scale example of such situations, prior to the 1981 riots, were, of course, the events at the Notting Hill Carnivals of 1976 and 1977. In the context of generally deteriorating relations between the black community and the police, what was regarded as an overbearing police presence at the Carnival itself made it very likely that *any* police action, including genuine attempts to apprehend pickpockets, would provoke a collective response. The result of such a situation is illustrated by the 1977 Carnival in which there were 170 police injuries, 217 arrests and reported crimes totalling 580!

The general dynamics of the self-reinforcing drift towards military policing are summarized in Figure 5.1. The general features of this vicious circle are clear. Initial moves in the direction of military policing result in antagonizing the older generation of blacks, and in a further reduction of the flow of information; the weakening effectiveness of other institutions of social integration result in more youngsters spending more time on the streets and in contact with the police, which reinforces the processes of stereotyping the community as a whole as crime-prone; and the propensity to collective resistance to arrest, when unchecked, threatens to make any attempt at policing a major military operation in the literal sense of the term.

Before we conclude this discussion it is worth asking a simple question: why has it taken so long – why, in fact has it taken the summer of 1981 and the threat of its repetition – to open

Figure 5.1. The self-reinforcement of military policing

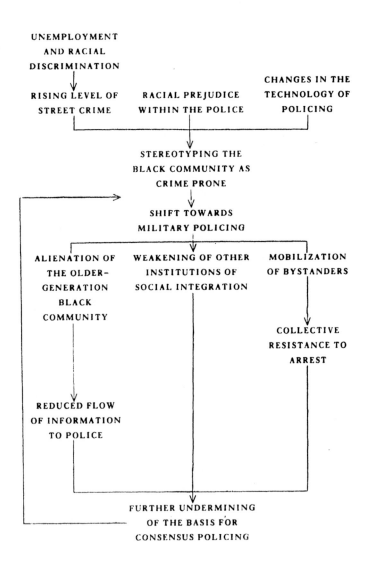

up a space for some serious political discussion of the nature
of policing in the inner city? There have been enough warnings
of what was to come. A decade ago the House of Commons
Select Committee on Race Relations and Immigration in its
1971–2 session report concluded that:

> To state that a sizable proportion of the West Indian community no
> longer trust the police is to confer a euphemism upon a situation which
> for many has reached a level equal to fear, and we are convinced that
> if urgent action is not taken to give effect to the grave issues at hand,
> violence on a large scale cannot be ruled out.

Why were the gathering storm clouds of the 1970s ignored?
One response, not uncommon on the left, is to see the move
to military policing, with its attendant risk of large-scale
violence on the streets, as more or less a conscious act of state
policy in order to bottle up the new generation of unemployed
youth in the inner city and counter, at the same time, the rising
militancy of the organized working class by the creation of a
'moral panic' concerning rocketing crime rates. There is an
important element of truth in this view. A generation of young
people surplus to requirements in the strict economic sense do
really pose new problems of social control. Some of the aspects
of this we shall look at in the next chapter. But to argue from
this that simply bottling up this population through military
policing and an escalating technology of repression culminating
in water cannon and plastic bullets is a conscious act of state
policy is to oversimplify matters considerably.

The broad aim of government policies in the late sixties and
seventies was to create, by state intervention, mechanisms of
integration into mainstream social and economic life for those
groups which the changing structure of capital accumulation
had excluded from it. This ranged from the Race Relations
legislation, through initiatives to persuade the trade unions to
take black workers seriously, to the various components of the
urban programme and the Manpower Services Commission

youth opportunity schemes. Such policies have been weak and
have failed by and large to influence the situation over the last
decade. They have failed, above all, through government
financial constraints, as well as opposition by employers to strong
anti-discrimination legislation.

It is the *failure* of central government policy to avert the crisis
of the inner city and unemployment among youth and ethnic
minorities which has created the structure within which the
development of military policing has taken root. The failure of
central government to stem deprivation has resulted in higher
crime rates. Other general social forces associated with economic
decay have fuelled the fires of racial prejudice in British society
and so some of the crucial factors setting off the vicious circle
of military policing have been generated. These processes have
taken the form of pressures to deal with an already developing
situation: pressure from police officers for more power and resources – witness the Police and Criminal Evidence Bill – and
from the judiciary to increase the scope of summary jurisdiction
to deal with crime rates.

From this standpoint it is easy to see how the warning could
be ignored and how the drift to coercive policing policies at
ground level could occur without great opposition from public
opinion. Three factors stand out. Firstly, the move to military
policing in the inner city among the ethnic communities has
been absent from the middle-class suburbs and their enclaves
within the inner city. Rather than the moral panic concerning
crime in the inner city being a deflection of rising struggles at
the 'core' of society, it has been precisely the fact that the consensus at the core has been secure *despite* increasing
economic crisis that has laid the basis for a move to a more
repressive policing policy at the periphery. As Brogden notes
(p. 205):

Consent to policing does not of itself necessarily imply support for
what police institutions actually do. Inner City residents believe that

police work is crime work and support policing in general ... Public
order police work is conceived of as a kind of accidental by-product
of the primary duties of police officers, engaged in the 'war against
crime' ...

But suburban residents recognize the objective function of police
work – maintaining social and public order. The concentration of police
officers in the Inner City, on public order duties, and on the prevention
of incursions into suburbia, are functions which fit that conception.

Secondly, the drift to military policing has taken the form, as
far as the majority of the British public have been concerned,
of a fight against crime, and street crime in particular. The niceties of the theorization of crime as a form of 'non-ideological
politics' escape the ordinary citizen concerned about his property
and personal security. But finally – and this factor will constitute
the starting-point of our discussion in the next chapter – the
population that has borne the brunt of military policing has been
largely a population *about* which we talk, but rarely a population
*with* whom we talk. A section of society has arisen that lacks,
in effect, one of the basic features of liberal democracy: a means
of expressing its grievances and interests at the level of national
politics. It is a population in our midst without a political voice.

# 6   Marginality and Violence

An important component of the vicious circle described in the last chapter was called the 'mobilization of bystanders'. Riots can be seen as an extreme form of such mobilization. Most riots, as we have noted, are triggered off by someone being stopped by the police and questioned or arrested. This is sufficient, given the state reached by police–community relations, to bring people on to the streets in massive numbers. People join in for a variety of reasons – unemployment, housing, social discrimination, resentment at police behaviour, and so on. But at this stage an important question has to be posed: why does this 'mobilization of bystanders' take the form of riot? After all, in democratic societies there are established procedures, it would seem, whereby group grievances can be voiced and attended to. One of the defining characteristics of modern democratic political systems is that both within and outside the state, social groups have the right publicly to organize and mobilize in order to press for or resist particular changes affecting their interests. The most obvious examples of this, of course, are the activities of political parties, trade unions and employers' associations. In drawing attention to the centrality of such processes in open democratic societies we are not subscribing to the view that questions of political power and domination in Western democracies can be exhaustively analysed in terms of these processes of pressure group politics or institutionalized conflict, but we are simply concerned to note that it is this system which historically has enabled a political process to take place with reference to opposed class interests but without habitual recourse to organized and widespread violence.

The historical preconditions for liberal democracy are not our main focus here, though we shall have to say something on the subject during the course of this chapter. Neither is an exhaustive treatment of the much-discussed crisis of the democratic political system, though, again, we shall have to touch on it. Indeed, we are dealing with one of its manifestations. In an editorial on the Home Office research study into the riots in Birmingham, the *Guardian* commented:

> It is not so much the poverty or joblessness that provokes street violence; it is the alienation that arises from a feeling that these hardships are being caused by institutions that are remote and uncaring. In other words there has been a chronic loss of faith in our political institutions, which has bred a dangerous cynicism and lost those institutions the support of the community. In such circumstances a breakdown of social control is almost inevitable. (8 June 1982)

It is precisely this question that we will address in this chapter: how is it that widely felt grievances among young people, such as unemployment and police harassment, have been the pre-condition for riot rather than organization and articulation through the existing channels of liberal democracy? In brief, our problem is the growing political marginalization of young people, and the younger sections of the ethnic minority communities in particular, from the political process of liberal democracy. It is this political marginality which both increases the propensity to riot as a method of expressing grievances concerning unemployment and policing, and which at the same time exacerbates the social conditions of rising crime rates which become a component of the drift to military policing. In the previous chapter we dealt with the latter side of the coin; now we turn to the former.

## Violence, Politics and Industrialization

The specific characteristic of the riots of summer 1981, like those of the United States in the late sixties, is that they are not attributable to some short-term peculiarity, such as sudden demobilization of soldiers or a period of intense industrial conflict. Rather, a long period of rising deprivation, deteriorating police–community relations, and failed social policy initiatives indicate that industrial societies are, in their maturity, beginning to reproduce some features analogous to those of their earliest stages of development. At first sight, violence in the streets does not seem to be a feature of British society which ever entirely disappeared with the onset of mature industrialization. Therefore, some type of classification of the different stages through which violence itself has passed is necessary if the particular characteristics of the riots of summer 1981 are to be put in context. We would identify three major stages through which riots and collective violence have passed in industrial societies generally, Britain included.

The first stage can be called violence associated with the process of incorporation of the working masses into the process of capitalist industrialization. Under this heading, of course, come many of the numerous 'riots' which characterize English history of the late eighteenth and early nineteenth centuries. A great deal of the violence of this period can be seen as popular attempts to stop the advance of capitalism by means such as Luddism and machine smashing or action against price fluctuations, which E. P. Thompson has characterized as 'a last desperate effort by the people to re-impose the older moral economy as against the economy of the free market' (p. 73). Historians such as Thompson find it easy to discern a clear political purpose behind the actions of the mob: defending traditional society and culture against the onset of capitalism. But the very fact that such violence so readily presents itself as a political phenomenon draws our attention to the second aspect: violence as a form of politics by those sections of society denied any other form of representation or articulation of their interests. Not only was the eighteenth-century mob resisting, from the standpoint of the rural periphery, the onset of urban capitalism, but it was denied any of the forms of political representation which later came to be associated with the stability of such societies. Violence was the only form of collective mass politics available.

The second stage, therefore, is that of the gradual incorporation of the masses into the process of politics: this has come to define the political organization of modern democracies, and at this stage violence as a political process becomes marginalized, exceptional and episodic, rather than the norm. Indeed, violence comes to be seen as the breakdown of politics *and* of any rational process. In this situation collective violence can easily be seen as a variant of other forms of more individualistic irrationality such as various forms of crime, even when it is not. The most visible aspect of the incorporation of the masses into the political process was, of course, the extension of the franchise. The essential dynamics of this process have been summarized by Poggi (p. 124):

For various reasons the subaltern strata could not long be prevented from obtaining the franchise and seeking to put it to their own use. The growing fiscal and military needs of the state were leading it to engage ever larger numbers of the masses in an increasingly direct relation to itself; and some degree of legitimate participation in the country's political process suggested itself as a counterpart to the burdens imposed. Also, the possession by the masses of basic civil rights ... required by the capitalist mode of production gave the disenfranchised a toehold in the larger society and a means of taking part in 'public activities' to the end of gaining political rights. Similarly, an increasingly sophisticated industrial technology made at least a minimum literacy a requisite of the work-force; but the resulting establishment of public education systems ... increased the workers' ability to organize and mobilize themselves. Finally, where even a rudimentary party-system involving competition for votes existed, the 'outs' were often led to promote the enlargement of the electorate in order to be rewarded at the polls by the newly enfranchised.

But the acquisition of the franchise was only one aspect of the process of incorporation of the working class into the political system of liberal democracy; at least two others were involved. First, the ability to form organizations which could represent the interests of working people, both in a day-to-day sense as regards employment relations, and in a more general political sense through political parties, often connected to trade unions. The second aspect was, of course, the development of a framework whereby the organized interests of labour, or sections of workers, could confront employers or the government in a process of political negotiation and compromise. It is this process, above all, which removed politics from violence and the streets and displaced it to a process of institutionalized class conflict, or, as George Woodcock expressed it, 'out of Trafalgar Square and into the corridors of power'.

These last two aspects, the development of working-class organization and participation in a stable framework of compromise politics, involved quite profound developments in the culture and social life of the working class. The acceptance of urban life, the separation of work from family and leisure, the acceptance of the rigours of the working day – these developments are crucial to the emergence of a stable, reformist, working-class politics. Their importance lies in the fact that by making uncontentious so many aspects of urban working life and capitalist discipline, they enable a very restricted conception of needs to become the basis for class politics. A set of needs fundamentally revolving around wage levels and the day-to-day aspects of work-place organization can become the basis for a compromise politics involving stable relations between workers and employers. A politics such as that of the earliest stages of the Industrial Revolution, revolving around the fact of the market economy, factory discipline *per se*, work, leisure and family life, cannot.

At the same time that capitalist industrialization, by re-organizing needs, provides the basis for a politics of compromise, it also lays the foundations for the organized strength of the working class to be exercised as part of that political process. The growing concentration of the work-force in large factories and the progressive development of trade union organization among new layers of workers are well known features of the expansion of capitalist industrialization. It is this combination of a restricted conception of needs – in the sense outlined above – and the strength and cohesion of working-class organization which is the mainstay of stable, reformist, working-class politics. Organization based on the work-place -and linked through national trade-union organs, and political parties either directly based on, or in political alliance with, trade unions, were the means whereby the working class incorporated itself into the political system. The process of negotiation and compromise over wages or general increases in the standard of living (the social wage) is a political process that calls for a full-time bureaucracy of leaders and organizers. The political participation of the worker is restricted to episodes: union meetings, rallies and demonstrations, strike action. Politics is not co-terminous with life itself. This is true only for the leadership which is constantly in a process of drawing up plans, sounding out alliances with other political groups, negotiating, etc. What power the individual union or party member has over his/her leadership is exercised through the franchise, the power to elect and reject the leadership.

These, then, in a very schematic and summary form – we are not writing a book on the history and development of politics – are some of the features of stable, working-class, reformist politics as they emerged in the later nineteenth and twentieth centuries. It is not our purpose here to criticize or evaluate this system of politics, just to point out that this political system was, historically, the means by which violence was largely replaced by a process of political compromise (and we are not suggesting that the compromises were necessarily equal on both sides) in the relations between the main social classes of workers and employers. The system is, of course, by no means immune from occasional recourse to violence. The system of compromise contains no mechanism whereby an outcome acceptable to both sides is guaranteed. At times of economic expansion the system is at its most stable, when the problems of sharing the cake are moderated by the fact that the cake is expanding. But at times of crisis, when workers are seeking to defend living standards against employers or governments intent on reducing them, violence is not ruled out. But the most important characteristic of such violence – which marks it off both from the violence of an earlier stage, the late eighteenth and early nineteenth centuries, and of the newer violence about which we shall speak presently – is that when it does occur, it comes as a stage in the process of political compromise, when that process breaks down. The long period of negotiations, the strike, the lock-out, the confrontation between strike pickets and the police, or the mass demonstration at which the trouble starts, are the most likely occasions when violence will occur: the violence is not itself the political process, but a response to the fact that the established machinery of compromise has been exhausted or has broken down. Violence is, at the most, a tactic or an episode in a political process which is defined predominantly in terms of its non-violent characteristics.

Before we leave this section it is useful, for the sake of later comparison, to emphasize some of its salient features. Above all, there is work. It is through participation in the process of production as worker (or, from the other side, as employer, though this is not our focus here) that participation in the political process we have been describing follows. This is not easy to grasp if the 'entry ticket' to the political system is seen simply as possession of the vote. The franchise is not tied to work; we do not lose the vote if we become unemployed. But the ability to vote in elections does not automatically confer the ability to participate in a process of policy formation and execution, the actual process of politics. The franchise merely confers the ability to check, periodically and in a very general way, some of the consequences of this process. Indeed, as numerous students of modern forms of democracy have pointed out (cf. Poggi), it is precisely the incursion of the organized working class into the political sphere which pushes the purely parliamentary aspects of democracy, the debate among elected representatives, to the periphery of the decision-making process, where it is replaced by the process of political negotiation and compromise between organized interest groups. It is participation in an organized interest group which in most democratic societies is crucially linked to participation in the process of production.

Participation in the process of production as worker results in two links between the individual and the political process. First, the individual is inserted into the system of needs around which political conflict centres, a system of needs which, as we have said, revolves around issues easily translatable into questions of money – wage levels, working speeds, etc. – and a more general but strongly linked set of social needs concerning housing, health care, education, etc. which can be translated into questions of public (state) investment in social welfare. In the transition from school to work the individual is conditioned into these conceptions of need as he or she picks up the accompaniments of adult working-class life: a house, a mortgage, a TV, concern about health, family responsibilities, all of which are invariably accepted as needs. As a result, the direct monetary needs around which his or her political sense will develop take on a real existence. Secondly, participation in work links the worker to those institutions which, in the system of pressure-group politics, are going to represent those needs in local industrial negotiations with employers, with national government and within the state itself. The definable set of needs, reducible to tangible questions of money and expenditure, and the political organization of trade unions and labour parties with their full-time bureaucracies dedicated to a politics of negotiation and compromise over precisely these questions are, of course, closely linked. Each reinforces the other; neither would be possible without the other.

The significance of what we have said can perhaps be seen by looking at the position in a political democracy of social groups excluded partially or entirely from participation in the production process. Women constitute the social group that comes most obviously to mind. Without wishing to suggest that participation in the labour-force should necessarily be thought as co-terminous with emancipation, it is quite clear that, in terms of political organization and the expression of needs and interests, lack of participation in the process of production has been one of the sources of weakness of women as a group and of the general marginalization of their needs from the central processes of political conflict in liberal democracies. Rather than suggesting that this in some way shows the peripheral nature of women's issues, we are suggesting that this highlights precisely the limitations of the system of representation of political democracy as at present constituted. Thus the women's movement has had to struggle to articulate its needs, to make political what in the dominant culture is very much taken for granted as a natural division between the sexes, and to find a political means for expression. The 'politics of the family', for example, has remained a peripheral issue, not from the moral standpoint but from the standpoint of its being translated into a set of demands backed up by organizational pressure within the political system. In terms of actual gains over the last ten years, apart from some influence upon the 'ideological climate' which can change very quickly (cf. *New Socialist* no. 6, July/August 1982), the pressure from the women's movement has been most successful precisely where its needs could be translated into those of workers in the production process and reflected in the policies of trade unions. Even the Equal Opportunities legislation, however, has a precarious existence (see Gregory).

What the women's movement illustrates is the relative political powerlessness of social groups who have no organizational basis in the process of production and whose needs cannot readily be articulated in terms of increases in wages or public spending. It needs to be added, of course, that access to the means of communication in modern societies can to some extent compensate for this. An articulate intelligentsia with access to mass media and communications can to some extent compensate for a lack of power and organization in the process of production. Again, the effect that the women's movement has had on the climate of ideas during the sixties and seventies is an illustration of this. But, to return to our main theme, what we have now is a social group which has access neither to the means of production nor to the means of communication: the growing army of young unemployed. The emergence of youth as a 'dangerous class' increasingly associated with crime and collective violence marks the third stage in our brief history of the relationship between violence and the political process in modern society.

The very existence of this third stage is not an issue that has been a major focus among sociologists or politicians, though the riots of summer 1981 will no doubt serve to concentrate thought on the issue. Until a few years ago most academic theorization was concerned with what was seen as the development of the second stage, the dynamics of the further incorporation of the (employed) working class into the system of consensus politics and into the cross-class cultural homogeneity that underlies it. Most of the debate was between those who, in one form or another, argued for the cementation of the stability of consensus politics by the reduction of the degree of conflict between the social classes in the 'affluent society', or were concerned with the degree to which terms like 'working class' had any meaning as a guide to political action, and those who argued either that there were new bases of conflict in the 'technological society' or that the return of general economic recession would re-awaken the older economic conflicts along basic lines of class cleavage.

In other words, while a lot of thought was given to the questions of the likelihood or otherwise of labour emancipating itself from capital, either in the classic form of the socialist revolution led by the working class or in more gradualist variants, rather less thought has been given to the revolution that has been and is proceeding at quite a pace, that of capital emancipating itself from labour. Certainly, the growing awareness of the impact of micro-technology has assisted a refocusing of concern upon those expelled from the process of production.

To characterize our 'third stage' briefly and schematically: what we are witnessing is the growth of a generation of young people in our inner cities and decaying industrial areas whose contact with the work process is, if existent at all, minimal and peripheral. A new core of young unemployed has arisen, a growing number of whom have *never* worked. That such a group exists and constitutes a growing social problem is, of course, not news. But what we want to emphasize is this: the growing army of young unemployed, among which the ethnic minorities are over-represented, is not just a social problem in the sense of deprivation and wasted lives and opportunities, but also a *political* problem, a simmering crisis for the political system of liberal democracy. This is because the marginalization of these young people from the process of production means marginalization from the process of interest-group formation and political compromise which we have described as a crucial stabilizing feature of democratic political systems. As we shall see, it is not inevitable that the processes of political group and interest formation in modern democracies should be based on participation in the production process, but in British society this is the case. Economic marginality becomes co-terminous with political marginality.

It is in this way that industrial capitalist societies in the late twentieth century have begun to reproduce features of the late eighteenth century: large numbers of people were greatly affected by industrialization but denied any effective channels for the expression of their interests in that society. The cause of this 'return to the past' is the changing dynamics of the industrialization process itself. The second stage, during which the incorporation of the working class into the political system was rapid, involved relatively labour-intensive industrialization drawing large numbers of people into the labour-force and the production process. Our third stage, which we have characterized as the emancipation of capital from labour, involves the decline of industrial relative to other types of employment in the tertiary sectors, the fragmentation of the working class into a small, highly paid, skilled industrial sector, a more rapidly growing sector of low-paid service and a new, small, manufacturing sector, the growth of middle-class white-collar employment in the public and private sectors, and the slowing of the rate of growth of employment itself. During the boom after the last World War the relative decline in industrial employment was covered up by the growth of employment in the service sectors, especially in the inner urban areas where industrial employment was declining as firms located new plants outside the inner areas. Recent years, however, have seen the decline of employment in public-sector services as slowing rates of industrial growth have generated fiscal difficulties for public investment, making 'Keynesian' solutions to economic recession problematic in most Western economies. Finally, the impact of micro-technology is not restricted to industrial employment and is therefore likely to have brought to an end the epoch in which the replacement of labour by machinery in the industrial sector can be compensated by the growth of more labour-intensive tertiary employment.

Why is the growth of unemployment especially concentrated among young people? What is important is not age *per se* but the fact that unemployment is especially heavy among those who have not worked, as opposed to those who have been expelled from the work process due to factory and plant closures, etc. Trade union strength, the desire of employers to hang on to trained labour till the last moment in hope of an upturn in

the trend of industrial production, together with the relative
rise in youth wages, the disappearance of 'young people's jobs'
through modernization, all help to explain the greater concentration of unemployment among those trying to get into the labour
market, who are predominantly young people. There are other
categories, of course, with extremely high unemployment rates,
especially unskilled workers who are easily recruitable and more
weakly unionized, women and ethnic minorities.

There are obviously some important differences between the
rioters of the eighteenth century and the young unemployed
of Brixton, Toxteth and elsewhere. What they have in common
are fundamental resentments and grievances relating to central
features of the industrialization process coupled with political
compromise. But there are two crucial differences. Firstly, the
rioters of the eighteenth century were attempting a last-ditch
stand against the consequences of an advancing industrialization
whereas the youth in the inner cities today are taking to the
streets to protest at the consequences of the retreat of industrialization and the decay, lack of opportunity, and deprivation
left behind by that retreat. Secondly, the rioters of the eighteenth
century were attempting to preserve a traditional culture and
way of life from the impact of urbanization and industrial life;
the young unemployed of the inner cities today are engaged
in constructing a new way of life, a sub-culture expressive of
the fact that they have grown up in and imbibed the expectations
and standards of life in industrial society but have been denied
the opportunity either to achieve those expectations or to
mobilize in some politically effective way to secure the means
to that achievement. It is out of these frustrations that collective
violence is returning to our streets. This second aspect – the
denial of means to achieve expectations, or relative deprivation
– coupled with the economic and political marginality of the
young unemployed, constitutes the main foundation of a growing
crisis for our political system.

## Economic and Political Marginality

To summarize a theme developed above, we argued that integration of the working class into the process of production paved the way for its incorporation into the political system by developing, firstly, a lifestyle and system of needs compatible with industrial society, and, secondly, a framework for political organization based upon the linkages and cohesion of economic life. This was reflected in the organ of traditional working-class politics, the trade union, which exists to pursue a set of clearly defined needs centring on wage levels around which political processes of negotiation and compromise can take place, and links the individual worker or the local working-class community into the national political system through the establishment of a political apparatus of leaders, organizers and administrators who conduct the political process on behalf of members. It is precisely this set of linkages to a stable political process that the new unemployed of young people and the ethnic minorities lack and which therefore forms a precondition for the re-emergence of riot as a substitute for politics.

The primary lack is a clear conception of interests around which a stable politics of negotiation and compromise could take place. As we have seen in our discussion of subculture, it is the transition from school to work which transmits to the individual the set of needs around which traditional working-class politics revolves. The working-class male leaves school, gets a job, gets married, buys a house, has children, gets a mortgage, etc., so he needs a stable job and an income that keeps up with the cost of living, in order to pay the bills and take the wife and kids on holiday once a year. The young unemployed person, out of school and on the streets with no fun and no future, inhabits what we have seen to be a subculture of despair built around ways of dealing with the resentment of unfulfilled expectations. These expectations, it is important to understand, are not a set of needs as precisely formulated as the married, employed worker's (otherwise it would be quite simple for the young unemployed to unite themselves around a reasonably coherent political programme and organization, as did some of the adult unemployed in the 1930s), but a much more diffuse set of feelings that the future ought to have been interesting, worthwhile, rewarding, and so on, when it manifestly is not.

The lack of a clear conception of interests, or, more precisely, the replacement of interests by the more diffuse set of resentments and grievances which have become woven into the lifestyles of subcultures, accounts for the lack of political mobilization of young people. Alongside this is the lack of any framework, which the production process provides, for linking the individual into a national organization. Not only are there no issues formulated precisely enough to sustain a permanently organized political pressure group, with a leadership and bureaucracy of its own, but the structure and cohesion are absent which the process of production provides for traditional working-class politics. The only terrain of organization for the young unemployed of today, the terrain upon which the contradictory lifestyles of subcultures are lived out, is that of the streets. The streets do not make for cohesion in the same way as the factory or industry. The cohesion of the streets is localized and expressive. For the employed worker the occupation of the means of production is a source of power; the potential and actual use of the strike weapon as part of the process of bargaining is a central aspect of working-class politics. As we have said, the use of that threat is part of a process of bargaining which has many components. For the young unemployed, however, the streets, the pop concert, the riot, the mass rally, are not weapons in an arsenal to be utilized tactically by a social movement whose cohesion and solidarity are already to be taken for granted; they are the means of constituting the movement itself and simultaneously its only form of collective action.

An important consequence of this is that in so far as organized political movements attempt to appeal to the young unemployed, they tend to succeed if they can adapt their methods of political mobilization away from the older conceptions of politics (meetings, membership, debates, resolutions, etc. – a 'rationalist' politics) towards the expressive, episodic mobilization of the riot, the demonstration, or the football crowd. In this it has to be said that, for a time at least, the far right developed more expertise than the far left. In their book *Knuckle Sandwich*, Dave Robins and Phil Cohen show how the nihilism and despair of white working-class youth was mobilized by the National Front. At meetings both of the far left and of the National Front, the kids were frustrated by the tameness and lack of 'action'.

Recently, however [1978], the Front has learned how to organize directly through some aspect of youth culture, for example, by gaining influence in football supporters' clubs and inculcating N F slogans through the medium of 'end' chants. (p. 170)

Thus a recent survey of young unemployed in Liverpool found that

85% of those interviewed had no political convictions at all; many were vehement in their indifference to politics. Half the group were even unwilling to define themselves as members of the working (or any other) class -- hardly fertile soil for extremist movements of the left.

The National Front is another matter because it offers a rather different outlet for frustrated energies. Street fights are more likely to strike a chord than organized political action. But it is well to remember that riots can be triggered off by all sorts of organizations or, indeed, by no organization at all. (Ridley, p. 124)

The obstacles in the way of far-right mobilization of white youth may be less the counter-activity of the left in relating to youth culture (though the Anti-Nazi League had some success in this area) than the fact that black youth culture has had a crucial input into the culture of white youth. Thus, as Paul Gilroy remarks (1981, p. 218):

Though it contains no guarantees of a progressive outcome, the fact that neo-fascist and nationalist attempts to win young whites have been forced to recognize the political power of black culture as an obstacle to their success indicates the relatively precarious nature of the youngsters' commitment to race and nation.

So, the economic marginality of the young unemployed today, by taking the form of isolation from forms of political organization and the style of political culture, which makes possible what has been defined, since the mid nineteenth century, at least, as the political process of liberal democracy, reproduces itself as political marginality. To talk of the political marginality of a growing number of young people is to try and reorient the discussion about the problem of youth which has followed the riots of 1981 away from a focus simply on deprivation and lack of opportunity coupled with police harassment. Looking at riots simply as the result of deprivation never quite fits until the riots are seen as caused not by deprivation and unemployment but by the lack of channels whereby young people feel they can draw attention to their position or mobilize in some constructive way to change it. It is important to be clear that political marginality involves two distinct components: isolation from the effective channels of pressure-group politics, and isolation from processes whereby political interests can be clearly and instrumentally formulated. Only a focus on both of these can lead to an understanding of the proclivity to riot or to other forms of mobilization such as those mentioned above in connection with the far right. Concentrating on only the first is the mistake so often made by the far left, as it persists in the notion that it is possible simply to go out and recruit youngsters to another political party which, this time, *will* give voice to their interests. This entirely begs the question of political marginality by assuming a clear conception of interests and the willingness of youth to participate in a type of political organization which exactly reproduces that of the older parties and organs of the employed working class.

More important, perhaps, is the tendency altogether to ignore the political aspects of marginality. This occurs for two reasons. Firstly, as we have mentioned already, the nature of political marginality can be missed by simply defining possession of the vote as a sufficient criterion for inclusion in the political system. The franchise is necessary but not sufficient. Political marginality is above all the exclusion from the ability to form co-ordinated, stable interest groups able to function in a process of pressure-group politics. Indeed, it is the marginality of youth in this latter respect which is reflected not only in the pent-up frustration of riot, but also – what is but the other side of the coin – the declining participation of young people in the formal, vote-centred, aspects of the democratic process. Alarming also was the MORI poll of August 1979 which showed an increasing propensity on the part of young people to sanction violence as an acceptable means of political change.

The second source of ignoring political marginality is to see youth simply as a transitional social group, so that lack of political participation could be seen not as a problem of political marginality but simply a prelude to the transition to adulthood – that is, to acquiring work and hence interests and forms of political participation. With long-term structural unemployment and the alarming prospect that 'by 1986 as many as 60 per cent of an EEC dole queue that could well number 15 million registered unemployed will notionally be under the age of 28 and will never have held a permanent full-time job in their lives' (Merritt, p. 102), the whole relationship between youth and adulthood becomes disconnected. Youth is no longer a transitional phase to political integration, but is artificially prolonged, well into the twenties in terms of age, by precisely the absence of opportunity to make that transition to adulthood by acquiring a steady job. It is at this point that youth become a distinct group and their exclusion from effective political processes becomes not just 'pre-entry' but political marginality; they form a growing social group with a developing identity and no political voice.

The problems that the increasing political marginality of young people poses for the structure of Western democratic political systems have to be clearly understood. There are two aspects we would like to emphasize. The first we have already spoken about at some length. Democratic political systems find themselves confronted by groups of the population who through political marginality are outside the forms of organization *and* the type of cultural expression of interests conducive to the process of political negation and compromise characterizing liberal democracy. But, secondly, the very fact of the growth of political marginality changes the character of the political system itself. It is not the case that those still part of the system carry on with a stable process of compromise politics as if nothing had happened, simply leaving a growing number of marginalized people outside knocking at the door. Take, for example, the trade unions: as the representative organs of a decreasing number of employed workers, they can expect in various ways to come up against government *administrative* measures designed to deal with the unemployed and marginalized strata of society. There is, for example, already some friction between the TUC and the government concerning Manpower Services Commission schemes for youth training. Unions have expressed concern over the wage rates paid to trainees and the extent to which MSC attempts to persuade businesses to offer places to trainees further restrict the opportunities for employment through the ordinary channels of the labour market.

The point can be made more generally. To the extent that social groups marginalized from the economy and from the forms of political representation and compromise in our society remain the concern of the state, their relationship to the state changes quite fundamentally. Although economically and politically marginalized they still possess a minimum of civil rights, and they remain the recipients of state education, welfare and unemployment benefits. They cannot, as social groups in society, literally be ignored. What happens, however, is that they become *objects* of state policy dealt with *administratively*, having no participation in the formulation of the policies which are applied to them. The growth of such groups, the young unemployed and the ethnic minorities, begins an incipient drift towards an authoritarian state of a particular type: one in which a vestige of democracy remains at the 'centre' between those social classes still involved in the production process, providing a continuity of democratic legitimacy to the state, on the basis of which increasingly authoritarian policies are applied to the social groups marginalized at the 'periphery' of political society. For these groups the basis of legitimacy of the state changes radically. Whereas at the 'centre' it is still the assent of the citizenry via the extant processes of political compromise that forms the basis of the legitimacy of state actions, at the 'periphery' it is precisely the adherence of the marginal groups to the administrative regulations of the state that qualifies the behaviour of such social groups as legitimate.

In the long term, this administrative solution to the problem of marginality is problematic and likely to be productive of increased rather than decreased violence on the streets. From our standpoint, the growth of collective violence is a response to both economic and political marginality. Being related to the state and the political system only through the dole office and the police station is part of a marginality which breeds violence. It is this culture born of a resentment at denied opportunities which marks off the marginality of young people today from the marginality of the eighteenth-century rioters attempting to defend a pre-capitalist way of life against the incursions of industrialism, or even from the ghettos and 'rookeries' of the nineteenth-century industrial city with their self-enclosed subcultures of the underclass. Young people today have been exposed to the values and standards of modern industrial society but are denied the means of achieving them; in other words, alongside political and economic marginality as the preconditions for the re-emergence of collective violence must be added a high degree of relative deprivation: the ghetto cannot be cut off from the rest of society. The culture of the ghetto is a culture born out of the recognition of, and resentment at, the consignment of a generation of young people to the social periphery.

## Relative Deprivation

Relative deprivation is the excess of expectations over opportunities. The importance of this concept is that it gets away from simplistic notions that try and relate discontent and collective violence to levels of absolute deprivation. The link between relative deprivation and political marginality is crucial for understanding riots and collective violence. Political marginality is unlikely to result in riot unless there is the added sense of frustration stemming from relative deprivation. A social group may be economically and politically marginalized, yet if it has no desire to participate in the structure of opportunities and social rights from which it is excluded, frustration need not occur. For the rioters of the eighteenth century the problem was not the failure to be included in a structure of opportunities stemming from industrial society, so much as the fact that an existing way of life was in the process of being destroyed by industrialization and its opportunity structure. In contemporary industrial societies social groups that have a high degree of economic and political marginality but a low sense of relative deprivation tend to be either deviant subcultures, particularly religious groups oriented to 'other-worldly pursuits', or first-generation immigrant communities. The latter, forced to take the worst jobs and the worst housing that industrial societies have to offer, may still, in the short term, be sheltered from a sense of relative deprivation by virtue of the fact that their standard of comparison is not so much the opportunity structure of the wider society from which they are excluded by racial discrimination or legal barriers, as the societies from which

they recently emigrated by comparison with which living standards are higher.

Conversely, of course, a sense of relative deprivation can co-
exist with the absence of economic or political marginality. This
is the situation with regard to the majority of the organized working class in industrial societies faced with a marked inequality
in the distribution of wealth and opportunities. Relative deprivation becomes the driving force of militant trade union and
political struggles to increase living standards through the
process of political negotiation and compromise. This distinction
between relative deprivation combined with political integration
and relative deprivation combined with political marginality enables us to understand some of the differences between the
1930s, with their relative absence of riots despite high levels of
unemployment, and the present period. During the thirties the
experience of unemployment was not linked as closely as it is
today with political marginality. Unemployment was concentrated in the older working-class communities centred in the
basic industries of the north, iron and steel, shipbuilding, coal
mining, etc. The experience of unemployment was often the
collective experience of a whole community related to the slump
of the industry around which the community lived and worked.
This meant that the institutions of class politics – the trades
councils, Labour Party and union branches – appeared to the
unemployed as the natural weapons of struggle. The attempt to
transfer these traditional methods of struggle *at* work into the
arena of the struggle *for* work, such as in the construction of the
National Unemployed Workers Movement, was an obvious
course of action for the unemployed, most of whom had spent
a period of their lives at work. Even the younger unemployed
could be drawn into this through the general status and influence
of labour-movement institutions in the cohesive working-class
community.

The present period presents two contrasts to this. Firstly,

the working-class community, particularly in the inner-city areas throughout the country – not just in the older industrial areas – is far less cohesive. The fragmentation of employment between older, industrial employment in decline, newer state employment in the public services, and new small firms relying on cheap labour, combined with a greater cultural and ethnic diversity as older sections of the working class have moved out of the area or just ceased to exist and new immigrant communities have been established, has produced a much greater diversity of levels and types of labour-movement organization. It is not that organization has not emerged in the inner cities, but it no longer constitutes the cohesive and unifying force in the working-class community that it once did. Added to this is the massive growth in the number of young people who have never worked and therefore are not familiar with the organization and attitude of working-class politics. The isolation of youth from work and from class political organizations combines with the reduced hegemony of working-class institutions in the community, by comparison with the 1930s, to produce an acuteness of political marginality probably never previously experienced by any section of British society since industrialization.

But the burden of our argument here is that this acute political marginality is, for the young unemployed, combined with a greater sense of relative deprivation than in the 1930s. It is this volatile combination that underlies the rising street crime and collective violence that we see returning to our cities. This sharp growth of relative deprivation follows from quite fundamental changes, again by contrast with the thirties, and even more with the nineteenth century, in the mechanisms determining the relationship between expectations and the opportunities for achieving them.

If we define relative deprivation as the excess of expectations over opportunities for fulfilling them, then it is easy to see a situation in which relative deprivation might be kept in check – one which undoubtedly corresponds to the vision of a stable society held by many belonging to what has come to be called the 'new right' in the Conservative Party, in which expectations and opportunities are generally determined by the same mechanism: the free competitive market. Where the competitive market exists not only as a mechanism for the allocation of society's resources but also as a 'moral force' in society, then expectations and opportunities will be brought into some sort of balance. People will not expect a higher income or standard of living than the sale of their particular skill or labour in the market brings, if it is generally considered that the standard of rewards obtaining from the competitive selling of labour or goods in the market is just. Also, in such a competitive society, if an individual does not achieve the same rewards as others from the sale of similar labour or goods, then that individual is likely to blame himself or herself on the grounds that this must be due to offering an inferior product for sale on the market.

Some politicians and academics would like to see this idealized world of *laissez-faire* present in society, in order to solve the problem of relative deprivation, but, to the extent that it actually functioned as a social force in industrial society, it did, and does, provide such a solution only for sections of the middle class. Under nineteenth- and early twentieth-century capitalism, the fact that the working-class community was insulated by both distance and communication from wealthier sections of society was a far more effective check on relative deprivation, especially coupled with the fact that remnants of pre-industrial religious and customary ways of thinking about society as an inevitable and justifiable hierarchy remained in the popular culture. As the working class became organized and the strength of trade unionism developed, the aims of working-class politics centred not so much around reaching the *same* standards of living as the employers and the ruling class as around the defence of existing working-class living standards, together with modest improvements.

What is even more important about the thirties is that, despite

the depths of the recession, militant discontent was never widespread. Wal Hannington, who led the National Unemployed
Workers Movement, had to concede, despite the claims he made
for the influence of his organization, that 'at no time has the
standing membership approached even 10 per cent of the vast
masses of the unemployed'. As Runciman notes (p. 64):

> The Depression imposed severe and sometimes intolerable hardship
> on large sections of the working class and many non-manual workers
> also; but it did not heighten their feelings of relative deprivation in the
> way that both wars did. Particularly severe wage cuts were, as one would
> expect, resisted, notably in the textile industry. But the disposition to
> grin and bear it remained much more widespread than the disposition
> to storm the barricades.

Particularly since the last war the growth of the Welfare State
has combined with the mass media and mass secondary education to produce a steady growth in relative deprivation. The
mass media have disseminated a standardized image of lifestyle
particularly in the areas of popular culture and recreation which,
for those unemployed and surviving through the dole queue, or
only able to obtain employment at very low wages, has accen-
tuated the sense of relative deprivation. The spread of mass state
secondary education has had a similar effect, not so much by
standardizing expectations of career patterns, living standards,
etc., as by raising the minimum expectation. During the period
of exceptional economic expansion of the fifties and sixties this
posed no problems. But now the phenomenon of 'over-edu-
cation' is beginning to appear. As Cloward and Ohlin (pp.
118–20) have pointed out, the excess of aspirations and opportunities can paradoxically lay the basis for social, racial and other
forms of discrimination:

> The democratic ideology of Equality of Opportunity creates constant
> pressure for formal criteria of evaluation that are universalistic rather
> than particularistic, achieved rather than ascribed – that is, for a struc-
> ture of opportunities that are available to all on an open and com-

petitive basis ... However, the democratic society, like other types of society, is characterized by a limited supply of rewards and opportunities. Although many are eligible for success on the basis of formal criteria, relatively few can succeed, even in a rapidly expanding economy. It is therefore necessary to make choices on some basis or other among candidates who are equally eligible on formal grounds ... In this situation, criteria based on race, religion, or class, that have been publicly repudiated in favour of achievement standards, are informally invoked to eliminate the surplus candidates. Thus the democratization of standards of evaluation tends to increase the competition for rewards and opportunities and hence the discrepancy between the formal and the actual criteria of selection for lower-class youngsters.

Finally, the Welfare State has had the same result. New concepts of need and minimum standards of living, coupled with a focus on the poorest sections of society have had the effect of raising the minimum expectation. The *Sunday Telegraph*, comparing the slump of the 1930s with that of today, grasped this well:

> Though unemployment is similar in scale, social security benefits today are not far short of average living standards then. Today's problem, though, is just as acute since expectations, fostered by television and advertising, are high and the frustrations generated by our own slump are vast and dangerous. (*Sunday Telegraph*, 21 February 1982)

The consequence is that expectations have become governed by a set of mechanisms much more loosely, if at all, related to opportunities. The latter are still to a large extent determined by the market mechanism coupled, of course, with the massive growth of state intervention and investment, which itself has had an effect on relative deprivation. As it has become perceived that the state has taken responsibility for major components of the opportunity structure through careers and employment in state services, as well as the general responsibility undertaken by post-war governments, until recently, for maintaining the level of employment, so the discrepancy between expectations and opportunities, now growing as a result of economic recession and cutbacks in state spending, becomes blamed on the 'system' rather than on the individual.

Meanwhile, another quite important change was taking place, the consequences of which are now much clearer. While the tendency, as far as expectations were concerned, was for greater standardization and raising the minimum, the nature of post-war economic expansion was to create a working-class opportunity structure which was increasingly differentiated in terms of wage levels and working conditions. The decline of manufacturing employment in general and the rise of new highly paid white-collar and technical occupations, combined with new sectors of low pay in services (often combining low pay and unsocial hours) and small firms, has produced a more diverse set of opportunities at the same time as expectations have been becoming more standardized. In the short run the solution to this problem in most Western industrial societies was immigrant labour. We have already mentioned how immigrant groups of the first generation may combine political and economic marginality with low expectations and hence low relative deprivation. The passivity of the early, post-war, immigrant communities was based on a combination of a cultural orientation towards the homeland and an expected short stay in Britain. This meant that immigrant workers were prepared to accept working conditions which would not be accepted by native workers, such as low pay and flexible shift systems involving long periods of night work. In addition, the legal barriers of alien status and racial prejudice of the native British population generally excluded immigrants from better paid forms of employment.

This situation has been brought to a conclusion during the seventies by the growth of a second generation of Britons of immigrant parentage. Going through the same education system (despite various forms of discrimination operating there), the children of immigrant families have grown up with the same spectrum of aspirations and expectations derived from the mass media and the education system as young people in general.

Expectations and opportunities, then, have been moving in opposite directions, relative deprivation has been increasing, and, as the state has increasingly been seen as the determinant of opportunities, the resentment of unfulfilled expectations increasingly takes the form of resentment against the state and its manifestations, particularly those, like the police, who are encountered on a day-to-day basis by the young unemployed.

Relative deprivation is not something that can be reversed. An extreme nationalist government could no doubt have some success in mobilizing elements of the resentment against an 'external' enemy. We already know from the experience of the 1930s that the connection between unemployment and war exists and it is by no means impossible that it could be repeated, as the Falklands episode illustrated.

# 7 The Struggle for an Accountable Police Force

It will be useful to begin this chapter with a general summary of some of the main points in our argument. Our analysis has centred around the ideas of marginality and relative deprivation. We have argued that the progressive economic marginalization of a generation of young people, among whom the ethnic minorities are heavily represented, coupled with a high degree of relative deprivation, has produced a youth subculture. This subculture, manifested in different ways among black and white youth and within different groups of black and Asian youth, is an attempt to come to terms with lack of achievement and denial of opportunity – that is, with relative deprivation. Such a subculture is contradictory: it combines the attempt to sustain dignity and solidarity with a highly individualistic predatory streak. It faces both ways, in the direction of a petty criminality that wears down the community, and in the direction of a unity and solidarity in the face of adversity.

Thus one consequence of economic marginality and relative deprivation is a rise in crime rates. This has become bound up with the vicious circle of the drift to military policing in the inner city which has become one of the central grievances of young people, blacks in particular, and ranks alongside socio-economic deprivation like housing and unemployment as one of the main ingredients of the riots of summer 1981. In particular, the drift to military policing emphasizes the solidarity of the community and tends to direct it against the police. Finally, the frustrations of the young and the black community reached breaking point, in the form of riot, because of the lack of any other effective channels whereby their grievances could be formulated and represented in the political system. This political marginality, we have argued, has been one of the consequences of economic marginality in a society in which the forms of political group formation are based on participation in the production process.

In the course of the argument we have hinted at certain solutions. In this chapter our argument will be that fundamental changes in policing, particularly in terms of local democratic accountability, are necessary to break the vicious circle and shift policing towards the consensus model. But first, what if nothing is done?

## Leaving the Inner Cities to Rot

In a paper to the British Association in September 1982, Ken Roberts, a sociologist from Liverpool University, argued: 'We are now learning that unemployment does not inexorably demoralize all its victims or propel potential victims towards extremist politics.' He envisaged a situation in which, as far as the education system was concerned, 'Careers education [would] prepare leavers for living without continuous employment [and] teach them to regard their initial years in the work force as a period of exploration.' The basis of such an analysis is this: in the theory of relative deprivation, it is necessary to have someone to compare yourself with who is better off than you are. A sense of relative deprivation for the unemployed is at its highest when there are people around them who are employed and who are manifestly enjoying the fruits of what is left of the consumer society. But as unemployment and deprivation become the normal experience of a whole generation, then, of course, it is reasonable to expect that the sense of relative deprivation of young people will to some extent become lessened: the unemployed individual would not be in a situation of being surrounded by people better off than himself or herself. Crime, of course, remains as a method of acquiring some of the good things of life, but to the extent that generalized frustration is decreased, crime and collective violence become less likely. Such a process could be used to explain why, for example, in the United States there have been no repeats on a large scale of the riots of the late 1960s despite the fact that during the subsequent decade conditions in the black ghettos have worsened rather than improved. The sixties' riots came after a period of rising expectations encouraged by the economic boom and a good deal of social mobility within the black community coupled with the expectation of beneficial effects from Equal Opportunity legislation. A sense of relative deprivation became more acute among the ghetto masses when nothing happened, despite the media razzle-dazzle of equal opportunities and new frontiers. Since the riots nothing has changed, but deprivation has become more generalized due to further worsening of conditions. People have forgotten the message of the sixties and no longer compare themselves to people who are getting somewhere, and so a mood of apathy has descended on the ghettos. They can be left to rot economically and socially without much threat of future conflagration.

Under such conditions police chiefs might well decide that the time has come for a rethink of policing strategies in the areas of mass unemployment and deprivation. Policy rethinks might involve a move away from military policing to one of not enforcing the law. Giving up on the war against street crime in the ghettos would reduce the necessity for road blocks and 'swamp' operations and leave the police free to concentrate on only the more serious crimes that affected the 'outside world', such as drug trafficking, stolen goods, etc. As regards street crime and other thefts and burglaries the community could be left to its own devices. This would no doubt involve the tolerance by the police of *de facto* alternative policing by the 'community' itself through vigilante squads and summary justice meted out on the spot by such gangs.

Learning to accept unemployment as a way of life and giving up the search for work does not, however, necessarily constitute a reduction of relative deprivation. There are two reasons for believing that the inner-city areas, and particularly the ethnic minority youth in those areas, are not experiencing a decline in relative deprivation. Firstly, one consequence of current Manpower Services Commission youth-training programmes may be to increase a sense of relative deprivation. This can happen in two ways. On the one hand, to the extent that the programmes do not lead to real skill training but simply forms of low-wage temporary employment, they raise expectations in young people which they are not able to fulfil in the long run. Secondly, to the extent that such schemes are not immune from racially discrimatory bias against young blacks, they further increase frustrations and a sense of relative deprivation among that section of unemployed youth.

The second reason for not expecting a marked decline in relative deprivation is the nature of the inner-city community itself. It was the traditional, cohesive working-class community which was the most conducive to the acceptance of unemployment as a natural fact of life and not the fault of the individual: 'Neighbours and others in the community where steep streets look down on to the empty shipyards recognize the interruption of work as part of the established routine of the trade' (Sinfield, p. 152).

In the inner cities, particularly in areas like London previously sheltered from heavy unemployment, the newness of the phenomenon coupled with the occupational and ethnic fragmentation of the community itself can lead to a considerable stigma being attached to unemployment. Ken Roberts, in another survey of young unemployed for the Department of Employment Gazette, found a very high rate of non-registration in London compared with other cities and concluded that 'Widespread non-registration is a phenomenon of times and areas of rising

unemployment blighting localities where it was previously uncommon, affecting families where some parents have spent
recent decades deploring "workshy scoundrels".'

Unemployment as the monolithic experience of an ethnically
homogeneous community does not yet, as a general rule,
characterize British cities. There are no black ghettos on the
scale of American cities. The existence of such areas acts to
reduce the immediacy of relative deprivation, but also as
a source of political demarginalization. In the States the number
of inner cities with black voting majorities with regard to mun-
icipal elections is increasing. This phenomenon allows a black
middle class to emerge in local government, something that
happened rapidly in the years following the riots of the late 1960s.

Such situations are the framework for a temporary stability;
but the temporary nature of that stability must be stressed.
Political participation brings a sense of power and the capacity
to influence events. If it becomes clear that political participation
is unable to redistribute resources to the inner city, then, of
course, in the long run, frustrations will increase again. If it
becomes clear that the only effect of participation in local government has been to enable a middle-class stratum to achieve some
status, prestige and resources for itself, but has not been able
to affect the lives of ordinary people, then the political marginality of the ghetto masses is reinforced rather than ameliorated.

To discuss the general dynamics of urban politics and development in American cities over the last, or the next, ten years
is beyond our scope, but reference to that situation serves to
highlight features of the situation in Britain which do not seem
conducive to the quietening down of the social problems and
the new phases in urban decay announced by the riots of summer
1981 and repeated in the odd sporadic outburst since. Rather,
the absence of cohesion among the deprived has been the salient
fact of inner-city politics over the last decade. Rising unemployment rates and the general deterioration of housing and social
services in the inner cities became the basis of political polariza-

tion on ethnic lines during the seventies far more than the basis for unity. The rise of the political extremism of the far right with a real basis of support among the white population of these areas looked at one stage likely to exert a substantial influence upon local government. By contrast, potentially unifying struggles, such as the mobilizations of the late seventies against cuts in hospitals and health services, failed to produce the mass movement that many of those who participated in them had hoped for.

In returning our discussion to the question of policing we are thus faced with the question: is the response of the inner-city community to rising crime – exploited as it is by the media, and periodically aided by the form of presentation of the crime statistics – any more likely to be a unifying force in the community than were earlier struggles over other aspects of the inner-city crisis? Before attempting to answer this question we shall try to review the main issues in the emerging debate on police accountability.

## Democracy and Accountability

The question of democracy brings together both themes of the book: effective policing responsive to the needs of the community, and the ending of the drift towards a political marginalization of the young unemployed. Our argument is that a much more organized and rigorous system of local democratic accountability of the police is vital for restoring mutual respect and trust between police and community, restoring the flow of information between the two, and at the same time for creating a political structure in which the most deprived sections of the working-class community can articulate their interests and grievances (which, in large measure, concern policing matters).

First, however, we must say in more detail what we mean by a political system. For some people, no doubt, the riots of 1981 constituted in themselves a form of politics of a very revolutionary nature. Thus, for example, for the authors of the pamphlet on the riots entitled *Riot Not To Work*, 'Brixton stands as one extreme case of people developing their own ways of getting money outside the official economy and their own ways of enjoying themselves outside of the official marketplace. It is the self-organization of non-work, or of unofficial work, which makes the entire culture extra-legal and labelled "criminal" by the state' (p. 36). From this anarchist standpoint the riots are to be seen as a sort of declaration by the riot areas of independence from the rest of society, rather like Third World countries imagining that they can escape from the grips of the international economic and monetary system simply by securing political independence from their former colonial rulers.

More seriously, the riots, as we have said, are a form of politics in the sense that they were constituted by collective mobilization and based on grievances denied other modes of expression; but by their very nature they were episodic and reactive. Riots only initiate changes and reforms in society to the extent that they force *others* (like Lord Scarman) to respond and, inevitably, to define the issues. Precisely because they remain a form of reaction, not a process whereby political changes and developments at the level of society as a whole can rationally be evolved, the riots signify that a large number of people are outside politics. The real issue of political reform facing us now is not that of how to define riots, but of how to adapt our political system in such a way that those previously driven to riot can be re-included in the organs of political discourse.

Many of the issues which communities without an effective political voice will wish to bring forward concern policing and the demand for effective policing. A reform of the system of police accountability to the public is the vehicle whereby these issues can be voiced and discussed. The consequences of a situation in which the local communities are able to discuss and formulate their needs as regards policing – and there will only be an incentive to do this if those policies can be carried into effect through the local accountability of police forces – will be that the relation between police and public will change from the present one verging, in growing areas of our major cities, on open warfare, to one of mutual confidence. This change in police–public relations is the only basis upon which a close sharing of information between police and public can be envisaged such as would make possible a form of consensus policing approaching that outlined in earlier chapters.

This is our view. But for such views to become anything other than wishful thinking a number of important problems, complications and counter-arguments must be effectively dealt with. The most important of these can be listed as follows:

(1) Local democratic accountability of the police opens up the strong possibility of the direction of policing falling under the influence of unrepresentative local interest groups. Conversely, the argument that policing policy can in any coherent way be placed under the direction of the 'local community' presupposes that there really survives such an entity which has been undermined precisely by problems of urban decay and fragmentation.

(2) Policing policy is to a considerable extent a technical matter requiring a degree of discretion to be exercised by chief constables and senior officers which would be seriously hampered by local democratic control.

(3) The undoubted advantages of close contact between the police and the local population whereby mutual trust and the exchange of information could be fostered can be achieved through the already existing mechanisms of community policing such as those pioneered by John Alderson and David Webb and recently embraced, in part, by Sir Kenneth Newman, without the disadvantages of local democratic control.

## Local Accountability and Local Interests

Local control, argue its opponents, makes policing vulnerable to the influence of local interest groups which may be able to put pressure on the police from purely sectarian standpoints. On the face of it, the same argument could be applied at a national level: both the direct accountability of the police to the national government and the indirect accountability of the police to the laws enacted by central government mean that the police could be vulnerable to the influence of particular social classes, particularly the owners of capital, whose interests may have a disproportionate influence upon the policy of national government. The argument for national, as opposed to local, control is at its strongest, therefore, if it can show that particular interests which are, at the national level, either insignificant or modified by the process of political compromise may assume an exaggerated importance and influence upon the local policing policy of particular areas and hence threaten the universality of the rule of law. For example, an extremist political group of little national significance may exercise a disproportionate influence locally and attempt to pressure the police to use their discretion in a sectarian manner. Particular interests in one part of a city may seek a policing policy which acts against the interests of people who come from the suburbs or outside the city to use its facilities: central city residents may be able to ruin the social life of people from outlying districts by getting all the cinemas and places of entertainment closed at an early hour in the interests of 'peace and quiet'; a group that engages in a widespread form of deviance in a particular part of the city may through the local political process secure the co-operation of the police in turning a blind eye to its activities. To the argument that recent revelations such as emerged from the 'Countryman' inquiry into the Metropolitan Police show that this flourishes under a situation where there is no local control, the opponents of local accountability would argue that the situation would only get worse under local control.

From this standpoint it can easily be concluded that in a modern democratic state anything but a national police force is a hangover from an essentially pre-industrial and predemocratic system. The residues of local control of the police in Britain would be seen as residues of the control of law and order by the rural squirearchy or the local bourgeoisie rather than as remnants of popular democracy which have been whittled away by the concentration of power in the hands of the central state. By contrast, in those industrial countries in which the state played a leading role in the promotion of industrialization, national centralization, including the development of a national police force (even if co-existing with local forces), was an essential aspect of the overcoming of locally based particularism and aristocratic or landed opposition to democratic reforms. A glance at recent American history might serve to illustrate the point about the resistance to democracy by local interests. In the 1960s it was the central federal government and its agencies which were in the forefront of the struggle to enforce Civil Rights legislation against the entrenched resistance of locally based groupings in the southern states. The picture of Federal Marshals, even on occasions assisted by Federal troops, enforcing school desegregation against the entrenched resistance of the white section of the local community – including the 'democratically elected' local police chiefs and sheriff's deputies – was a familiar one on our television screens and in our newspapers and can be used to underline the point about the dangers of local control. Transfer the picture to Britain now, in the 1980s, and we get a frightening picture of local police, supported by the more unsavoury elements in the white community – in an electoral majority – launching a reign of terror against local ethnic minorities.

It might seem that the connection between local control of the police and justice and the rule of law in a multi-ethnic urban Britain is somewhat tenuous. It might seem that firm central control by Parliament rather than the 'local community' is the only way to guarantee a just and effective policing in accordance with the rule of law. Such an argument, in juxtaposing national to local accountability, makes, of course, the crucial assumption that the former works. Yet a general characteristic of modern democratic societies, noted at least since the turn of the century, has been the increasing autonomy of the executive from the legislative branches of the state. The problem of popularly elected legislatures trying to control an increasingly powerful professional bureaucracy is thoroughly familiar, and a powerful case for the progressive decentralization of state functions can be, and has been, built upon the foundation of this fact alone.

But in addition to this, the process which we have called political marginality – the marginalization of deprived communities and above all the unemployed from the process of effective political representation of interests – provides a second challenge to the effectiveness of national accountability. The argument that, whereas particular sectarian interests may predominate in a locality, at the national level all significant social interests are articulated and engaged in a process of political compromise has long been recognized on the left as hollow. Marxists have tended, however, either to stress how the class background of the Civil Service can effectively result in the sabotage of radical programmes by popularly elected governments (this is not to suggest that all popularly elected governments are necessarily of the left), or to show that the objective restraints of the capitalist economy 'necessitate' the abandonment of radical policies in the face of the 'harsh reality' of the International Monetary Fund or international bankers. The emphasis we wish to make is that long before such factors come into play, or quite apart from their operation, the process of political compromise which takes place both inside and outside Parliament leaves out, except as an object of benevolent concern, the interests of the deprived, and in particular those who are presently bearing the brunt of 'military' policing. Thus a police organization accountable solely to national processes of political life is likely to be minimally accountable to those sections of society who are being most policed. So even if there is a danger of local account-ability rendering policing liable to particular pressures based in some localities, it is no answer to point to national account-ability as 'obviously' more representative. In addition, if the argument rests here, nothing changes. The marginalized com-munities continue their processes of decay and frustration, riots or mini-riots always remain on the horizon, crime rates soar, and the vicious circle of police and community alienation con-tinues unabated.

The most important issue that has to be faced is: precisely what do we mean by the *local community* under whose control we are proposing that many aspects of policing be placed? It is one thing to argue that the national political process excludes significant social interests; it is quite another to argue that the locality can somehow be constituted as a political entity with sufficient coherence to control its own policing policy. We have yet to answer the argument that such local control would make policing policy the tool of whatever political interest group might gain temporary ascendancy. Indeed, what sort of control would an inner-city population, many of whose members have, no doubt, at some time either participated in, or sympathized with, those who have been involved in some form of criminality, be likely to exercise over policing policy? For many people, not only conservatives, the question has only to be posed in this way to produce the conclusive answer that the only way to preserve law and order in the inner cities is through firm central con-trol, perhaps allowing a measure of consultation so that the police may ascertain the views and concerns of the community for which they are responsible.

Writers of both the right and the left have recognized that the breakdown of the cohesiveness of the traditional working-class community has proceeded apace since the last war. Writing from a left-wing standpoint Ian Taylor has argued that 'Working-class support for the police has appeared to increase the more that the traditional social controls of the working-class community have been dislocated by post-war social and economic changes' (p. 151). Indeed, with the fragmentation of the community through unemployment and rising crime and the very fact of ethnic diversity itself, 'sections of the white working-class population living in particular parts of London in particular have in recent years come to demand the kind of reactive fire-brigade policing that is provided by the Special Patrol Group' (ibid.). This emphasizes the basis of the argument that locally controlled policing would be unlikely to produce a consensual policy acceptable to all social and ethnic groups living in the area. From the right of the political spectrum the American criminologist James Q. Wilson associates the demand for tougher policing with a breakdown of community cohesiveness occasioned by the flight of middle-class people – those most concerned 'to maintain standards' – to the suburbs. 'Communal social controls tend to break down either when persons with an interest in, and the competence for, maintaining a community no longer live in the area, or when they remain but the neighbourhood is not sufficiently distinct, territorially, from areas with different or threatening lifestyles. In the latter case especially, the collapse of informal social controls leads to demands for the imposition of formal or institutional controls – demands for "more police protection" ' (p. 40).

What both these writers exhibit is a particular conception of community, one defined predominantly in terms of *cultural* cohesion. One can, of course, and many conservative thinkers do, conceive of the national political community in predominantly cultural terms. And it is from precisely such a perspective that the presence of different cultural groups, particularly if some are of recent immigrant origin, is seen as a threat to the stability of the political system. However, at the level of national political systems there is enough evidence to point to the fact that in order to constitute a political community, capable of running its affairs with a reasonable degree of stability, a national state need not be culturally or ethnically homogeneous. One has only to think of Switzerland or the United States.

Turning back to the local community, it is reasonably obvious that the old cultural homogeneity of the traditional working-class community, to the extent that it existed, has passed away for good. Can the local community be reconstituted as a political entity despite the decline in cultural homogeneity and the fragmentation characterizing the present period? The answer is yes. And the only way to develop, or rather re-develop, the local community as a political entity is to create the institutions for local democracy. It is no good looking first to see if the local community has properly constituted itself with a degree of political responsibility and only then contemplating the decentralization to the locality of decision-making procedures previously concentrated in the national state. As John Stuart Mill wrote a very long time ago, 'A democratic constitution not supported by democratic institutions in detail but confined to central government not only is not political freedom but often creates a spirit precisely the reverse' (p. 358).

Democracy, in other words, has an educative and an integrative function in itself. It is through participation in decision-making on matters that affect our lives that we learn political responsibility, the respect for other people's right to their point of view, and the acceptance that the final decision will have to be a compromise between differing points of view. That was the classical argument for democracy. It is as relevant today as it was two hundred years ago particularly because, as we have seen in previous chapters, the present crisis is the re-emergence, in a new form, of course, of an old problem: the problem of marginality and its connection with violence and rioting. Just as many conservatives today will throw up their hands in horror and denounce us as a 'dangerous tendency in public life' for arguing that the 'riff-raff' should be given more political power, they only echo their forefathers who, generations ago, threw up their hands in horror at the thought of the extension of the franchise to 'riff-raff' who, they felt, could not possibly learn the habits of civilized politics. But that is exactly what happened, though in becoming politically civilized the working-class movement at the same time changed what politics itself was about: from the polite discourse of men of property to a system of political confrontation and compromise between organized social classes based on the system of capitalist produc-tion. Now the rapidly changing nature of that system of produc-tion has placed another change upon the agenda: that of changing the democratic system from one which reflects only the com-promises between those social classes rooted in the system of production to a system in which the interests of the new strata of people marginalized from production can find a voice.

Such a political system, it should be clear, has to be far more decentralized. The tendency to centralization, speeded up over the last decade, and the reduction in the effective powers of local government have to be reversed; the ambit of the powers of local government has to be extended, crucially to include policing. Unless local democratic control is secured over the institution that, above all, in a constant daily sense, affects the lives of the marginalized, then the incentive to participate is reduced, and local democracy becomes, or remains, simply the manoeuvring of local party groupings.

## Technical Aspects of Policing

It might be argued at this stage that while we have given some very general arguments for increased democracy in local affairs which might well be applied to things like health-care, housing allocation, education and transport, we have ignored the quite special characteristics of police work that make it the exception.

We have noted before that the modernization of policing over the last decade and more has given it an increasingly technical nature. The complexity, it may be argued, places any rational discussion of policing policy beyond the capacity of the elected local representative. The increasingly sophisticated range of specialist units, computers, different types of vehicles, and combinations of manpower, makes decisions as to when and in what combinations to deploy such resources only really determinable by people with a great deal of expertise. Therefore, the only viable type of accountability is to national government at which level technical and political discussions can be entered into with the requisite levels of expertise available from both sides.

Secondly, part of this technological revolution within policing has been the increasing proportion of police services that can only be provided on a national as opposed to a local scale. This is especially true of computer information and forensic services. The development of Regional Crime Squads was a reflection of this. Local control, from such a perspective, becomes less and less of a viable proposition: witness the decline in the number of police forces in Britain, through amalgamation, from 123 in 1945 to forty-one at the present time. And with that amalgamation has had to go a decline rather than an enlargement of the immediacy of local democratic supervision.

The final argument under this heading concerns the unique role of the police as the enforcers of law. The rule of law requires that an individual committing a particular crime stands an equal chance of being prosecuted for it irrespective of where he or she commits that crime. A rigorous local control of police practice would, therefore, undermine the rule of law by opening up the possibility of a local police committee adopting a very different prosecution policy from that of other such committees.

The translation of questions which are basically political into questions of technique to be dealt with only by experts is a familiar process within bureaucracies either at the national or local level. Often the starting-point for the redefinition of a political problem as technical is that the political process has either omitted to discuss it or fails to produce any clear directions. The experts then step into the vacuum and redefine the problem their way. Policing is no exception. Indeed, something like the opposite has tended to occur. The increasing technicality of policing has gone hand in hand with an increasing politicization of senior police officers. If a previous generation of chief constables remained faceless men behind the scenes getting on with the job, the current generation, beginning with Sir Robert Mark of the Metropolitan Police, and including men like David McNee, John Alderson and James Anderton, are, by comparison, public political figures. They do not all have the same political position: John Alderson and James Anderton are certainly pointed in different political directions.

The relation between the increasing role of technology in policing and the increasing politicization of senior police officers is an interesting one. Its roots lie, it seems to us, in the fact that the technology has not done the job. Success rates are still disastrously low and in many cases falling. More policemen, more vehicles, computers and specialists have not overcome, but, indeed, become part of, the crisis in police–public relations exemplified in the drift to military policing. The increased use of technology, as we have noted previously, is both a contributory factor, through distancing the police from the public, and at the same time a response, the predilection for computers being to a considerable extent a response to the drying-up of information from the public, which is the current crisis of policing. Questions of technique are inextricably bound up with questions of police–public relations, which is a profoundly political matter, and no doubt one of the motivations for chief constables increasingly to seek to address the public directly.

Many 'technical issues', such as whether to deal with a public disorder with vanloads of men armed with nightsticks or a smaller number of unarmed foot constables with some knowledge of the local population and local terrain, or to place permanently armed squads on the streets as James Anderton did in Manchester in April 1982, are not in fact very difficult for lay persons to grasp, especially when they are drawn from the population being policed. But the real issue about policing and technology is the extent to which many of the technical developments are at all advisable. At least one chief constable in the recent past instructed his CID officers to destroy irrelevant information on members of the public stored in their files. A move in the direction of consensus policing, a situation in which there was mutual trust between police and community and a higher flow of information, would reduce the necessity for 'fire-brigade' and high-technology policing. They would become aspects, or reserve options, in a form of policing based much more upon close links with the locality. The temptation to store massive amounts of information in computers based on the surveillance of ordinary citizens going about their lawful business would certainly be reduced. It is also likely that the size of police forces could profitably be reduced under such conditions even though certain services, of course, such as forensics, would be much more efficiently provided on a national scale (see Baldwin and Kinsey).

A further argument mentioned above concerned the fact that consistent national criteria for prosecution might be interfered with by strong local control. There is an important assumption here, that police work can be defined predominantly in terms of prosecution of those suspected of having committed crimes. But the 'prosecution' model of policing assumes the existence of consensus policing. That is to say, it assumes that in the general regulation of public order the community either regulates itself or accepts as quite legitimate the 'non-prosecution-oriented' activities of the police, such as directing traffic, regulating public gatherings, etc. These situations may involve the police in making prosecutions, but that is not the reason for their presence in the first instance on such occasions. To the extent that consensus policing is absent or weakened in the way described in our 'vicious circle' argument, and the very presence of the police, irrespective of what they are doing – investigating a crime *or* directing the traffic and crowds at some public event – becomes a problem and a potential occasion for disorder, then the key issue becomes not whether the police are free to enforce universal criteria of prosecution, but the restoration of the legitimacy of police presence in an area. Only when this is established does the question of whether or not the police are free to use consistent prosecution criteria become the important question.

Thus the argument for democratic local accountability remains precisely an argument for the method whereby the legitimacy of police presence in an area and the willingness of the public to co-operate with them can be restored. As to prosecution policy, it is important to separate out two distinct issues. As far as the use of consistent criteria for prosecution are concerned, there is a strong argument for taking the responsibility for prosecution out of the hands of the police and making it the responsibility of independent Crown prosecutors. Such individuals should be responsible to the Crown. This was, in fact, recommended by the Royal Commission on Criminal Procedure. It was not, however, included in the Police and Criminal Evidence Bill currently (1983) before Parliament. There is little point in prosecutors being made responsible to local democratic police committees since their task is precisely the enforcement of consistent criteria nationally.

Police discretion, however – the problem of where to direct resources when there are few policemen and many laws and offenders – is another matter. The direction of resources by a local police committee representing a particular faction would be no improvement on its arbitrary direction by senior police officers. However, as we have argued above, if the framework of local democracy can establish a meaningfully representative system of local control – we shall say more about this below – then there will be an improvement.

But there is an important grain of truth in the opposing argument. Police discretion can never totally be controlled on a day-to-day basis by a democratic police authority. Nor is it really desirable that it should be. Within a system of laws laid down by national government, a local police committee may decide from knowledge and agreement among its members that the particular problems of the locality demand a concentration of police resources on the enforcement of some laws more than others. For example, if a large number of the inhabitants of the area live in tall, badly lit housing estates and, because of work patterns, have to walk home late at night, then the police committee may decide that officers should be patrolling such an area at a late hour rather than being engaged in other duties. In another locality the situation may be quite different. Experience leads to the conviction that under the present system of either no public accountability, as in London, or very ambiguous accountability, as in other parts of the country (of which more below), local police commanders by no means take full account of community wishes in distributing their resources. General policy direction is about as far as a viable system of local accountability could go, and very necessary it is.

Even within such a framework, however, police discretion will have to be used in at least three quite obvious sets of circumstances: first, to decide when an offence has been committed and under what category it falls; second, to decide who initially is to be suspected of such an offence (the notion that all citizens can be equally suspect of any type of offence is quite ludicrous and would be very oppressive to the public if a police force tried to act on it). Third, quite irrespective of policy laid down by the police committee, individual members of the public may call upon the police – and they are more likely to do so when, as a result of local accountability, relations between police and public are good. This will involve discretion (for instance, in evaluating the seriousness of the complaint), and may lead police resources in directions which deviate from the general policy laid down by the local police committee. Of course, in the long run, the local police will bring this to the attention of the committee and discussion may enable the re-evaluation of local priorities. But this does not alter the fact that a *degree* of discretion is a necessary and unavoidable aspect of policing in a democratic society (cf. Kinsey and Young).

## Community Policing and Police Accountability

The crisis in police–public relations culminating in the riots of summer 1981 about which we have had quite a bit to say in this book has led to a renewed interest in 'community policing'. Many of the features of community policing appear at first sight very similar to the type of changes we are advocating, so we will concentrate on emphasizing the differences between community policing and democratic police accountability. The aims of advocates of community policing are basically similar to our own: to restore trust between police and community and thereby the flow of information from community to police, reversing the drift in the direction of military policing. Lord Scarman's report on the Brixton riots of 1981 gave a tremendous fillip to the advocates of community policing who were urging that a statutory duty be placed upon the Metropolitan Police to institute police–community consultation procedures. Although the Association of Chief Police Officers (ACPO) opposed Scarman's recommendation (we shall look more closely in a minute at why they did), such a clause is contained in the Police and Criminal Evidence Bill. A body already exists for the Lambeth police district to look into this and its initial meeting was chaired by no less than the Home Secretary himself.

There are two elements in 'community policing': first what one of the foremost advocates of the system, John Alderson, calls 'the community constable'; and secondly, the local police–community consultative or liaison committee. The notion of a community constable can, of course, mean nothing more than a few more men on foot instead of in Panda cars. But properly carried through in combination with consultation procedures in which the views of the representatives of the public can be made known and the police have an obligation to explain their policies for the locality, the aim of community policing is a restoration of good relations and with it the flow of information between community and police.

There is one crucial difference between community policing and democratic police accountability: the absence of control by the local community over the activities of the police. Local representatives will have a right to consultation, and in Scarman's view the scheme for London should include the police complaints system and inspecting local police cells, but what local representatives will not have the right to do is *decide* local policing policy. To quote Lord Scarman: 'Neither will consultation always produce an agreed result: in the end it will be necessary for the appropriate police commander to take a decision' (p. 65).

Nevertheless, it might be felt that even if decision-making power in the last analysis should rest with the local police commander rather than an elected police authority, as long as the former displays mature judgement and behaviour with regard to the consultation process, and does not attempt to ride roughshod over local opinion but is careful to take it into account and patiently to explain and discuss his decisions, then the advantages of a close relationship and trust between police and community can be established without the disadvantage or danger of the police becoming the tool of local political factions. But the type of locality in which success is most likely is one in which the police and the community already share quite articulated conceptions of the nature and priorities of the policing process: in a phrase, where consensus policing actually exists. If we look for the type of locality in which 'community policing' might be expected to work we are led to the middle-class suburb, or the established neighbourhood of the 'respectable' working class. Where we most definitely are not led is towards the inner city and the marginalized populations of the younger unemployed and ethnic minorities, which are precisely the areas in which the crisis in police--public relations is at its worst and in which the drift to military policing is furthest advanced.

Consider for a moment the reason why the ACPO opposed Scarman's call for statutory liaison committees. One of the things that concerned them was the form of representation on such committees: they did not wish to be saddled with an obligation to consult (let alone be controlled by!) 'community leaders who are not in fact community leaders'. This point goes right to the heart of the issue. As we have seen, one of the salient characteristics of the inner-city communities is that, through massive unemployment and weakening of the connections with the older forms of working-class local representative institutions, to a great extent they lack a political structure in the traditional sense of the term. This means that when a police--community liaison scheme is established in such an area there can easily be a problem of who the representatives actually represent: they can end up representing small sections of the community or even no one but themselves. Police commanders in the localities will sense this and will certainly not wish to tie their hands with too rigid a system of consultation.

That is one side of the coin. The other is that community policing initiatives such as the Home Office is currently encouraging in London occur in a situation where there is already widespread hostility to the police. Fragile consultation machinery and more foot patrols will be unlikely to change this state of affairs in the short run. So local commanders will continue to rely, even if less frequently than in the past, on the type of saturation policing operation exemplified by 'Swamp '81', which in a matter of hours can undermine months of patient work from those involved in community relations. Local police commanders cannot be expected to suspend the war against rising crime rates and low clear-up rates until better police–community relations are established.

As we see it, therefore, the weaknesses of community policing as a strategy underline the need for a system of democratic accountability. The key issue is the establishment of the machinery of democracy as a way of re-establishing the sense of community. In other words, only if there is a general public debate concerning policing priorities in which all sections of the local community feel that they have an incentive to participate, will community representatives, as properly elected delegates, come to represent the community. And all sections of the community will only have an incentive to participate in the democratic process if they know that the police themselves are answerable to that process.

In the absence of proper accountability the newly constituted liaison committees will be in a position of searching around for significant groupings or representatives of the local community to consult. So, for example, the Home Office guidelines for the constitution of such bodies stipulate that membership should include the local Community Relations Council representatives. The CRCs were originally established to 'promote harmonious community relations', to act as forums in which different ethnic groups could establish dialogue and compromise. Yet more than a decade of experience has shown that such institutions have been able to achieve relatively little in the field of race relations. As early as 1971 a survey of the work of CRCs concluded that they did little more than channel off middle-class elements from the ethnic minorities into a political vacuum and certainly were in no position to act as effective representatives for the black community as a whole, with the consequence that only a relatively small percentage of the black community studied had even heard of the CRC (Hill and Issacharoff). In their study of Birmingham in 1979 John Rex and Penny Tomlinson saw little reason to change this estimation. It is true that during the seventies the ethnic minority communities developed more articulate pressure groups and to a small extent began to enter local government politics. But for the unemployed youngsters in the black community neither the machinery of local government nor the particular institutions of CRCs have much appeal for the expression of their problems. The former exerts very little control, and in London absolutely none, over the one institution that affects their lives on a daily basis: the police. The latter are non-starters because they have absolutely no political power either as regards policing or any other aspects of local affairs. It is hardly surprising, therefore, that they should become largely the enclave of middle-class elements. The same considerations apply to the relationship between the young white unemployed and the institutions of local government.

Despite the ambiguities of, and police opposition to, Scarman's recommendations for statutory police–community liaison, the police themselves have put a considerable amount of effort into such schemes, particularly in areas like Brixton. This can be seen partly as an attempt to short-circuit the growing campaign of a future Labour government, and partly as realization that the drift to military policing is indeed counter-productive.

The police are claiming success in Brixton. The community policing initiative there was launched in November 1982 and combined a number of elements. In addition to closer dialogue with community representatives through a community liaison committee backed by the Home Office, Sir Kenneth Newman, who took over the Metropolitan Police in October 1982, introduced what he called 'targeting' which, though future operations of the 'Swamp '81' type were not ruled out, was obviously intended to be an alternative to the reinforcing tendencies of 'military' policing by which such operations alienate the community. Reported in the *Evening Standard* (6 April 1983), the chairman of the community–police liaison committee, Canon Charles Walker, claimed the new 'targeting strategy' as one result of police–community liaison: 'I think we have encouraged the police to go in for careful targeting of criminals to catch the naughty boys and to discourage them from indiscriminate action and anything that looks like saturation policing. We've also encouraged them to get men on the street to relate to people and do that patient business of cultivating an area.' Not surprisingly, Newman found the crime statistics for Lambeth district encouraging: 'L' district as a whole showed a rise of 3.4 per cent in violent crime, but the Brixton division, from December 1982 to February 1983, showed a 9.4 per cent drop on the same period of the previous year. There was a similar trend for muggings. The police commander, Alex Marnoch, commented: 'I think it is the combination of a number of factors – the new policing initiative in the area together with better direction in the use of plain-clothes officers in surveillance and targeting operations and the support of the community as a whole in an effort to reduce the crime rate in Lambeth.' Police-community liaison has been encouraged by the Home Office since the Scarman Report and, of course, existed before. It will become a statutory duty in the Police and Criminal Evidence Bill now (1983) before Parliament.

Sir Kenneth gave a press conference in January 1982 at which one of the express priorities announced was to 'make the force more responsive to the needs and feelings of the local communities'. As if deliberately contradicting ACPO responses to Scarman's recommendations for community consultation which focused on the alleged non-representative nature of community groups, Newman's approach explicitly confronted the fact that: 'In recent years there has been a substantial increase in the number of formally constituted associations and groups representing a range of special interests. In many districts, commanders and their senior officers have to take in contact with at least forty representative and pressure groups.' Also recognized was 'a growing problem for the police in the decline of positive co-operation from the public.'

What Newman's new strategy involved was nothing less than

the recognition that police–community liaison was a vital part
of crime prevention:

> The crime prevention thrust will have two main facets, the rational-
> ization and redeployment of manpower, and the utilization of con-
> sultative committees as a vehicle for directing the overall strategy. Dis-
> trict commanders will be responsible for deploying their resources as
> dictated by their own professional judgement, taking full account of
> the views of the local community. Problems identified locally will be
> tackled systematically by co-ordinating the contributions of police,
> public and local agencies. The concept of a corporate strategy is vital.

Newman goes on explicitly to recognize 'that the police alone
cannot make a major impact on crime and that major resources
for crime reduction reside in the community itself and in other
public and voluntary agencies.' Among the proposals are
included: a focus on consultative committees to discuss and
develop the reduction of criminal opportunities and develop
crime prevention by asking District Commanders to identify
specific problems to the committees; and specific steps to obtain
the public's views on policing needs and priorities through consultative committees and other liaison groups, and through surveys of public opinion.

The first thing that is obvious from a reading of Sir Kenneth's
press release is that he has listened to and taken some notice
of the public debate on police accountability that has gone on
over the last few years and which focused around the riots of
1981. Gone is the reliance on technology and fast response, and
in its place is a recognition of the community as a source of
information and crime control and the need for the police to
have a close relationship with community groups, if they are
to be effective. Even the most hard-nosed senior officers feel
that public hostility coupled with appallingly low clear-up rates
for crime is a situation that cannot be allowed to continue.
Another likely reason is a felt need to short-circuit the GLC
initiative and the police committees established by a number

of Labour Boroughs in London. Despite having no legal powers, these bodies have made quite a public impact, and in some cases the police have taken them very seriously, sending officers along to discuss matters and be confronted by groups from the community in an environment which is entirely new and not on the police's own terms.

An optimist might say that the tide had turned, and that the need to press for a system of police accountability to democratically elected representatives is now less urgent. In our opinion it is more urgent, for the following reasons. Sir Kenneth's press conference is only one aspect of the post-Scarman developments in police matters. The other is the Police and Criminal Evidence Bill. At the time of writing this Bill is still before the House of Commons. If it is enacted, it will be against a wide coalition of opposition. Though the Home Secretary has dropped provisions which would have enabled the police to search confidential medical records and those of other 'caring' agencies, the police will still gain powers to enter the houses of individuals who have committed no offence to search for evidence relating to a 'serious arrestable offence' committed by others. In addition, police stop-and-search powers will be extended, as will the right to set up road blocks and to hold people for questioning for ninety-six hours as opposed to the current twenty-four, without charge. Journalists could be forced to surrender their confidential notebooks, address books, tape recordings, etc. Finally the age for fingerprinting will be reduced and the police will not be obliged to apply to a magistrate should a suspect object to fingerprinting.

Though the Bill will also make police–community liaison a statutory requirement, once again an opportunity to introduce an independent element into the investigation of complaints against the police will have been passed over. This Bill is the result of the Police Evidence to the Royal Commission on Criminal Procedure appointed by the Labour administration in 1978 which, incidentally, explicitly recommended such an

independent element, and also – something very important in
bringing the planning of policing policy under democratic
control – the separation of prosecution from the policing function. Thus, alongside Kenneth Newman's initiative lies a
draconian increase in police powers, in precisely those areas of
activity which feature heavily in military policing. The fact that
the police see these powers as necessary in a period following
Scarman and apparently have recognized the need for closer
community liaison shows the police asking for the impossible:
greater information flow from the community without a fundamental change in policing style, and without answerability
to those who employ them.

Under such circumstances, police–community 'liaison' by
means of a few representatives drawn from CRCs and local
government which at the end of the day leaves policy-making
exactly where it was to begin with, firmly in the hands of the
police themselves, does nothing to end the political marginalization of the young unemployed. It is hardly surprising, therefore,
that the bulk of the local community should see little point in
participation in such enterprises and that the police should feel
hamstrung by consultation procedures tying them to talks and
discussions with local individuals whose representative
credentials they regard as highly suspect.

Accompanying police–community liaison, indeed as one of
its components, Sir Kenneth's new strategy makes use of
'Neighbourhood Watch' systems in selected areas of London.
These began to get under way during 1983, alongside other
innovations against burglary, such as property marking. Neighbourhood Watch involves the creation of a network of citizens
who keep their eyes open for any irregularities in a particular
area, and report directly to the police. Such schemes are a direct
import from the United States where they have, in certain
instances, had great success.

One of the more successful schemes in the United States was
the Crary-St Mary's project in Detroit. The area was racially

mixed and had a high and increasing burglary rate. The young people of the area were predominantly black whereas the elderly were largely white. A control neighbourhood a few miles away was closely monitored as part of the experiment. The result: crime in the Crary-St Mary's area was reduced by 58 per cent over the period 1977–9, whereas in the control neighbourhood which had similar demographic characteristics it fell by only 11 per cent.

The background elements to this scheme are quite interesting. Firstly, in 1976 a radical black mayor, Coleman Young, appointed a new police chief, William L. Hart, with the explicit task of combating crime with new initiatives. Hart's programme included the setting up of a major crime prevention service and the creation of a police force which more adequately reflected the multi-ethnic character of Detroit. He also established 'shopfront' police stations to serve the community explicitly, and set up an independent police complaints panel. Neighbourhood Watch schemes were part of this package of innovations. They were set up through the existing network of community action groups, a network that was particularly strong in Crary St Mary's and which had a representative multi-ethnic membership in that area.

Sir Kenneth Newman's initiative exhibits a number of features which contrast sharply with the Detroit version of Neighbourhood Watch. Firstly, there is the total absence of democratic accountability of the Metropolitan Police. There is widespread criticism of the lack of representation of ethnic minorities in the police force, and of the inadequacies of the police complaints system. Furthermore, the scheme has not been introduced in co-operation with an existing network of community organization. This is presumably because the police feel that such a form of co-operation would threaten their monopoly of control of the scheme. Indeed, the only Neighbourhood Watch scheme in London to be explicitly based on a local tenants' organization has been established quite independently of the

police, by the London Borough of Islington. Islington introduced its own 'Crime Watch' scheme in October 1983 and was
not greeted with enthusiasm by spokespersons for the local
police.

What are the likely effects of Neighbourhood Watch schemes
in London? Because of the lack of democratic accountability it
is hardly likely that they will do much to reduce public suspicion
of the police. Indeed, the danger is that, by creating an auxiliary
force of 'snoopers', they will only increase public alienation from
the police. Secondly, because they are not based on any existing
community organization, they will have quite a low potential
for gathering information about crime. Thirdly, they will probably work better in middle-class suburbs where there is a high
degree of support for the police than in working-class inner-city
areas. These middle-class areas generally have a low crime rate
and the problem of lack of communication between police and
public is less evident. They may also have a measure of success
in middle-class enclaves within the inner city, areas which border
on the deprived areas and which have high crime rates. The
effect in such areas of Neighbourhood Watch may well be simply
to displace crime into the working-class areas which border them
and so increase the already high crime rates in such parts of
the city.

In Detroit, crime fell in the city as a whole; crime fell particularly sharply in the Neighbourhood Watch areas, people's
fear of crime dropped, their confidence in the police increased
and, perhaps most important of all, the sense of community
increased. All this was carefully monitored. In London, Neighbourhood Watch is being introduced completely outside such a
context. Our predictions are that for this reason it will generally
increase rather than reduce the problems of inner-city policing.

## Conclusion: Three Views of Police Accountability

The current debate about, and political struggle for, police accountability has become very complex. In Manchester, the struggle between James Anderton and his Police Authority has flared up yet again, this time over the question of firearms. In London, the GLC and Labour Boroughs are engaged both in a struggle for a Police Authority to replace the Home Secretary's control of the Metropolitan Police and at the same time various actions to try and call them to account for particular actions or inactions. The death of Colin Roach in Stoke Newington, the complaints about policing strategy in the King's Cross area, and complaints by Islington tenants concerning inadequate police presence on housing estates are all current issues upon which action is being attempted. To make sense of what is going on, and to keep a sense of political direction, it seems useful to try and separate out three distinct views of the nature of police accountability.

## The Conventional View: Politics Versus Administration

People living in London sometimes forget that in the rest of the country there exists some sort of police accountability to elected representatives of the local community. It is, however, a system that has long been in crisis. The fact that the Police Authorities are only partly democratic – one third of their membership are unelected magistrates – is one aspect of the issue. But what has really become clear over the past few years, particularly since the riots of 1981, is that where policing is considered a fundamentally technical question, above politics (what could conceivably be political about the most efficient method of catching criminals?), then the role of accountability is thoroughly ambiguous. Many people have commented that the 1964 Police Act left the Police Authorities in a completely powerless position. They are required to maintain an efficient police force, yet all operational matters are under the control of the Chief Constable, who can only be removed from his post by the Police Authority with a great deal of difficulty. James

Anderton is by no means a typical Chief Constable, but he illustrates all the problems because of his extremism. He puts armed
squads of officers on the streets of Manchester and claims it
is purely his professional judgement and, furthermore, implies
that the fuss created by the Labour delegates on the Police
Authority may endanger his officers by drawing attention to
their new armed status. The problem behind all of this is that
in the conventional view there is no real answer to the question
of what is a matter of legitimate democratic concern and what
is a matter of organizational strategy for police expertise. This
unresolved issue has pushed the conventional system into
crisis under the new conditions of the eighties. For this reason
alone the struggle in London for a Police Authority as such
is not, and cannot be, simply a demand to be like the rest of
England, Wales and Scotland. This is where the need for clarity,
particularly on the left, comes in. It's useful to distinguish two
current attitudes to police accountability on the left, which often
differ in emphasis rather than substance; we might call them
idealism and realism.

## Left Idealism: Keeping the Police at Bay

Left idealism starts from a straightforward Marxist view: the
state is a class state, the police as a state organ are concerned
with the repression of radical struggle, and much 'crime' is in
fact radical struggle 'criminalized' by the state and the media.
After the revolution there will be no need for a police force
anyway, and in the mean time the issue is to keep the police
out of working-class communities and constantly expose and
publicize their repressive actions. Apart from the political
analysis involved, there are some practical problems with this
view. While monitoring police actions *is* an essential part of police
accountability, taking it as the main issue means, firstly, that
the monitoring body simply responds to police actions. It takes
up issues of illegal police behaviour which may affect particular

individuals or even sections of the community. The rest of the community is not involved and, worse, may even approve of police action. The police, in turn, will regard the monitoring group as an extremist and interfering body unrepresentative of the community at large. They will be tempted to become more explicitly political themselves and appeal over the heads of the monitoring group to what they see as the 'silent majority' which, they feel sure, has no reason not to support them. So the danger, if monitoring is seen as the main issue, is always that the group will become isolated. An important assumption of this view is that the community really exists as a politically cohesive entity standing behind the monitoring group. In reality, the *building* of such cohesion is one of the tasks that any struggle for police accountability has got to take on board: it does not yet exist.

## Left Realism: A Policing Policy for the Community

Left realism starts from the following assumptions: we need a police force because crime is a real problem. There is a lot of it and it harms the working-class community. Working-class crime is directed against working-class people. Vandalism, rape, mugging, burglary, etc., constitute just one more factor in the burdens that working-class people have to suffer. The issue is to get a police force that will deal properly with these problems. Democratic control of policing is a necessary pre-condition for such efficiency for three reasons. Firstly, only the local community knows its policing needs. There are many technical aspects to police work but in the crucial area of where to distribute resources the police have discretion. It is this that the community must control because only it knows what its crime problems are. A community-wide debate on crime and public order, traffic problems and so on would enable the community to draw up a clear account of its policing needs. This is very different from a fragmented process of 'con-sultation' of particular community groupings by the police.

Secondly, such a debate would provide a new source of cohesion in the local community as different groups discovered that they faced similar problems and had similar needs. In this way a positive plan for the distribution of police resources could be drawn up. Of course, the police should participate in this debate: as practitioners they have invaluable experience and information to contribute. But it should be the case that the *community consults the police as part of the process of formulating its needs, not that the police consult the community in formulating its strategy*. It is the community and not the police which is the ultimate repository of information on its needs *and* of information which can lead to the solution of crimes. This brings us to the third point. The accountable police force will be one that is trusted by the community, and, of course, this accountability must include a 'monitoring' element: an effective complaints procedure involving the public and the visitation of swift justice on officers who commit illegal acts. A force trusted by the community will be one to which the community will be prepared to yield a high flow of information concerning crime. It is this flow of information and *not* the numbers of police or the high-powered technology at their disposal which is the most important single factor in solving crimes. A democratically accountable police force would have a higher clear-up rate.

In conclusion, there are two issues of current urgency: first, given that democratic accountability requires, at the very least, legislation by a future Labour government, it might be felt that, in fact, monitoring is about all that can be done at present. Secondly, Kenneth Newman's policy for the Metropolitan Police raises the issue of what should be the attitude of police committees in Labour Boroughs to the new community liaison initiatives? On the first issue, some boroughs are going ahead with the idea of a victimization survey conducted by the police committee. This is of considerable importance: it generates an alternative set of statistics about the incidence of crime to the police arrest statistics or statistics for victim-reported crime (much crime is unreported where it is felt that the police could not be bothered anyway). These can be used as part of a public debate about policing needs. Such surveys can also include questions not normally considered relevant by the police, such as the incidence of domestic violence, illegal acts by police officers, and the specific problems of ethnic minorities. The community can then get a clearer picture of what it is facing than it can from the police statistics. This brings us to the second issue. In our opinion it would be a mistake to try and ignore the police liaison schemes. Rather, the borough police committees should use the resources they have and the roots in the community they have already established to enable the representatives of the liaison scheme to present a united and well worked-out position. This will make the case for democratic control of policing stronger: the clearer the line taken by community representatives even on police-operated liaison schemes, the more a police refusal to follow the 'advice' will demonstrate the need for control. The worst scenario would be if the police committees boycotted the liaison schemes, while community groups, tenants, etc., anxious to have at least *some* dialogue with the police, supported them. This would undercut the police committees from their public support and the tenants and community representatives would be deprived of the back-up which police committees could provide: the only victor would be the status quo.

# 8 A Realistic Approach to Law and Order

We have attempted in this book to outline a realistic strategy about crime and policing from a socialist perspective. In doing this we have heeded the appeal that Ian Taylor made in his *Law and Order: Arguments for Socialism* (1982) to transform the vacuum in left-wing thinking and concern on the matter. Under the impact of the Women's Movement socialists quite correctly began to realize the problems of violence against women and their sexual harassment. The struggle against fascism galvanized particularly by the Anti-Nazi League and continued by numerous monitoring groups brought home to the Labour movement the extent and severity of racist attacks. But concern about crime stopped at these points. There was a schizophrenia about crime on the left where crimes against women and immigrant groups were quite rightly an object of concern, but other types of crime were regarded as being of little interest or somehow excusable. Part of this mistake stems, as we have noted, from the belief that property offences are directed solely against the bourgeoisie and that violence against the person is carried out by amateur Robin Hoods in the course of their righteous attempt to redistribute wealth. All of this is, alas, untrue. Indeed, the irony is that precisely the same kids who break into the next-door neighbour's flat sit around the estates wearing British Movement badges and harassing Asians.

But in adopting a realistic perspective on crime we must avoid finding ourselves in the ranks of the law-and-order lobby; a correct perspective is needed, but is extremely difficult at present. There is the story of a seminar in North London where one week the students, reeling from the impact of a description of the deplorable results of imprisonment on inmates, decided to abolish prisons. But then the next week, after being, quite correctly, informed by a speaker from the Women's Movement of the viciousness of many anti-female offences, decided to rebuild them!

An important corollary of the breakdown of community is decrease in accurate knowledge about crime. In a tight-knit social setting not only is there more unanimity of communal interest and an ability to stigmatize offenders, there is also greater knowledge about what is going on and what deviance is about. As social splintering occurs there is a decrease in direct knowledge about crime, but, although the quality of information declines, the actual quantity increases. As has been well documented, one of the key selling-points of Western mass media is its coverage of crime and social problems (Cohen and Young). A commercially oriented media bent on maximizing sales and audience ratings supplies news coverage which, although based on a rational kernel of public fear, has few curbs on its excesses of sensationalism. The only limits on this process are good taste and the limited knowledge that journalists have of crime. Thus we come to the crux of the matter. To recapitulate, in our time, relative deprivation and hence discontent have increased. This, combined with unemployment and community breakdown, has not allowed such discontent to be channelled into political forms. Instead, the most obvious solution is that of crime. Meanwhile, community breakdown facilitates crime by drastically undermining the informal process of social control. The same forces which make for the increase in crime fuel a moral panic about crime. That is, the real fear about crime is intimately related to the moral hysteria about crime. It not only provides a rational kernel for alarm, but its genesis lies at the same source; and the mass media serve and exaggerate such public fears. The demand for crime news is great; the media reporting of crime and policing foments and exaggerates this appetite. This atmosphere carries with it a corresponding politics, but the law-

and-order campaigns, such a familiar monopoly of the right, are an area in which the left has had very little to say except when it is on the defensive. Thus, at precisely the time when there is the greatest need for a rational approach to crime, the greatest level of irrationality occurs. Just at the time when there is a need for a humane and realistic political intervention from the left, such a movement is lacking. Let us conclude by spelling out the basic premises of left realism in the areas of crime and the police.

## 1 *Crime Really is a Problem*

In contrast to the beliefs of left idealists, working-class crime really is a problem for the working class. This is not to deny the impact of crimes of the powerful or indeed of the perfectly legal social problems created by capitalism. Rather, left realism notes that the working class is a victim of crime from all directions; that one sort of crime tends to compound another, as one social problem does another; and furthermore, that crime is a potent symbol of the antisocial nature of capitalism and is the most immediate way in which people experience other problems, such as unemployment or competitive individualism.

Left realism examines the problem of crime seriously; it does not enter into the moral panics of the mass media or the blatant denial of left idealism. It clearly separates out moral panic from moral realism, and moral indignation from material conflict. With this in mind, it assesses the impact of crime on different victims and sections of the population. Furthermore, it carefully appraises the impact of crime, materially, politically and ideologically, on the maintenance of capitalism. For fear of street crime helps the disintegration of the working-class community and thus engenders a breakdown in the ability to fight back. It divides the poor against the poor both in a real sense and in the distorted ideological sense repeated by the mass media that the real enemy is crime and not the inequitable nature of our society.

## 2   *We Must Look at the Reality behind Appearances*

Left realism does not simply examine crime on the level of its immediate appearances. Conventional criminology notes the antisocial nature of crime; in this it is correct, but it ignores the social basis of its genesis. Left idealism, in that it notes how crime is a form of rebellion, is also correct, but by failing to go further than a discussion of its causes, is seriously myopic about the reactionary nature of its impact and the conventional nature of its mode of operation.

It is vital to realize the contradictory nature of working-class crime. Its cause is seeing through the deception and inequality of the world; its direction is towards that of selfishness. Its cause is righteous, its direction individualistic. The political energies that could have been harnessed for a transformation of society become channelled into ensuring its inertia. As Jeremy Seabrook has argued (p. 64):

> This process is a deforming, a deviation, of all the energies that might have gone into the collective struggle for change; and is a measure of the capitalist appropriation of all the socialist or utopian or imagined or dreamed-of other worlds and societies, and the marketing of them through the filter of market-priced commodities and consolations. If there is violence, wrecking, arson and looting in the places where the poor live, it doesn't really matter. The cargo of tormented humanity which the ambulances and police wagons fetch each day out of North American ghettos piles up in vain.
> This will not change anything, because, unlike traditional political reactions, these have been effectively isolated from the actions of the rich and powerful. After all, the rich are themselves on the side of the poor: they too want to get richer in order to help the poor become a little less poor. In this way, a perfect symbiosis of rich and poor has been reached, a kind of harmony re-established that the Western world hasn't known since the end of feudalism.

## 3  *We Must Take Crime Control Seriously*

Left realism is in fundamental disagreement with conventional and left-idealist approaches to crime control. The draconian penalties advocated by the law-and-order lobby, by amplifying and hardening criminals, simply serve to make matters worse. A fundamental irony is that the policies of the 'hard-on-crime' advocates in fact only serve to increase crime. They do not take crime seriously. On the other hand, the idealists with their myopia about crime simply turn their back on the problem. They leave crime alone and help create social mores where no one seems to care.

Realism instructs us that the problem is crime and not the criminal; that the vast majority of crimes are minor, amateurish and of little consequence in isolation; and that the average offender is not committed to crime but drifts into illegality sporadically and compulsively. But if one pinprick is of little significance, a thousand, repeated daily, certainly are! For this reason the keynotes of a left realism crime control programme are as follows.

(a) Demarginalization: Instead of marginalizing and excluding an offender, realists would argue for alternatives to prison which help to integrate rather than separate the offender. They would, therefore, advocate such measures as community service orders, victim restitution schemes, and widespread release from prison. The marginalization of the offender which occurs at the present does not involve just the physical and social exclusion of the offender in the prisons, but it also crucially involves his or her ethical alienation: a severance of the moral bond with the community. The institutions that are involved in controlling crime and criminals must epitomize justice – not, as they do at the moment, create veritable havens of lawlessness.

(b) Pre-emptive deterrence: To deter crime before it is committed is infinitely better than to attempt to intervene by punishing the culprit after the event, with the aim of deterring his future activities or perhaps those of others. Environmental and public precautions against crime are always dismissed by left idealists and reformers as not relating to the heart of the problem. They are distractions from the real concerns and, furthermore, because they do not get at the causes of crime, are largely irrelevant. Conventional criminology *and* left idealism are united on this score. On the contrary, the organization of communities in an attempt to pre-empt crime is of the utmost importance. Citizen groups cooperating with the police, ranging from elderly observers during the daytime and more youthful patrols in the evening, could vastly improve the conditions in many housing estates and working-class areas.

(c) The minimal use of prison: Prison should only be used in those circumstances where there is extreme danger to the community. The development of weekend prisons which permit people to maintain their jobs and social relationships is important, but where full-term imprisonment is necessary it should restrict itself to civilized forms of containment. Life inside prison should be as free and as 'normal' as possible. Such a demand is not humanitarian idealism – it is based on the simple fact that the result of prison experience is to produce either pitiful inadequates or hardened criminals. Any hospital which made the people more sick than they originally were, and where each visit made the next more likely, would have been shut down years ago. Moral outrage against crime should not be directed merely into fuelling the circumstances which create the indignation in the first place. The control of crime is an area where we have constantly to be on guard against irrationality and where righteous indignation only too often swamps the real interests of the community.

## 4   *We Must Look Realistically at the Circumstances of Both the Offender and the Victim*

Two abstract systems of justice dominate our penal and sentencing system. One, epitomized by the adult trial (for example, in the Crown Court), has the notion of the free-willed, responsible agent. Mitigating circumstances are allowed as random, unsystematized, marginal excuses; they only peripherally enter the realm of free choice which citizens as offenders are presented as inhabiting. All people, in this scheme, are held equally responsible for their deeds, and the seriousness of the offence is judged against a scale of well-intentioned but rather ill-defined notions of social harm. The other system is quite the opposite: the individual is viewed as a product of circumstances. This mode of justice is seen in the Juvenile Court.

Both systems of justice have opposite yet equally abstract notions of evaluating social harm. In the first case, harm is judged, if it is property, by cost. £500 worth of theft is considerably more important than £5 worth. Who the victim of the theft was is of little importance. In the other the degree of social harm is deemed inconsequential. What is considered important is not whether a delinquent stole £5 or £500, but the basic problems which he suffers in terms of his personality and social skills, of which the theft is a mere symptom.

A socialist system of justice would seek to put both offender and victim into context. We must emphasize that people really do have choices and thus are responsible for their actions. But we must realistically appreciate that such freedom exists in very determinate and variable circumstances. To judge an unemployed youth stealing £50 as equal to an accountant fiddling £50 on income tax is invidious. Secondly, the impact of crime is very different for different victims: £50 stolen from an OAP is very different from £50 stolen from Woolworths. Both the choices available to the offender and the effects of the offence on freedom of the victim are vital variables in terms of justice. So to explain a criminal event in terms of the total system is not to excuse it. It is to provide mitigating circumstances on a systematic level which the present system of law does in an arbitrary and individualistic fashion. This is not to advocate a hard law-and-order approach, but neither is it to provide a blanket excuse, as in much socialist thinking on crime. Rather, it recognizes the vital necessity for intervention, firstly, because – as we have argued – much criminality is essentially contradictory and strong intervention can – if it comes from the right direction – 'resolve' these contradictions; secondly, because crime is a demoralizing force within the community, which saps the strength of any political organization within the most depressed areas of the city. To recognize that there is this element of choice in crime is to accept that it is necessary to counter crime with force – realistically guided by knowledge of the circumstances involved.

## We Must be Realistic about Policing

The paramount fact is that the police need the public and that the effectiveness of policing is dependent on the extent to which we transform, as Steve Bundred of the GLC Police Committee put it, 'the police force into a police service'. The arrogance and autonomy which the police evidence towards those who pay their salaries must be got rid of. It is essential to impose a system of positive public accountability in which the needs of the community direct the activities of the police. Arguments about the need to maintain autonomy in operational tasks should clearly note that much of what the police deem operational is in fact directly political. The police demand to keep politics out of policing is only too often an argument for giving the political decisions to them. But we must not shirk the problems of democratic control. There is no reason for suspecting that a free vote on policing would protect the ethnic minorities, would stop the harassment of the young, would be tolerant of the dosser, and would direct police attention to the corruption among local councils or corporate executives. One of our constant nightmares is that if there was a completely democratic control of police in areas such as Hackney, the resulting police force would look exactly the same as the present Hackney police force. The irrationalities engendered by the mass media, the real and divisive difficulties which people face in their everyday life, the breakdown of community and 'obvious' sources of collective interest, all militate against this. But a crucial function of party politics in a democracy is not to be a mere cipher of public opinion but to attempt to try and convert the fearful and to create the circumstances for greater rationality. We must, in this context, also be realistic about the difficult position of the police. Their capacity to clear up crime has fallen to an all-time low. In the Metropolitan Police District, Walter Easy, Head of Camden Police Support Unit, has calculated that only 6 per cent of burglaries are successfully cleared up by the police. Part of this is due to rank police inefficiency, part is the lack of co-operation of the community, but the most difficult part is the breakdown of a working-class community which could possibly provide such instruction and information. We have argued that public involvement in a politics which is concerned with control of crime and antisocial activities within their areas will be dependent on the bringing of the police within democratic control and thus enhancing the co-operation of the public. But it will also serve to recreate the community.

## 6 *We Must be Realistic about the Problem of Crime in the Present Period*

Although for the last century crime has been a perennial problem for working-class people, we feel that there are certain key factors about the present period which are of great importance. Firstly, the degree of relative deprivation engendered by education, the mass media, the Welfare State and the inconsistencies of the market has constantly risen. Secondly, such discontent, instead of focusing on political objectives, has constantly been splintered as a consequence of the breakdown of community and the fragmentation of employment. Such a situation of discontent without a political outlet creates a criminal response which the left are, by tradition, extraordinarily inept at dealing with. Yet the whole possibility of a new community politics which unites people at a grass-roots level depends on this. If we return to our equation that crime is a result of economic discontent without political alternatives, then the implication for socialists is clear. Not only is crime control a material necessity for the working class and therefore an essential part of any socialist programme, but the absence of an alternative politics for marginalized youth that can give their lives meaning and potential contributes substantially to the creation of crime and disorganization. Jeremy Seabrook (p. 64) puts this eloquently:

> The young poor see no meaning in the fight for a better world: the better world exists already, in such close parallel to that worse and unbearable one which they inhabit. They are thus cut off from any sense of collective hope and action. Hope lies only in individual escape – the big win, the massive haul, the lucky stroke, the windfall, the right number, a winning ticket.
>
> Because the better life has been taken over and redefined in terms of the capitalist version, all the struggles of the Labour movement have been eclipsed for the poor, another mangled and shadowed hope. The rich are no longer guilty; just successful. The poor have been refashioned in the image of the rich. For as long as they remain in opposition to them, collective hope – an alternative, in fact – remained.
>
> It is because these visions of an alternative have been occluded that the dispossessed turn on each other. The poor prey on the poor; and this is an act of political despair. There is plenty of evidence that our inner cities are coming to resemble those of North America: violence, depravity and cruelty can be contained in the ghettos where the poor can be safely left to attack each other. The rich, meanwhile, can sleep safely in their beds.

We must be involved, then, for material, political and ideological reasons: materially, to pursue the cause of justice in working-class communities; politically, to provide an alternative politics which will harness the energies of the marginalized, thus diminishing the causes of crime while providing a humane and efficacious crime control. Such politics of crime control are part of the wide sweep of grass-roots politics: the control of pollution, industrial safety, traffic control, environmental improvements – representing, in fact, the united interest of a divided community. In this process of seeking out a common political interest and exerting public control, we will recreate a sense of community both in consciousness and in muscle, rather than resurrect a mythical entity which has long since disappeared. Lastly, ideologically, we will combat the tendency of a divided and disillusioned public to move to the right, to construct a quasi-community out of shabby nationalism and racism, and replace the 'war against crime' notion of conventional politics with the notion that the fight against crime is one that combats the material deprivation of capitalism and the rank individualism of its values. It is with this aim in mind that we have written this book. For too long the politics of law and order have been a monopoly of the right. Yet the left have every reason materially, politically and ideologically to intervene in this area. We are too paralysed by our own preconceptions easily to take up the challenge which is demanded of us. The opportunities for an initiative from the left are enormous; we must not shirk the task.

Let us conclude with a quote from Eileen Fairweather's article which graphically sums up the predicament we face:

> In the street old Sal asks me was I too woken up by last night's shouting, the screams and then the sirens? What do I think of it all? Useless to tell Sal that it's slums and poverty which cause crime. She's been poor all her life and never hurt anyone. Useless even to tell her that the pros are her sisters in struggle. They jostle her in the street, shock her with obscene oaths, laugh at her little dog.

So hang 'em and flog 'em all! cries Sal. She's become a Tory not because she's reactionary, but just because she's so weak and so damned scared.

Strong-arm solutions appeal when you are powerless and nobody seems to be offering anything else. Night after night, when I have been kept awake by the pushers' cock-rock and drunken parties I've been consumed with terrible, vengeful fantasies about how one day I'll castrate, then kill them, torment them as they've for so long tormented and terrified me.

Being female, of course, I'll do no such thing. But I do now understand how the law of the jungle infects and corrodes even those who try to resist it. 'The reason I want off this estate,' a woman neighbour confides, 'is that I swear to God it's turning me into a fascist. And I've been a socialist all my life.'

# Bibliography

Alderson, J. (1979), *Policing Freedom*, Plymouth: McDonald and Evans.

Armstrong, G., and Wilson, M. (1973), 'City Politics and Deviancy Amplification', in I. and L. Taylor (eds.), *Politics and Deviance*, Harmondsworth: Penguin, pp. 61–89.

Baldwin, J., and Bottoms, A. (1976), *The Urban Criminal*, London: Tavistock.

Baldwin, R., and Kinsey, R. (1983), *The Police and Police Powers*, London: Quartet.

Balkan, S., Berger, R., and Schmidt, J. (1980), *Crime and Deviance in America*, California: Wadsworth.

Blom-Cooper, L., and Drabble, R. (1982), 'Police Perception of Crime', *British Journal of Criminology*, pp. 184–7.

Bowlby, J. (1946), *Forty-Four Juvenile Thieves*, Balliere: Tindall and Cox.

Box, S. (1981), *Deviancy, Reality and Society*, London: Holt, Rinehart and Winston.

Bridges, L. (1983), 'Extended Views: The British Left and Law and Order', *Sage Race Relations Abstracts* vol. 8, pp. 19–26.

Bridges, L., and Gilroy, P. (1982), 'Striking Back', *Marxism Today*, pp. 34–5.

*The British Crime Survey* (1983), M. Hough and P. Mayhew, Home Office Research Study no. 76, London: HMSO.

Brogden, M. (1982), *The Police: Autonomy and Consent*, London: Academic Press.

Chapman, D. (1968), *Sociology and the Stereotype of the Criminal*, London: Tavistock.

Clark, R. (1970), *Crime in America*, New York: Simon and Schuster.

Clemente, F., and Kleinman, M. (1977), 'Fear of Crime in the United States', *Social Forces* 1977, pp. 514–31.

Cloward, R., and Ohlin, L. (1960), *Delinquency and Opportunity*, New York: The Free Press.

Cohen, S., and Young, J. (1981), *The Manufacture of News*, London: Constable.

Conklin, J. E. (1975), *The Impact of Crime*, New York: Macmillan.

Cowell, D., *et al.* (1982), *Policing the Riots*, London: Junction Books.

Damer, S. (1976), 'Wine Alley', in P. Wiles (ed.), *The Sociology of Crime and Delinquency*, vol. 2, London: Martin Robertson, pp. 193–201.

Demuth, C. (1978), '*Sus*': *A Report on the Vagrancy Act 1824*, London: Runnymede Trust.

Engels, F. (1969), *The Conditions of the Working Class in England*, London: Panther.

Fairweather, E. (1982), 'The Law of the Jungle in King's Cross', *New Society*, 2 December.

*Final Report of the Working Party into Community/Police Relations in Lambeth* (1981).

Friend, A., and Metcalf, A. (1981), *Slump City*, London: Pluto Press.

Garofalo, J. (1980), 'Victimization and the Fear of Crime', *Criminology Review Year Book*, vol. 2, pp. 647–64.

Geis, G. (1978), 'Deterring Corporate Crime', in M. Ermann and R. Lundmann (eds.), *Corporate and Governmental Deviance*, New York: Oxford University Press.

Gilroy, P. (1981), 'You Can't Fool the Youths', *Race and Class*, vol. 23, pp. 207–22.

Gilroy, P. (1982), 'The Myth of Black Criminality', in *Socialist Register*, London: Merlin Press, pp. 47–56.

Gilroy, P. (1983), 'Police and Thieves', in Centre for Contemporary Cultural Studies, *The Empire Strikes Back*, London: Hutchinson, pp. 143–82.

Gregory, J. (1979), 'Sex Discrimination, Work and the Law', in NDC/CSE, *Capitalism and the Rule of Law*, London: Hutchinson, pp. 137–50.

Griffiths, C. (1981), 'Black People, the Police and the State', *Haldane Bulletin*, pp. 10–13.

Hain, P. (1983), *The Democratic Alternative*, Harmondsworth: Penguin.

Hall, S., *et al.* (1979), *Policing the Crisis*, London: Macmillan.

Harman, C. (1981), 'The Summer of 1981: A Post-Riot Analysis', *International Socialism*, vol. 2, pp. 1–41.

Harman, C. (1982), 'The Law and Order Show', *Socialist Review*, pp. 18–21.

Harrington, M. (1963), *The Other America*, Harmondsworth: Penguin.

Hewitt, P. (1983), *The Abuse of Power*, Oxford: Martin Robertson.

Hill, C., and Issacharoff, R. (1971), *Community Action and Race Relations*, Oxford: University Press.

Hobsbawm, E. (1964), *Labouring Men*, London: Weidenfeld and Nicolson.

Humphrey, D., and John, G. (1972), *Police Power and Black People*, London: Panther.

Jackson, G. (1970), *Soledad Brother*, Harmondsworth: Penguin.

Jefferson, T., and Clarke, J. (1974), 'Down Those Mean Streets', *Howard Journal*, no. 14, pp. 33–42.

Johnson, E. H. (1978), *Crime Correction and Society*, 4th ed., Homewood, Illinois: The Dorsey Press.

Kinsey, R., and Young, J. (1982), 'Police Autonomy and the Politics of Discretion', in Cowell *et al.*, pp. 118–34.

Kittrie, N. (1984), *Rape: The American Crime* (mimeographed).

Lambert, J. (1970), *Crime, Police and Race Relations*, Oxford: University Press.

Landau, H. (1981), 'Juveniles and the Police', *British Journal of Criminology*, vol. 21, pp. 143–72.

Lea, J. (1980), 'The Contradictions of the Sixties' Race Relations Legislation', in NDC, *Permissiveness and Control*, London: Macmillan, pp. 122–48.

Lea, J., and Young, J. (1982), 'The Riots in Britain 1981: Urban Violence and Political Marginalisation', in Cowell *et al.*, pp. 5–20.

Lundberg, F. (1968), *The Rich and the Super Rich*, New York: Bantam Books.

Maguire, M. (1980), 'The Impact of Burglary upon Victims', *British Journal of Criminology*, pp. 230–44.

Mannheim, H. (1940), *Social Aspects of Crime in England*, London: Allen and Unwin.

Mapes, G. (1970), 'A Growing Disparity in Criminal Sentences Troubles Legal Experts', *Wall Street Journal*, 9 September.

Marcuse, H. (1971), *Soviet Marxism*, Harmondsworth: Penguin.

Matza, D. (1964), *Delinquency and Drift*, New York: Wiley.

Mawby, R. (1979), *Policing the City*, Farnborough: Saxon House.

Mawby, R., and Batta, I. (1980), *Asians and Crime*, National Association for Asian Youth, Southall.

McClintock, F. H. (1963), *Crimes of Violence*, New York: St Martins Press.

Merritt, G. (1982), *World out of Work*, London: Collins.

Mill, J. S. (1910 edn), *Utilitarianism, Liberty and Representative Government*, London: Dent.

Mills, C. Wright (1956), *The Power Elite*, New York: Oxford University Press.

Morris, T. (1957), *The Criminal Area*, London: Routledge and Kegan Paul.

Musgrove, F. (1963), *The Migratory Elite*, London: Heinemann.

Pearce, F. (1973), 'Crime, Corporations and the American Social Order', in I. and L. Taylor, pp. 13–41.

Pitts, J. (1979), *Changes in the Control, Prevention, Anticipation and Surveyance of Youthful Disorder in England and Wales* (privately circulated).

Platt, T. (1981), 'Street Crime: A View from the Left', in T. Platt and P. Tagaki (eds.), *Crime and Social Justice*, London: Macmillan, pp. 13–29.

Poggi, G. (1978), *The Development of the Modern State: A Sociological Introduction*, London: Hutchinson.

Pratt, M. (1980), *Mugging as a Social Problem*, London: Routledge and Kegan Paul.

Pryce, K. (1977), *Endless Pressure*, Harmondsworth: Penguin.

Reiman, J. (1979), *The Rich Get Rich and the Poor Get Poorer*, New York: Wiley.

Rex, J., and Tomlinson, P. (1979), *Colonial Immigrants in a British City*, London: Routledge and Kegan Paul.

Ridley, F. (1981), 'View from a Disaster Area: Unemployed Youth in Merseyside', *Political Quarterly*, vol. 52, pp. 123–41.

Riot Not to Work Collective (1981), *Riot Not to Work: The 1981 Brixton Uprisings*.

Robins, D., and Cohen, P. (1978), *Knuckle Sandwich*, Harmondsworth: Penguin.

Rose, D. (1982), 'Estate of Siege', *Time Out*, no. 614.
Runciman, W. G. (1966), *Relative Deprivation and Social Justice*, London: Routledge and Kegan Paul.
Runnymede Trust Bulletin, No. 143 (1982), *Race and Immigration*.
Samuel, R. (1981), *East End Underworld*, London: Routledge.
Scarman, Lord Justice (1982), *The Scarman Report*, Harmondsworth: Penguin.
Seabrook, J. (1983), 'The Crime of Poverty', *New Society*, 14 April.
Silberman, C. (1980), *Criminal Justice*, New York: Vintage Books.
Sim, J. (1982), 'Scarman: The Police Counter-attack', *Socialist Register*, pp. 57–77.
Sinfield, A. (1981), 'Unemployment in an Unequal Society', in A. Sinfield and B. Showler (eds.), *The Workless State*, Oxford: Martin Robertson, pp. 122–67.
Sivanandan, A. (1981), 'From Resistance to Rebellion', *Race and Class*, pp. 111–52.
Sivanandan, A. (1982), *A Different Hunger*, London: Pluto Press.
Smith, S. (1982), *Race and Crime Statistics*, Race Relations Fieldwork Background Paper no. 4, London: HMSO.
Sparks, R., Genn, H., and Dodd, D. (1977), *Surveying Victims*, Chichester: Wiley.
Stevens, P., and Willis, C. (1979), *Race Crime and Arrests*, Home Office Research Study no. 58, London: HMSO.
Tarleng, R. (1982), 'Unemployment and Crime', *Research Bulletin* no. 14, London: Home Office.
Taylor, I. (1982), *Law and Order*, London: Macmillan.
Thompson, E. P. (1978), Introduction to *Review of Security and the State*, State Research Collective, London: Julian Friedmann.
Tuck, M., and Southgate, P. (1981), *Ethnic Minorities, Crime and Policing*, London: HMSO.
Veblen, T. (1922), *Theory of the Leisure Class*, London: Macmillan.
Whitlock, F. (1971), *Death on the Road*, London: Tavistock.
Willis, P. (1977), *Learning to Labour*, London: Saxon House.
Wilson, J. Q. (1975), *Thinking about Crime*, New York: Basic Books.
Winslow, R. W. (1968), *Crime in a Free Society*, California: Dickenson.

Wolfgang, M., and Cohen, B. (1970), *Crime and Race*, New York: Institute of Human Relations.

Wright, E. O. (1973), *The Politics of Punishment*, New York: Harper and Row.

Young, J. (1971), *The Drugtakers*, London: Paladin.

Young, J. (1975), 'Working Class Criminology', in I. Taylor *et al.*, (eds.), *Critical Criminology*, London: Routledge, pp. 63–94.

# Index

Alderson, J., 181–2, 242, 246, 247, 275
Anderton, James, 242, 243, 258
Armstrong, G., 41, 275
Association of Chief Police Officers (ACPO), 246, 248, 251

Baldwin, J., 40, 275
Baldwin, R., 182, 243, 275
Balkan, S., 43, 275
Batta, I., 130, 277
Berger, R., 43, 275
Blom-Cooper, L., 106, 163–4, 275
Bottoms, T., 40, 275
Bowlby, J., 81–3, 275
Box, S., 19, 275
British Crime Survey, 17–19, 25, 28, 275
Brixton, 143, 145, 146, 162–4, 167, 175, 210, 250–51
Brogden, M., 170, 205, 275
Broken homes, 82–3
Bundred, S., 269
Burglary, 24–5, 29, 34–5, 46–7, 86–7

Capone, A., 43
Carib Club, 144
Chapman, D., 15, 68, 275
Chicago School, 132–3
China, crime in, 88
Clark, R., 30, 275
Clarke, J., 130, 134, 276
Clemente, F., 27, 36, 275
Cloward, R., 65, 222–3, 275
Cohen, B., 113
Cohen, P., 213, 278
Cohen, S., 49, 263, 276
Community (local), 234–40

Community Relations Council (CRC), 141–5, 188; *see also* Police–community liaison
Community Relations Councils (CRCs), 249–50, 254
Community Service Orders, 102
Conklin, J., 29, 54, 276
Consensus policing, 169–72, 186
Corporate crime, 66–73, 89
Cowell, D., 276
Crime
  and marginalization, 27, 30–31, 37–49
  in the United States, 22, 26, 51–3
  professional, 39, 43
  race and, 135 *et seq.*
  upper-class, 11–12, 66–8, 72
  victim-reported, 139–40, 144, 145, 146
  working-class, 11–12, 41–5, 89
Crime rate
  of old people, 89
  of women, 90
  of the working class, 100
  Jews, 128, 132
  Italians, 132–3
Criminal area, 38–45, 171, 174, 180
Criminal statistics, 12–17, 135 *et seq.*
Criminal values, 42–4, 72–5, 96–7
Crutchley, J., 113

Damer, S., 41, 276
Dark figure of unreported crime, 17–21, 25–6, 146, 156
Davis, A., 65
Dodd, D., 20, 279
Drabble, R., 106, 163–4, 275